Adam On: Projects (Volume 1)

50+ Axioms on the Art and Science of Managing Projects of All Kinds - Adaptive, Predictive and Organic

Adam Russell

Adam On: Projects (Volume 1)

50+ Axioms on the Art and Science of Managing Projects of All Kinds - Adaptive, Predictive and Organic

Adam Russell

ISBN 978-0-6458573-0-6

Published by **BrainJuice.Media**

BrainJuice.Media is an imprint of Tiligent Pty Ltd

https://tiligent.com/

BrainJuice feeds your professional brain

For more **BrainJuice.Media** publications, visit https://www.brainjuice.media

To Peter Burrett, who first got me into Project Management.

Also By Adam Russell

The Deliverables Management Handbook
Axioms of Project Management
Adam On: Advanced Excel Outlining with TreeWiz
Adam On: Advanced Excel Table Management with TableWiz
Adam on: ChatGPT - The AI Appliance
Adam On: Advanced ChatGPT Application Primer
Advanced ChatGPT for Agile Project Management
Project Teaming Principles
Adam On: Projects - Agile Edition
Adam On: Projects - Quotations Edition
Adam On: Projects - Volume 2
Principle-Based Project Leadership

Contents

CONTENTS

Getting Engaged with this Book and its Author

Now that you have your copy of the book, bootstrap its value by getting engaged with other people and resources on the same topic.

1. **Message**: You can post me a comment or question via my publisher (BrainJuice.Media) using their ***Feedback Form***[1]. Ask me anything. I'll answer as quickly as I can. (Remember to select the book in the "Topic" field)
2. **Facebook Group**: Join my private ***Facebook Group***[2] which is for anyone who is interested in the topics I'm writing about. That's the main place I interact with folks.
3. **Author Page**: My ***My BrainJuice.Media Author Page***[3] is the jumping point for all my current content, both published and "in the works".
4. **Blog**: I publish blogposts on Medium.com on my ***AdamOnProjects Blog***[4].
5. **Mailing List**: If you haven't already joined, sign up for my ***mailing list***[5], on Brainjuice.Media's website (my publisher). You'll get information on new books, courses, and other content when I make it available. I'll update you on interesting deals, as well as information on upcoming events and other activities in the world of **Adam On Projects**.
6. **Social Media**: you can track me down on the internets:

- ***X (formerly known as Twitter)***[6]
- ***LinkedIn***[7]

7. **Adam's Axioms** (New): Visit my Companion Website, ***Adam's Axioms***[8], for more information on the axioms. This is where I'll publish additional material between book updates, plus additional resources that may not be suitable for book form.

---

[1] https://bjl.ink/contact
[2] https://www.facebook.com/groups/adamoneverything
[3] https://bjl.ink/adam
[4] https://adamonprojects.com/
[5] https://bjl.ink/engage
[6] https://twitter.com/adamonprojects/
[7] https://www.linkedin.com/in/adamonprojects/
[8] https://adamsaxioms.com/

Notes about this version

This is Version 1.10 the book.

Updates in this version:

- Various Editorial fixes.
- Introduced axiom numbering across all editions. I resisted this for a long time, but it just makes cross referencing easier as well as referring to axioms from outside the AOP multi-verse.

Introduction

Who is this book for?

This book is for project managers at any level of experience who want to continue the endless journey towards mastering the art and science of project management. PMs who want to move as far away from the "Suck Zone", as Kathy Sierra calls it, and progress towards expert-level performance.

If you're in the early stages of your career, this book and its siblings - a collection I like to call "**Adam's Axioms**" - will raise many questions. That's okay because questions are good. Questions are the pathfinders that will guide you to improvement.

If you've got some solid experience under your belt, I can see you nodding in agreement at some things, violently disagreeing with others, and maybe scratching your head in other places. This is also good.

Whether you agree, disagree, or just want to ask me a question, then please reach out and tell me. I'd love to hear your side of the story. Please check out "**Getting Engaged with this Book and its Author**" for contact channels.

My perspective on Project Management

When I talk about "project management", I take the broadest possible perspective on the meaning of both those words. For me, any goal-seeking human endeavour is a project, regardless of the goal, how many people are involved, its duration or how it is managed.

My perspective on how to manage projects is to take a contingency approach, which is to say match the management strategy to the specific project you're managing. If they truly are unique, then we manage them with a unique combination of strategy, process, and tools.

Of course, there are patterns that we re-use, but use is dictated by circumstance. *"Form follows function,"* as the Bauhaus folks used to say.

I'm not particularly interested in "methodology shootouts" and have little time for "black hat, white hat" comparisons of this approach with some other approach.

That said, I don't oppose the concept of *"Bodies of Knowledge"* or *"Branded Methodologies"*. I'm more concerned about the unquestioned adoption and excessive evangelism of their promoters. The IT industry is a battleground of methodologies, but success relies more on our ability to think freely and apply the right tools in any given context.

The content

This book contains a collection of assertions about the practice of Project Management, drawing on my 40+ years of experience in Information Technology (IT) project management. See **"About the Author"** for more detail on my experience.

Because I hold that projects need a contingency approach, and anything can be a project, project managers need to know how to **"think their way around"** any project so they don't get captured by context or situation or pre-conceived ideas.

By understanding these axioms, readers can gain insight into the underlying nuts and bolts of project management, enabling more effective navigation of their challenges.

Most axioms are my original formulations, some are adaptations of others' ideas, and a few are direct quotes.

Despite being "axiomatic", they are not indisputable facts, but my judgements, opinions and experience, written up assertions. They offer a reference point for consideration and analysis. Agreement, disagreement, or even disproving these axioms equally proves their value.

You'll probably find some duplication in theme and content across the different axioms. This is the product of structuring the content as assertions that don't fit into the traditional structures of projects. I've tried to minimise this and put cross-reference links to relevant topics, but some duplication is inevitable.

Parting Thoughts

I invite your engagement and differing opinions, underlining the dynamic nature of project management wisdom. I encourage you to reach out using one of the contact channels I've listed here: **"Getting Engaged with this Book and its Author"**.

Above all, I invite you to think.

How to Read This Book

What this book is—and is not.

This book is not a prescriptive guide or a textbook on project management methodologies. There is no test for you to pass, and no certification to put on your resume. The value in this book is whether it challenges you to ***"think your way around a project"***, independently of whatever methodologies or toolsets they may be using.

This book is a compilation of my perspectives on rules, heuristics, and observations showing how projects run in the real world and how project managers should approach them.

What do you mean by "Axiom"?

Each axiom contains a nugget of "**truth**", as I see it, about some aspect of Project Management. The axioms are mid-level: not low-level detailed instruction or explanation of some technique, and not high-level generic commentary that is hard to match to a PM's lived experience.

The axioms highlight critical aspects of projects that apply to multiple situations and types of projects, though they may not apply universally.

The axioms are written using the same structure:

- **The Axiom**: the axiom in a sentence.
- **The TL;DR**: the "Too Long; Didn't Read" overview of the axiom.
- **The Back Story**: the background, experiential or theoretical basis for the axiom.
- **The Bottom Line**: the conclusion or takeaway.
- **The Tags**: a set of keywords that help you search for similar references.

Sometimes, I'll follow these sections with a story or anecdote that was too long to fit nicely into the other sections. Or I may include a "tip" for a specific technique or approach that could help in implementing the rule.

Whilst the axioms are essentially stand-alone, they often cover similar ground as other axioms, but from a different perspective.

The Project Management Version of "The Knowledge"

One way to think about "Adam's Axioms" is as a project management equivalent of **"The Knowledge"**[1] used by London taxi drivers.

Just as "The Knowledge" ties together multiple facts and facets of London's streets and landmarks, the axioms, and their corollaries in this book connect various aspects of project management processes.

"The Knowledge" uses a pedagogical device of 26 "runs" or specific routes through London. As candidate taxi drivers learn these runs, they accumulate the vast factual detail attached to each run. And more importantly, they learn how to adapt to changing conditions in the face of traffic problems, construction, and other impediments.

In a similar way, I've grouped these axioms into higher-order themes that look at a topic from a common perspective.

What would a Guru Project Manager do in this situation?

By understanding these axioms, readers can gain insight into the underlying nuts and bolts of project management, enabling more effective navigation of their challenges.

I envisage project managers facing a situation they hadn't encountered before and looking for advice. The PM can look up one or more axioms and read what I say about that situation.

If you're in a situation in one of your projects, and you ever ask yourself, *"What would an experienced PM do?"* or *"What would a project management expert say about this situation?"*, then these axioms are designed to be a guide.

As such, I didn't intend for you to read these axioms serially from start to finish. Just dig in anywhere that relates to your current thinking on a project.

In the future, it would be good to group them as a complete slice through the different stages of a project's lifecycle - much more like the 26 "runs" in "The Knowledge". But I'll probably do that in the online material I'm working up for readers of this book.

---

[1]https://en.wikipedia.org/wiki/Taxis_of_the_United_Kingdom#The_Knowledge

On Project Success

The primary goal of any project is to achieve success. However, success can have various interpretations. For instance, plan-based or "waterfall" projects are deemed successful if they are delivered within the scope, schedule, and budget.

Conversely, agile projects must meet the "Definition of Done."

However, ultimately it is the end-users and stakeholders who evaluate whether a project is successful or not, regardless of whether the project's deliverables meet these various definitions of success. The end-users of a project's outputs don't live in a world called "Scrum" or "PMBOK". They live in their reality, so success is defined in their terms.

This section examines the concept of success from that perspective.

1. The source of project success.

Project success flows from people thinking and working naturally together.

The Axiom

Project success flows from people thinking and working naturally together.

The TL;DR

This axiom is the foundation of successful goal-oriented human endeavours. Successful project outcomes are dependent on leveraging the ancient forces of human cognition and social bonding, which is one foundation of the Agile Manifesto. The highly-efficent, highly-autonomous, and egalitarian traits of early human and Hunter-Gatherer societies guide how current project teams work. Cooperation and sharing were critical for survival. By leveraging our social nature and unique cognitive abilities, we can overcome obstacles, push the boundaries of what is possible, and achieve great success. However, the last 500 years of political, social and organisational development were intended to suppress or thwart these innate human tendencies even while - in more recent times - organisations gave lip service to these characteristics. In reality, most organisations don't honestly want them working at scale.

The Back Story

Project success flows from people thinking and working naturally together. This is my project management "North Star" and guides how I approach every project.

This is the foundation of all successful projects, regardless of technology. It applies across all lifecycle models and methodologies. For any manager, understanding this axiom differentiates the truly great from the good or mediocre ones.

This concept embodies the intent of the Agile Manifesto and every team-focused management construct: they are all dependent on the ancient forces of human intelligence and social bonding that truly enable motivation and success.

In our current world of fads and short attention spans, the word "ancient" is both scary and highly relevant. While modern management theory and practice emerged approximately 300 years ago, and formalised traditional project management is over 50 years old, this axiom leverages capabilities and imperatives baked into the human genome for about two million years.

But what does all of this have to do with modern project teams and, in particular, why we have so many issues with modern projects?

Let's look at a very selective slice through two million years of agile practice.

First, we learned to plan (1m+ years ago)

While nobody knows what happened two million years ago, we can interpret the fossil record and durable surviving artifacts, and the last 20-30 years have improved researchers ability to analyse cellular and genetic structures.

Our hominid ancestors developed our uniquely structured and very large cerebral cortex around 1.5 million years ago. Researchers believe that this development enabled these emerging humans to use tools and plan for the future.

These abilities led to the development of social bonds and, ultimately, the emergence of modern humans. These highly adaptive characteristics enabled humans to evolve and dominate other hominid species until now.

Then we formed cross-functional teams (100k years ago)

To understand this, we must look at the core characteristics of Hunter-Gatherer societies and how they apply to modern teams. Hunter-Gatherer societies represent as close as possible to "naked" human beings, relying solely on their natural human resources and characteristics.

Anthropologists have studied modern Hunter-gatherer societies for over a hundred years, often representing First Nation peoples who existed for tens of thousands of years before the great age of European colonisation.

The traits of Hunter-Gatherer societies are highly relevant to understanding current project teams. These societies had a relatively egalitarian structure, with individuals having a high degree of autonomy and independence. Cooperation and sharing were critical for survival in these societies, suggesting that people in these societies may have been more naturally inclined to think and work together in a supportive and cooperative manner. These characteristics form the basis of "people thinking and working naturally together," a critical element of project success.

Robert Greene, in his book "Mastery" argues that two key aspects of human evolution have been critical to human success: social forces and vision. Greene writes that our social nature flows from multiple human capabilities:

- Advanced language abilities.
- Ability to form complex social networks.
- Capacity for empathy and altruism.
- Ability to work together to solve problems.

All of these must be nurtured and fostered in our project environments to maximise the benefit of a group endeavour.

Our advanced visual capabilities have allowed us to create and innovate in ways that are unique to our species. By leveraging our social nature and advanced cognitive abilities, we can overcome obstacles, push the boundaries of what is possible, and achieve greatness.

Applying these insights to project teams, we can see the potential benefits of creating a culture that promotes *"people thinking and working naturally together."* By leveraging the natural dynamics of group behaviour, we automatically enable an environment that displays cooperation, communication, and social learning. Understanding these two aspects of human evolution can unlock our full potential and help us achieve mastery in our chosen fields.

Then we invented companies, and threw it all away (~500 years).

But why are these characteristics so hard to develop now, and why are they so scarce? This is a complex question with many answers, but the essence is that they have been trained out of us for hundreds of years.

The establishment of modern corporations was based on the need for long-term predictability and outcomes for investors, which required very focused control of human work and behaviour over long periods.

In a nutshell, the last 500 years of organisational development, and the political support required to enable it, have trained people to suppress these innate human tendencies.

While organisations give lip service to the value of these characteristics, very few honestly want them working at scale.

Now, we're trying to build it back (50-100 years)

The Agile Manifesto wasn't the begining of our attempt to reclaim our innate human ability to operate in an agile fashion. Depending on who is measuring what aspect of human society this process began in the late 19th century and was accelerated by the devastating armed conflicts of the 20th century.

And more recently in 2022 and 2023, after the enormity of Covid-19's impacts on our society, it is interesting to hear the shrill demands of organisations insisting that workers return to the office, to be - once again - observed and managed in our work.

This imperative is far too important to think about it being only about software development, or a collection of methodologies, however funky their brand names sound. You'd better take an interest in this because it will determine the future of work.

The Bottom Line

Two million years of agile practice must have taught us something! By understanding the importance of *"people thinking and working naturally together,"* project managers can foster a culture that maximises the potential of their teams, ultimately leading to project success.

The Tags

#projectsuccess, #socialforces, #principlesofprojectsuccess, #agilemanifesto, #humanbonding, #agency, #autonomy, #socialnetworks, #sharedmentalmodels

2. Successful projects? We've got both kinds!

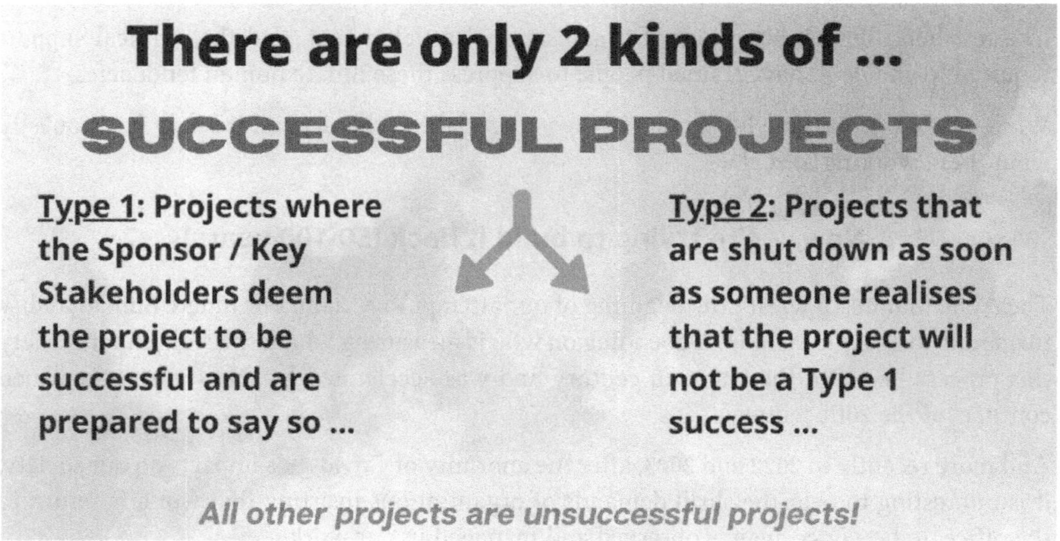

The Axiom

There are only two kinds of successful projects: sponsor signed off and explicitly shut down.

The TL;DR

The concept of successful projects is remarkably prominent in the project management narrative. You will find copious quantities of material about success factors and successful projects in books and blogs. But much of it is noise. In reality, there are only two kinds of successful projects. In the first kind, the Sponsor / Key Stakeholders decide that the project is a success. Not only are they happy to "sign off" on the project, but are willing to say so to their peers and promote the project as a success to stakeholders. In the second kind, stakeholders promptly shut down projects that are obviously not the first kind. All other projects are unsuccessful projects!

The Back Story

The unbearable lightness of value

Most projects prioritise deliverables over the desired outcome. Not only are projects focused on deliverables, but the project team rarely has a clear understanding of the business benefit.

This is not surprising: often the real business benefit is frustratingly fuzzy to all stakeholders. It's something that emerges over time.

But most project team members are builders, and it's difficult to code something fuzzy. Until AI came along anyway, but that's a different story.

> *(Note: if you're interested in AI and Project Management, please check out my book called **"Adam On: Advanced ChatGPT for Agile Project Management"**[1] for a detailed look at how to apply Generative Artificial Intelligence to your projects, using OpenAI's ChatGPT.)*
>
> For more of Adam's publications see the page: **"More from Adam Russell"**

And so when the goal is fuzzy, our brains switch focus to things that are definite: in projects these are the deliverables.

The conventional narrative of projects is that they are systems of concrete processes, inputs and outputs. But projects are about the "art of the possible"; how can we craft something of value in the face of uncertainty? In another axiom, we see projects are a *"bridge to an unknown future"* because we rarely know the result. Please see the axiom "**# 24. A project is a bridge**" for the origin of this concept.

The rolling assessment of value

The problem of a deliverables focus is that - as we see time and time again - deliverables mean nothing if they don't enable business value. But if you don't know the final business value until late in the project, how do you avoid the "deliverables myopia" that affects most projects?

The answer is a rolling assessment of value and working with as detailed a view of end-state value as possible. You relentlessly assess the value that the project can bring to your

[1] https://bjl.ink/chatgpt4apm/

stakeholders. You recalculate the value approximation whenever the project undergoes changes, such as delays or finding new knowledge about the problem domain.

Responsibility for value assessment

As PMs, we balance this rolling assessment of what is achievable against the likely cost which you can use to assess the project's viability. But who makes that judgement? It's not the project manager or project team. The responsibility for reassessing the expected enabled value lies with the project sponsor and other key stakeholders.

The project manager and team can play a significant role in this value assessment.

Effective stakeholder management involves managing expectations and proactively seeking hidden value. You can ensure a successful and satisfying project conclusion by co-creating value that wasn't immediately apparent.

> *"Just because something doesn't do what you planned it to do doesn't mean it's useless."* — **Thomas Alva Edison**

Bringing home the bacon

How do we bring a project to a close? Is it through a "project finalisation process"? No. Your sponsor brings the project to a close, preferably on your recommendation.

Ultimately, whatever projects or deliverables your sponsor "signs off" are deemed successful.

And I don't mean the salesperson-style *"you hold the pen and I'll move the paper"* sign-off - one in which the sponsor is persuaded, cajoled or even forced with a *"pistol to their heads"*.

Type 1 successful projects

Type 1 successful projects are characterised by the sponsor's genuine satisfaction with the outcome, even if it deviates from the original objectives. The sponsor provides a whole-hearted sign-off and is enthusiastic about promoting the project to their stakeholders and yours.

Ideally, there is a significant alignment between original expectations and eventual results, so the Type 1 success result is unsurprising.

But sometimes, the sponsor or end users get more than they expected or find an unexpected benefit from the project and see a successful outcome. Achieving a "Phase 1" output grows everyone's understanding of later phases as being unachievable or too risky. A successful project result can include cancelling "Phase 2" or beyond. The sponsor often sees this outcome as "dodging a bullet".

Type 2 successful projects

The other type of project success (Type 2) occurs when stakeholders explicitly decide to shut down a project because they recognise that achieving Type 1 success is not feasible.

Type 2 successes do not include the projects where we agree to narrow the objectives but still have a positive outcome.

You might wonder why this is considered a success. The answer is twofold:

First: avoided cost. Projects that will produce no beneficial result but are shut down early to avoid as much expenditure as possible.

Second: - and most important - it demonstrates a process success in managing the project and the relationship between the project team and the key stakeholders. Not only do we know enough about the project to make these decisions, but we also have a positive and open relationship with our stakeholders so that we can make these decisions and move on.

The project kill switch

In his August 2021 email newsletter, renowned agile author Mike Cohn called this concept the *"Project Kill Switch."* He explained:

> *"To avoid letting the scope creep up to where it does take [xx] months to deliver, you should set a kill switch at the very start of the project. If a kill switch is triggered, the project is cancelled."* — **Mike Cohn** in a subscriber email.

Mike's example of a type 2 successful project:

> *"a minimum viable product that doesn't achieve a certain goal—which could be usage, revenue, attention, or any of a number of other metrics. In this case, the kill switch could trigger cancelling the project outright or merely pivoting."* - **Mike Cohn**

But how do you work out when to trigger the kill switch?

The right way to estimate projects for success of either type

By understanding the value equation of your project, which includes the realisable value generated over time, you can determine the appropriate level of investment required to sustain that value.

This equation is fundamental investment analysis.

This analysis will give you the maximum budget your organisation is willing to invest to derive the value that your project plans to enable. Beyond this, your project is irrecoverably in the red. But you wouldn't want to use anything near that maximum. Your total budget for the entire project should be set at something less. From this budget you can also derive the component budgets for critical subsets of the budget, e.g., a prototype or MVP.

These financial targets serve as one trigger for your kill switch. If the project exceeds the predetermined sunk cost metric without achieving the required level of completion, it is a sign to trigger the kill switch and terminate the project.

The other kill switch trigger is stakeholder confidence: if you lose the confidence of your key stakeholders, your project is a "dead man walking."

The Bottom Line

The conventional measure of project success is meeting original expectations. However, this definition does not consider the numerous changes and variations that can arise during the project lifecycle. In reality, successful projects encompass not only those that meet the initial expectations, but also those that encompass multiple other achievements.

The Tags

#projectsuccess, #successfulprojects, #twokinds, #enablement, #stakeholders, #stakeholdermanagement, #projectkillswitch, #mikecohn, #thomasalvaedison, #fastfail, #mvp, #prototype

3. Why do projects fail?

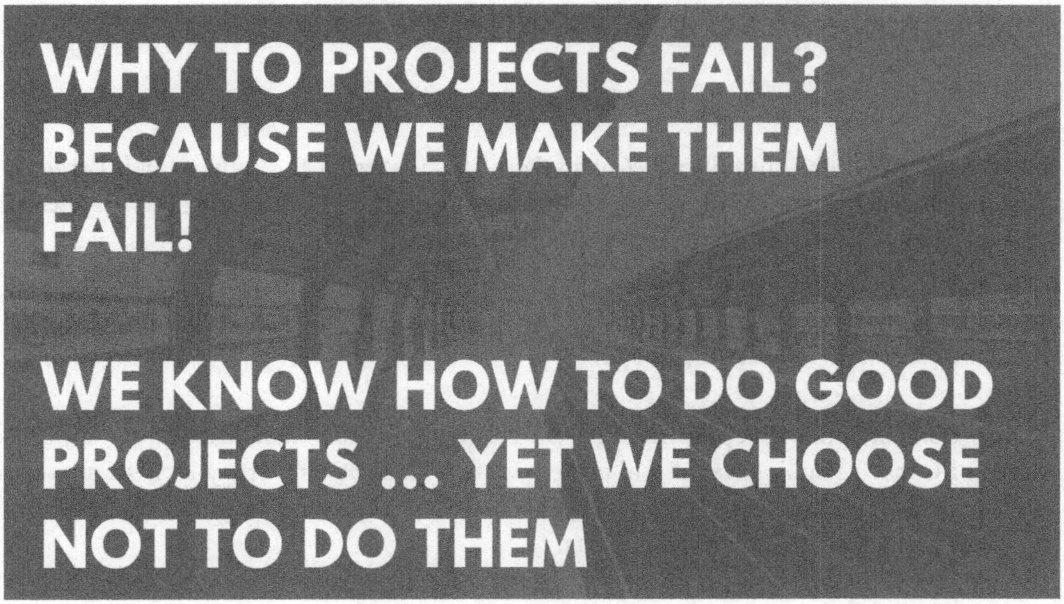

The Axiom

Projects fail because we make them fail!

The TL;DR

Projects fail because we make them fail! We know how to do good projects, yet we choose not to do them. In other words, the most common cause of project failure is our own actions and decisions. Projects continue to fail despite the widespread use of Agile methodologies and project management education. This suggests that there are underlying reasons why we choose not to implement successful project practices. The root cause is often generic, such as not engaging the right people with the right skillsets, not validating vendor assertions, starting projects without knowing requirements, and not having the proper governance. We make our projects fail by not addressing these fundamental problems. It's not easy, but unless we do, we'll continue to perpetuate ***Cobb's Paradox***.

The Back Story

What is ***Cobb's Paradox***? Who is Cobb and why is this "paradox" paramount to successful project management.

Cobbs Paradox

In 1995, Martin Cobb introduced *"Cobb's Law,"* also referred to as the *"Cobb Paradox."* This law highlights the perplexing question of why projects continue to fail despite our understanding of the reasons behind their failure.

> *"We know why [programs] fail; we know how to prevent their failure—so why do they still fail?"* - **Martin Cobb** (1995)

Martin Cobb was the Chief Information Officer (CIO) for the Secretariat of the Treasury Board of Canada. Cobb gave an oral presentation to CHAOS University in 1995, at which the Standish Group analysed the top ten most complex IT projects they had studied in the previous year (1994). Of these ten projects:

> *"... eight were over schedule, on average, by a factor of 1.6 and over budget by a factor of 1.9; the other two were cancelled and never delivered anything."* — **J.W. Carl and G.R. Freeman**, 2010 in "Nonstationary root causes of Cobb's paradox."

Extending the Paradox

Carl and Freeman's analysis is significant as it distinguishes between "stationary" and "nonstationary" environmental factors in a project, shedding light on the challenges faced by project management. A "nonstationary" factor changes over time, whereas a stationary factor does not change other than perhaps to reduce in intensity due to conscious effort by the project team.

> *"Nonstationary environmental factors prevent requirements from being established early with the thought that they will not change. They will certainly change independent of the degree of discipline and process maturity on the part of the system developer."* — **J.W. Carl and G.R. Freeman**, 2010. "Nonstationary root causes of Cobb's paradox."

In recognising nonstationary project factors, we see the genesis of Agile lifecycle models and the numerous questions they asked traditional project management. But, to this day, we still have the same puzzle: projects fail despite the massive growth of project management education and the pervasive use of Agile methodologies.

It's not random

Despite having access to extensive information on the root causes of project failure, projects still fail or face significant challenges. This raises the question of why projects continue to fail despite the existence of methodologies, tools, and techniques aimed at preventing failure.

It's almost as if we deliberately set out to fail by setting up and running projects based on concepts that we know will result in failure.

Again, we ask, "Why"?

The answer is that most projects fail because we make them fail.

We make projects fail by doing the things we know - or should know - will impair them. Or we make projects fail by omitting the things we know will feed success. Projects are still being run by teams and stakeholders who ignore the fundamental truths at the foundation of project success. Projects still get funding based on crazy premises.

This proposition on project failure is not a segue into a debate about Agile vs traditional projects. I'm not talking about adopting some methodology or other as some "silver bullet". In fact that debate is a positive indicator of teams that will make their projects fail.

How do we make them fail?

Many sins of commission and omission can lead to project failure or hinder their progress. These include:

- Not engaging people with the right skillsets and enough of them.
- Accepting vendor assertions about product capabilities without sufficient validation.
- Starting projects without knowing even the most basic requirements, having a vision or knowing how to develop either of these.
- Believing that a vendor or software package will reverse engineer your requirements for you.
- Buying and rolling out tools and methodologies we don't understand or can't use.
- Forming (and imposing) arbitrary timeline or cost constraints.

- Operating only in the solution or technical space and ignoring the problem / business domain.
- Not having the proper governance to help steer the project through difficulties.
- Not asking the hard objective questions that cut through the BS.
- Not engaging with user stakeholders and users and creating a sense of engagement and accountability.
- Reliance on simplistic ceremonies or process artifacts as if they were "magic potions" that can change the world simply by saying their names.
- Allowing or even facilitating ineffective team dynamics that result in team dysfunction.

I could go on and on - we haven't really scratched the surface of these project impacting issues.

By not addressing these fundamental problems, we make our projects fail.

In my experience, the number of projects that fail for these and similar reasons overwhelmingly outweighs projects that failed due to some "Black Swan" event or terminal change. Of course these happen, but not so many.

False choices

The root cause of all this - apart from ignorance (wilful or otherwise) - is that decisions are made based on stereotypes, memes and false dichotomies.

One of the most detrimental false dichotomies in project management is the belief that projects must choose between being fast and nimble or slow and process-driven.

This false trade-off can lead to dysfunctional behaviours, for example if teams (and their managers) believe that they know best and don't need to consult with business users about requirements. Or they develop the mindset that any form of process or formal technique will only "slow the project down" and "get bogged in red tape".

There are plenty of examples where that sort of thing happens, painful process mapping or requirements elicitation sessions that nobody uses or poor testing constructs that consume vast amounts of time and money with little effect on overall quality. These memes are fed by real experience.

But these examples are just more cases of doing things wrong, or worse, doing things dumb.

All that this type of approach proves is that there is a real dichotomy - the range of behaviour between "smart" and "dumb" - and that they are on the "dumb" end of it.

Pros and Cons of different lifecycle models

While there are debates about the pros and cons of different lifecycle models and project structures, it is crucial to focus on the core truths that underpin successful project management. I hope (and believe) that this collection of axioms distills some of those core truths.

It's really pretty simple.

Projects that are conceived or executed badly or stupidly tend to end badly or stupidly.

The Bottom Line

Despite the belief that we have made progress in ensuring project success, projects continue to fail because of common mistakes and oversights. I'm sure many practitioners think that in 2023 and beyond, we've taken steps to ensure every project succeeds. Sadly, it's not very sexy or easy to address these fundamental factors. But unless you do, you will just be promoting Cobb's Paradox for future projects and generations of project managers. Don't do it.

The Tags

#projectfailure, #projectsuccess, #cobbslaw, #cobbsparadox, #projectmanagementapproach, #failureaccountability, #martincobb, #chaosreport, #jwcarl, #grfreeman, #stationarycauses

---

4. If you want your project to succeed, move your ass!

The Axiom

Elapsed time is the most significant source of risk in most projects.

The TL;DR

Projects are complex beasts that require careful management to ensure their success. Elapsed time is one of the most significant factors impacting project success.

Time is not just a measure of duration but also a proxy for many other risk factors, such as changing project scope, external factors, lack of resources, and ineffective project management practices.

In this post, we will explore aspects of elapsed time and the risks that accrue as time goes by. We'll also look at the detrimental effect of the S-Curve concept, and use the ideas behind Critical Chain Scheduling to illustrate the problem.

The Back Story

Projects are such complex beasts that any mathematical model would be enormously challenging to calculate and understand. But we can simplify the complexity by using approximations and simpler models.

The probability of success

A good place to start is basic probability of success over time.

Let's start by considering the example of a coin toss: the simplest probability model - at least in concept. We know that the notional probability of getting heads or tails is approximately even - 50%. If you toss a coin 1000 times in a row, the likelihood of getting a head on the last toss is precisely the same as on the first. However, the probability of getting a particular sequence of heads and tails over a 1000-toss series is tiny: 2 to the 1000th power.

Similarly, in project management, time is a measure of probability. Every day is a coin-toss that a risk event will or won't occur. Imagine that a "head" coin toss is that the risk event doesn't occur. So, if you toss a "tail" you get a risk event. In many cases the probability of risk events is much less than 50%, but there are far more events. So, conceptually, you are daily tossing hundreds, thousands or more "risk event coins" hoping for a "head" on each one, each and every day.

The longer a project takes, the more "risk event coins" you have to toss, and the greater the likelihood of you tossing some tails and something going wrong.

If we extend the thought experiment a little, your risk event profile consists of many potential events with a wide range of probabilities and a wide range of impacts. You're pretty sure that some of those "risk event coins" will come down tails, but you're hoping that they are all low-impact events.

A project that takes six months is more likely to face unexpected challenges than a project that takes three months. Therefore, reducing elapsed time can help reduce the likelihood of project failure.

You might think that time is only one risk out of many, but it has its unique dynamic and is a proxy for many other types of risk. One example of a contributor to project delays is the "S-Curve".

S-Curve is a false concept

The S-Curve is a well-known concept in project management that suggests that the project starts slowly and gains momentum over time. Strictly speaking, the S-Curve tracks project expenditure — one of its many weaknesses — and is based on an outdated concept that maps expenditure to value. But it's so common in project management as to be a meme taken at face value. The S-Curve can be misleading in its abstract form, leading to a false sense of security. In reality, the early stages of the project are often the most critical in terms of defining scope, identifying risks, and establishing a solid foundation for project success.

In my opinion, engagement of the critical business and technical resources immediately at the start of a project is more urgent and vital than later. This urgency is because the number and size of the unknown are much more significant at the beginning, and assumptions about business value and technological capability must be validated as early as possible. My experience tells me that these assumptions are frequently invalid in whole or in part. Unless these errors are removed early on, they become part of the team's and stakeholders' incorporated expectations.

For a different perspective on the S-Curve, refer to Axiom "**# 91. Forget all about the S-Curve!**" in "**Adam On: Projects (Volume 2)**"[2],

Critical Chain Scheduling as a reference concept

Critical Chain Scheduling (CCS) is one approach that directly highlights the elapsed time issue.

I'm not introducing CCS to sell a technique but to use its approach to illustrate the elapsed time risk to projects. Amongst other aspects of CCS is that it requires teams to build a baseline schedule and then halve the elapsed time of their tasks and hand that time back to the project manager. The premise behind this is that all baseline schedules, no matter how many times they've been reviewed, are overestimated, specifically:

1. Every estimated task includes a hidden buffer, whether deliberate or accidental.
2. Every project is over-scoped.

The project manager retains the 50% buffer in CCS, and the published project completion date remains per the baseline schedule. If teams have problems with their CCS schedule, the PM has a cushion to assign them after a detailed review of the delay causes.

[2]https://bjl.ink/aopv2

As with many techniques, you can follow them religiously or use them to get accurate alignment and visibility. From my perspective - the reason for raising it here is- the latter.

So, if you are looking at alternative solutions or project approaches, and all other things being equal, choose the option that results in the shortest duration. And when you are running the project, do everything you can to drive it forward quickly. Always assuming, of course, that you want the project to complete.

The Bottom Line

A project is far more complex than a series of coin tosses. And as Project managers, we think we have a level of control over the outcome that will help improve our chances of success. But in reality, we know far less in practice than we think. The tools and processes give us a sense of "false concreteness" that disguises the variability that lives underneath the surface. The biggest thing you can do to control the outcome is to reduce the number of coin tosses, i.e., reduce your duration. So, keep your projects short and sharp, and you massively increase their chances of success. Or, to put it bluntly: *"Move your ass."*

The Tags

#projectmanagementapproach, #projectmanagermindsets, #risk, #schedule, #projectschedule, #deadlines, #scurve, #CriticalChainScheduling

---

On Projects and Project Management

The concept of a 'project' varies widely depending on your perspective on industry, profession and even general life paradigm. A formally trained professional project manager sees projects in one way, and an Agile-certified practitioner sees them entirely differently.

Dozens of definitions of 'project' are phrased to further the interests of a particular perspective.

Yet the concept of a 'project' at its most generic is the seminal organising framework for all human goal-seeking endeavours. Projects are the natural way people think and work together.

5. The power of the dog.

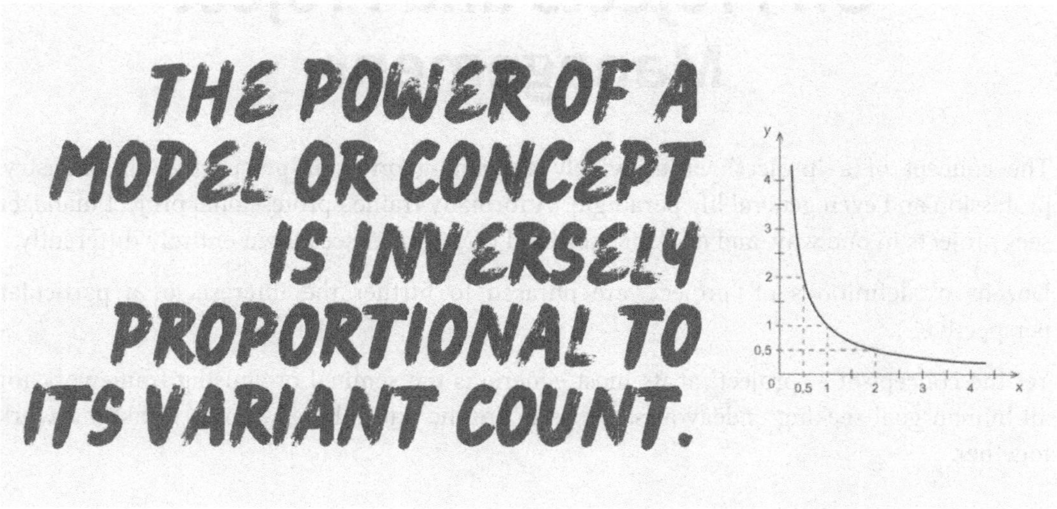

The Axiom

The power of a model or concept is inversely proportional to its variant count.

The TL;DR

Various concepts and ideas pervade traditional and Agile project management, some interesting and others weak. We also find that some ideas have many variations, such as the definition of a project or the "**Iron Triangle**". Why is this, and how does this eventuate? One answer is the use of "**memetics**" to analyse units of cultural information ("**memes**"). By comparing genetic variations with adaptive memes, these units of cultural knowledge can help their "owners" succeed in an organisational context. Groups of cooperating memes - "**memeplexes**" - ensure the survival and propagation of multiple memes. I observe that highly adaptive memes have few variants, regardless of their accuracy. The "Iron Triangle" and the definition of a project are ideas with many variants and are less potent. Tuckman's Model of Team Formation is a successful meme. Relying on strong but inaccurate memes can derail project success.

The Back Story

Why do some ideas stay around for years, but others die out or splinter into multiple variations that are each less successful than the original? And why are the concepts that sometimes thrive turn out to be flaky, incorrect, or even mythical?

Memes and the Memeplex

Stephen J Whitty (Whitty, 2011) hypothesises that ideas can be like genes in biological evolution: they can help or hinder their "owner" to compete in their respective environments. Adaptive genetic variations enhance the survival and reproduction of their "host" organisms in their environment. Memes - or cultural information units - are adaptive when they contribute to the success of their owners and are subsequently transmitted to others. Such transmission often occurs when the holder of the meme holds authority or influence.

Whitty describes "memeplexes" as collections of memes that work together to ensure their survival and propagation. The field of Project Management appears to be one such "memeplex".

The evidence of a strongly adaptive gene is that it passes from generation to generation largely intact. Weak genes are removed from a population quite quickly when their "owners" fall to competition. And in the middle are genes that are not strong enough to survive but which spawn variations in an attempt to find a more adaptive form.

Such is the case with an evolutionary view of memes.

An Example - Tuckman on Team Formation

This example might be the most successful meme ever given that it transcends project management and is used in every field of human activity where small teams form.

This is **Tuckman's Model of Team Formation**. If you've ever investigated or studied team formation, Tuckman's model will be familiar to you.

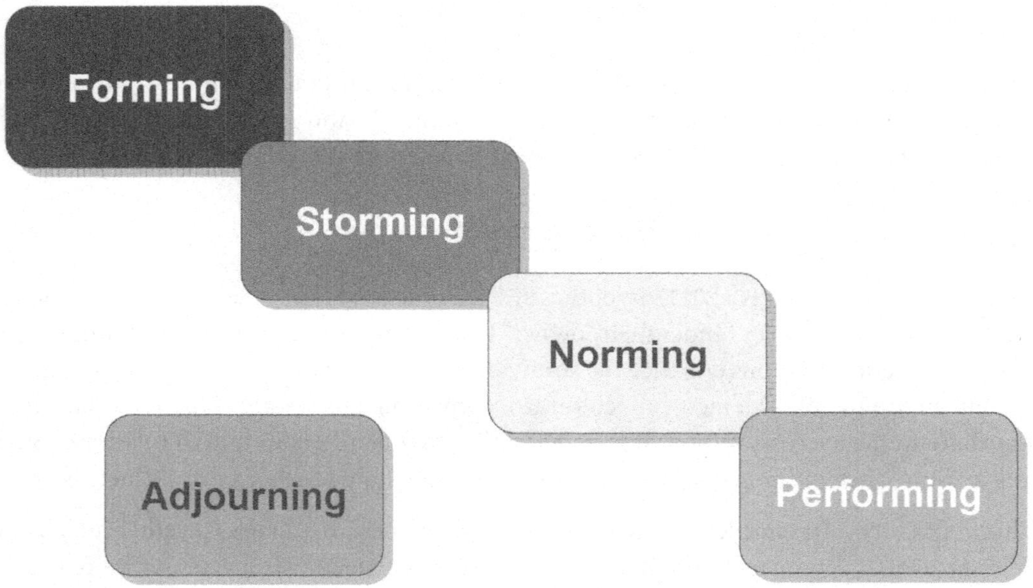

Figure 1. Tuckmans Team Formation Phases (Source: Knight, 2007)

Sometimes called the "Tuckman Ladder, the model proposes teams must pass through several distinct stages on the journey from "just formed" to "high efficacy". These stages are called "Forming", "Storming", "Norming", and "Performing".

Tuckman's model has been remarkably successful in business circles since it was coined over 50 years ago. It has become so popular that it is accepted as fact in most management circles. It was even included in the Project Management Institute's PMBOK Edition 7 as a Project Team development model. This model has few variants; the most significant variant is an addition (the "Adjourning" stage) that Tuckman proposed himself.

The enormous success of this "meme" comes although Tuckman developed this theory based on literature research with no direct, hands-on research of his own. According to one paper (Bonebright, 2010), the model was the result of an assignment given to Tuckman by his supervisor at the Naval Medical Research Centre in Bethesda, Maryland, who had collected articles on group development and asked him to review them.

The original names for these stages were unexciting to everyday readers: *"1) testing and dependence, 2) intragroup conflict, 3) development of group cohesion, and 4) functional role relatedness"* (Tuckman and Jensen 1977). Tuckman created the simplified names in the article summary. Tuckman himself called out the limitations of the study in a follow-up paper, Tuckman and Jensen (1977). In addition, the model hasn't been replicated by any other researcher since. One study (Knight, 2007) clearly identified that small-group behaviour did not follow the pattern defined by Tuckman. The diagram below shows two distinct activities of "Forming" and "Performing" as per the theory, but also shows "Storming" as a more or less constant background activity, and "Norming" also tracks in parallel to most activities.

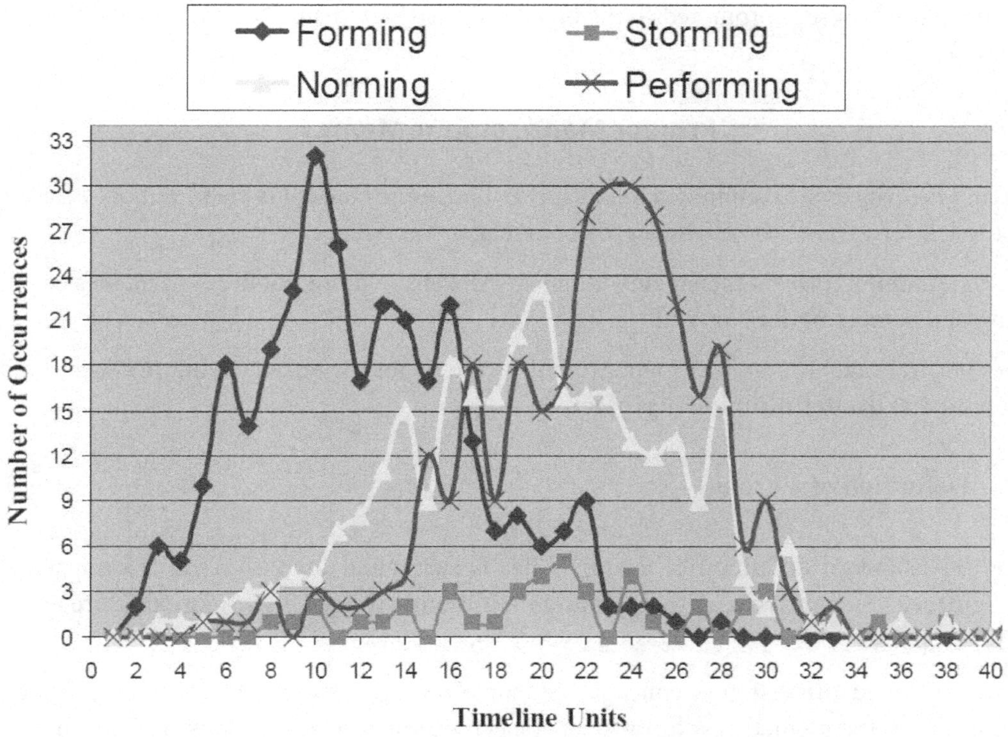

Figure 2. Teaming activities mapped to Tuckman Phases (Source: Knight, 2007)

So, with all these factors that limit the applicability of Tuckman's model, why has it become so pervasive? This is the power of a meme to survive, created by the following attributes:

1. Simple concepts (compare the one-word names to the original academic titles).
2. Easy to explain to others (critical).
3. Plausible (it sounds reasonable).
4. When explained and applied, it is adaptive for the explainer.

These four attributes explain why other concepts have succeeded, even if they were sub-optimal or even wrong.

For more on team formation, see the axioms, "**# 47. How do teams self-organise?**" and "**# 56. Invest in alignment!**".

I have gone into some detail on Tuckman to illustrate the memetic evolutionary concept: ideas can be successful because they are adaptive for their "owners" not because they are core truths. In other words, in the management domains where Tuckman had most applicability, the people who used, promoted, built upon and distributed survived and thrived in their domain.

Project Management Memes

Having described one example in detail above, I hope the concept is clear. In this section I'll just touch on some of the obvious project management memes.

The "**memeplex**" project management includes dozens — if not hundreds of memes cooperating and competing for survival.

The first example of a project management meme is not the strongest but it's where most people start: the **definition of a project**.

1. **Definition of a Project**

The PMI standard definition of a project has been around for years and is compact and straightforward. But there are many other definitions - thirty (30) or more that are used in different places.

It would be adaptive if this concept — "meme" — of a project construct were strong. According to the memetic evolutionary perspective, one interpretation is that the "project" meme is strong enough to survive but not strong enough to survive unchanged: it has adapted over time in a struggle to find a more adaptive form.

2. **The Iron Triangle**

Another example is the "**Iron Triangle**". If you google this meme, you'll find dozens of variations, each presumably created by a practitioner who felt that existing versions didn't meet their needs or match their lived experience.

3. **"The Waterfall Lifecycle"**

Waterfall is another meme. Single-pass Waterfall became the dominant lifecycle methodology for decades and is still in use today. This despite the huge body of work that showed that it did not work. Iterative and Incremental Development was widespread before management became so enamoured with Waterfall. For more information on why the Waterfall model is wrong, see the axiom, "**# 97. What if there never was a 'Waterfall'?**" in "**Adam On: Projects (Volume 2)**"[1].

4. **Work Breakdown Structure**

The "**Work Breakdown Structure**" is another one yet again - it still hasn't recovered from the "work really means product" repositioning - probably because all the examples include work and other elements.

5. **The S-Curve**

And the "**S-Curve**" has so many variants that it's hard to understand what it is trying to achieve. It is based on the premise that financial expenditure is a proxy for project completeness, and originated in population studies in ecology. You can read more about this in the axiom, "**# 91. Forget all about the S-Curve!?**" in "**Adam On: Projects (Volume 2)**"[2].

Broader Management Memes

If we want to abstract a little from project management tools, Whitty (2011) enumerates an entire collection of management memes that derive from Puritan beliefs and ethics, including:

- the Protestant Work Ethic.
- Managerialism.
- Reductionism.
- Efficiency (and from that we derive Productivity).

Each of these memes spall into an enormous set of variations, doctrinal schisms, and factional interpretations. The adaptive strengths of these memes is demonstrated by their continued prominence in the management narrative.

[1]https://bjl.ink/aopv2
[2]https://bjl.ink/aopv2

The Bottom Line

The scarcity of variants often indicates the power and influence of an idea – a "meme". However, this does not mean that it is correct. Tuckman's model was founded on little or no research and has not been replicated by other researchers. And yet it has withstood the test of time. If we base our planning and execution of projects on strong memes that prove wrong, is it any wonder that our projects go awry?

The Tags

#projectconstruct, #projectdefinition, #enablement, #principlesofprojectsuccess, #memes, #memeplex, #informationmanagement, #pmi, #projectmanagementinstitute, #agile, #memetics, #adaptive, #stephenjwhitty, #tuckman

The References

1. **Bonebright, D. A. (2010).** 40 years of storming: a historical review of Tuckman's model of small group development. Human Resource Development International, 13(1), 111-120.
2. **Knight, P. (2007).** Acquisition Community Team Dynamics: The Tuckman Model vs. the DAU Model. Proceedings of the 4th Annual Acquisition Research Symposium of the Naval Postgraduate School. Naval Postgraduate School
3. **Tuckman, B. W., & Jensen, M. A. C. (1977).** Stages of small-group development revisited. Group & organisation studies, 2(4), 419-427.
4. **Whitty, S. J. (2011).** On a new philosophy of project management: An investigation into the prevalence of modern project management by means of an evolutionary framework. International journal of managing projects in business, 4(3), 524-533.

6. What is a project?

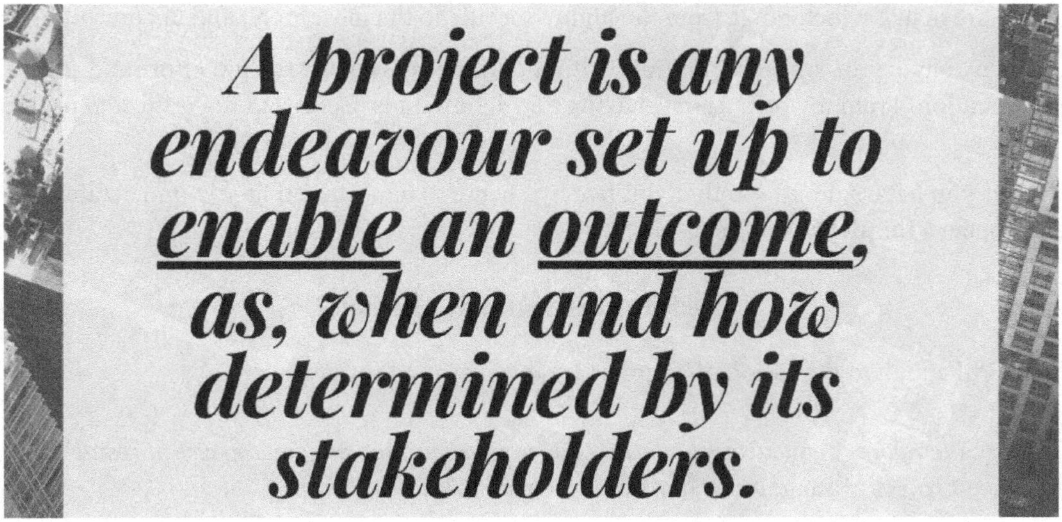

The Axiom

A project is any endeavour established to enable an outcome, as, when and how determined by its stakeholders.

The TL;DR

The only thing fixed about the definition of a project is that set up to enable an outcome, and everything else is determined by its context and stakeholders. In the traditional project management narrative, we must do projects in a specific way. They must be "one-off" or structured, have a project manager, or conform to the "Iron Triangle". However, despite this fixed perspective of a "project," there are dozens of definitions of the term. Still, none are generic enough to include all goal-oriented human endeavours. This axiom defines the project without all the methodological scaffolding. Projects must be infinitely flexible in their setup and execution to address a limitless range of problems combined with an endless combination of people and circumstances.

The Back Story

For some PMs and stakeholders, there is only one standard definition of a project. For others, there are many, which range from the highly specific to the most broad and unconventional.

Perhaps having an agreed definition is unimportant and not worth the effort and mental aggravation. From my perspective, having one definition is useful, but not critical to project success.

But, if you have a definition that you live by, then it is important that you understand why you believe this definition to be true.

The "Gold Standard" - or is it?

The PMI standard definition of a project has been around for years:

> *"A temporary endeavour undertaken to create a unique product, service or result"*
> — **Project Management Institute** in PMBOK Ed 7

This definition appears compact and straightforward, but it is bound into the traditional view of a project. Two simple words lock this definition into the entire historical body of knowledge. The words "**temporary**" and "**unique**" bind this simple definition into a vast cascading set of other definitions, assumptions, and implications for managing projects.

For example, "**temporary**" locks in the concept that project resources are only ever assigned while their skills and efforts are required. The term "**unique**" ties down the idea of a project into "one-off" outputs that are not repetitive.

These and other linked concepts come as one bound-together "lump" you must accept. They are founded on the need to differentiate project management as a distinct management practice. Those promoting project management needed to differentiate their newly emerging discipline from other management disciplines by creating wedges that split existing concepts into two categories: "**general management**" and "**project management**".

However, strategic usefulness does not equate to correctness or value.

Do we really need 30+ definitions of "Project"

A personal rule of thumb about concepts is that the less understood they are, the more alternative definitions or representations there will be for the concept. I expand on this in the axiom "**# 5. The power of the dog**".

The concept of "**project**" and, by extension, that of "**project management**" is a prime example.

Look through the definitions in Max Wideman's "Project Management Glossary[3]", which lists thirty-four of them when I last looked. Pick up any book on project management: you're just as likely to find a new one as one of Max's. Not only does the collection highlight the vast diversity of definitions, but Max also provides helpful editorial commentary and an interesting analysis of the origins of many of these terms[4].

This collection of definitions is only those arising from plan-based or "traditional" project management.

Do we need thirty or more definitions for the term "project"? Most of these definitions are similar; some are interesting or even weird. But they all use many elements that are not definitional. Most seem to pack as much into the definition to nail down some specific vision.

Are all these definitions talking about the same thing?

Creating an unbound definition

Creating a definition of "**project**" that is not bound into specific interests and stands alone is very simple. Just remove all the project-specific attributes, domain terminology, and methodological vested interests. And this is what you get:

> ***Any endeavour established to enable an outcome.***

Add in the necessity that your stakeholders determine almost every aspect of any project: how it executes, what it builds and its lifecycle model.

Thus, we have this final definition (and this axiom):

> ***A project is any endeavour established to enable an outcome, as, when and how***

[3]http://www.maxwideman.com/pmglossary/PMG_P12.htm#Project
[4]http://www.maxwideman.com/musings/name.htm

> ***determined by its stakeholders.***

This definition aligns very much with the Contingency model of projects: there is no fixed or perfect approach. Construct the project according to need and context. This contingent definition of what is needed for each specific project is co-constructed by its stakeholders.

It's that simple, and that's all you need to describe and differentiate projects from other human activities.

Projects then and now range in size, complexity, and the underlying materials used to deliver the results, be it whale carcass products, steel, or software. A project could be as simple as weeding a garden or vast and complex: a minutely planned and controlled endeavour that will launch the next mission to Mars (and bring them back), lasting over decades.

If you think about your experiences in everyday life, you'll quickly identify many projects you routinely carry out that are not considered projects according to traditional definitions, but which naturally fall into the definition in this axiom.

What makes a project is not project management tools and processes. Social forces, societal history, and knowledge enabled a collective endeavour in which people thought and worked naturally together. These are the common elements of all projects.

You can always add the tools and processes if you find you need them.

A whimsical definition

After looking at all the detail and practice-technicalities, I want to leave you with this whimsical definition from Max Wideman:

> *"a chaotic venture to some unknown destination - a randomised voyage of discovery with a total absence of management"* - **Max Wideman**[5]

If Max's contention is correct, which I believe it to be, anything can be a project.

What do you think?

[5]http://www.maxwideman.com/papers/institutional_context/perspective.htm

The Bottom Line

We don't lose anything with this definition, which includes all traditional projects, agile initiatives, and any different endeavours to which we want to apply project management perspectives, techniques, and tools. It makes simple projects easy and complex ones possible.

The Tags

#projectconstruct, #projectdefinition, #enablement, #principlesofprojectsuccess

7. Be the right kind of project manager.

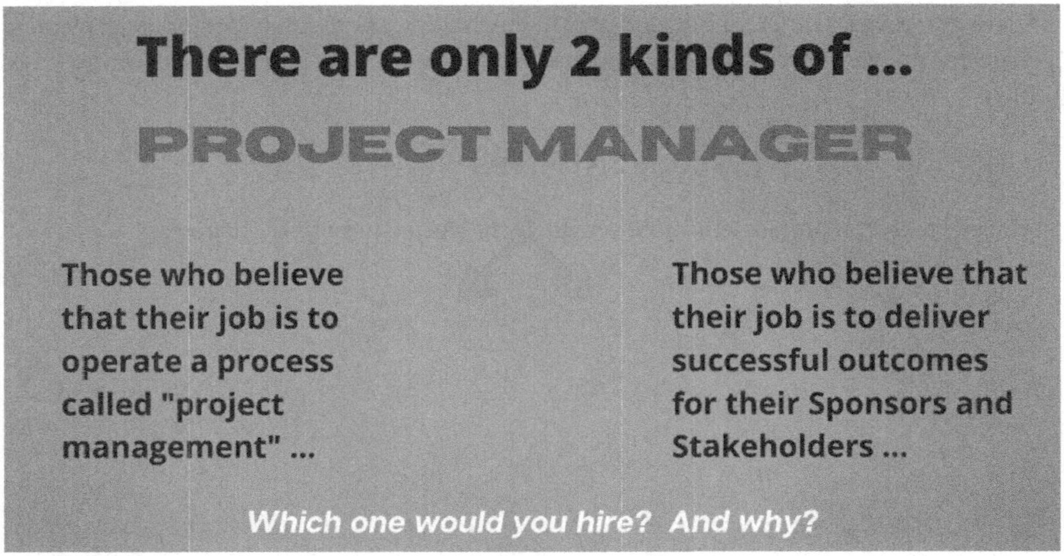

The Axiom

Be the kind of project manager who believes their job is to enable successful outcomes for their stakeholders.

The TL;DR

Project managers and the people they work with think of the PM in terms of many specialised aspects of their work, e.g. what lifecycle model they work in ("an *Agile Project Manager*"), or the software package they work with ("an *Oracle Finance Project Manager*"), or the domain practice they build solutions for ("a *CyberSecurity Project Manager*") and so on. But at the most fundamental level, there are only two kinds of project managers. Firstly, those who believe their job is to operate a process called "**project management**" and, secondly, those who think their job is to enable successful outcomes for their Sponsors and Stakeholders. Be the second kind.

The Back Story

There are many different kinds of project manager measured in all variety of dimensions: nationality, personal style, levels of experience, and many more.

But where it counts most, the world is divided neatly into two types.

Why do many project managers focus on tools and processes?

Why are so many project managers prone to focus on processes, tools, and outputs instead of people and outcomes?

This question never really goes away.

It could be because that's how project management was framed way back when it was carved out of the general management domain. The mechanism for defining project management was to express it through processes. But were the people who created those frameworks doing it because that was the way project management worked naturally? Or was it because their mindsets — their dominant "Paradigm Zero" — inclined that way?

Paradigm Zero may explain why

I define "Paradigm Zero" as the most fundamental paradigm anyone adopts: it is used to view reality and knowledge. Please refer to the axiom **"# 113. What is Your approach to documentation?"** in **"Adam On: Projects (Volume 2)"**[6], for more information about "Paradigm Zero". In summary, people with a "Hard" Paradigm Zero believe that reality is fixed and context-free and that all knowledge pre-exists, waiting to be discovered. On the other hand, people at the other end of this spectrum believe that reality is not fixed but depends on the context and that knowledge is co-created with other people. I describe these folks as having a "Soft" Paradigm Zero.

In any case, the vast bulk of material written or said about project management supports the "Hard Paradigm Zero", and this pretty much defines the landscape of project management.

There have been changes since Agile was born and became successful. Twenty years of market success, academic research and practitioner experience have pushed project management towards the "Soft" end of the Paradigm Zero scale. Except that the traditional authors of the project management narrative still frame "soft" characteristics in "hard" ways - it's like they can't help themselves.

[6]https://bjl.ink/aopv2

Simplified, normative training drives the "hard" perspective.

Why is this?

I think it is driven partly by historical inertia and partly due to the explosion in the certification business.

The economic engine of certification demands more customers to continue its growth. The best marketing tool is a proliferation of successful candidates. So, the courses must have a reasonably high pass rate. Not everyone, of course, but enough to make it attractive. So students develop high expectations of passing and getting their "cert".

As numbers grow, the accreditation delivery needs to be more streamlined. More resources move online and adapt to the needs of the engine. Online examinations require relatively simple test models: multiple-choice answers and open-ended text responses usually need more time and expensive resources to assess.

So, the content that supports the course material - which professional associations call "Bodies of Knowledge" or "Standards" have to change their intent. Their purpose becomes less about how to solve project management problems and more about defining the boundaries of a profession. And the professional boundaries define certification as a significant element of qualification. So, these bodies of knowledge evolve away from solving real-world, messy problems and more towards simplified and generic use cases. To support the certification process, the content must converge students concepts not diverge - it must be both **"learnable"** and **"testable"**.

The material that makes up professional standards adapts to the needs of certification exams, and it becomes more codified and prescriptive. Nuances and complexity are lost, replaced by long lists of simple statements and learnable facts.

What do we end up with? A body of knowledge more designed to support a lucrative certification process with reasonably high pass rate expectations. Employers look to these certifications as evidence of competence, which drives a "signalling" process in job candidates who believe they must highlight their certifications to improve their job prospects. As these credentials appear more often as job requirements, more candidates are driven to sign up to a course.

So, the certification tail wags the process guideline dog.

The Bottom Line

Anecdotally and in my experience, this is borne out by the project managers I see who emphasise this axiom. The project manager who wants to operate a methodology or framework will never be able to deal with the complexities of real-world projects. The other kind of project manager sees their role to enable their Sponsor's value ideas. They may also know methodology or framework but only care about them if they help achieve the goal.

The Tags

#twokinds, #projectmanagementskills, #projectmanagermindsets, #mindsets, #agile, #pmbok, #certifications

---

8. Practice Minimal Responsible Intervention.

> Project managers must practice **Minimum Responsible Intervention** - don't push any process or technique onto your team that does not solve an identified problem ... don't do or decide anything that your team members can do or decide ... don't call a meeting that is not absolutely required ... unless there is a specific reason to intervene, let them get on with it.

The Axiom

The overriding management principle for a Project Manager must be Minimum Responsible Intervention.

The TL;DR

Project Managers are trained to manage: to exert influence, to persuade, to direct, to intervene. They often see themselves as the centre of the endeavour; the "CEO" of the project. However, project managers should be slow to insert themselves into the team's working processes unless required. Only suggest — and if necessary, inject — tools or techniques when they offer specific benefits to the project team, and there is no alternative way to achieve a particular outcome in the project. Trust your team's abilities — and their ability to evolve and grow — but support them when needed. This practice is called Minimum Responsible Intervention (MRI).

The Back Story

Many Project Managers (PMs) insert themselves into their team's activities and decisions. Sometimes, PMs cannot help themselves. But one attribute of an excellent Project Manager is someone who only intervenes when necessary.

This axiom is expanded in "**# 9. The last resort custodian**".

What is Minimum Responsible Intervention?

Minimum Responsible Intervention (MRI) is a management approach that encourages and facilitates teams to work together effectively and efficiently using their innate abilities. Managers should be slow to intervene in the team's processes and be there to support when needed. Any tools, techniques, or guidance injected by a PM should only happen when there's a clear value proposition for their addition to the project.

I often tell my teams, *"Your productivity goes up when I leave the room."* This statement, half-serious and half-joking, highlights the core idea behind MRI – giving teams the space to grow and excel on their terms.

MRI fosters an environment where team members can naturally think and work together, leveraging their complementary strengths and allowing social bonding and ethical principles to guide their collaboration.

What is Intervention?

"Intervention" is the project manager injecting themselves into the day-to-day working of a team. In many projects, Project Managers intervene with their teams frequently and in multiple ways. The traditional concept of "managing" is founded on intervention – how managers interact with their teams to get them working on and completing their work as agreed.

An intervention is any action a manager takes that changes the way a team goes about its work, such as:

- Calling a meeting to obtain the status of work.
- Setting the priority or sequence of work, individually or for the whole team.
- Telling someone they should do something in a particular way or using a specific technique or tool.
- unilaterally deciding to hire a new person to join the team.

- Committing the team to achieve some work in a particular timeframe, with little or no consultation.

Does Management Intervention Help the Team?

Management Intervention is common — I'm sure very few people would say any of the above actions are uncommon.

But is intervention helpful to the team? I don't think so. At least not unless is has been explicitly requested by the team, or the circumstances warrant overriding the team's workflow.

Even if the manager has the power to do these things, the question is whether they increase the team's efficacy. Efficacy means not only the ability of the team to produce the desired result but also that this is done sustainably — the team binds and grows in the process.

Once a manager intervenes on a topic or issue, the team will likely expect the manager to take the lead. This is often true even if the manager is less skilful than the project team or does a worse job. Once they start "owning" - even partially - a process or decision, then they are stuck with it. Following intervention on a topic or issue, the team is likely the manager to take the lead on subsequent occurrences of that topic.

Often a manager - and I'd say I've been in this category - intervenes because they think that they are the most highly skilled person at a particular task, and that if they don't do it then an inferior quality job will be the result.

What that manager doesn't realise is that:

1. The power of task ownership gives great motivation.
2. The satisfaction of achievement builds awesome morale.
3. There are many ways to do a task that will result in a satisfactory outcome.
4. With most jobs there is high tolerance for variance and outcome - it simply doesn't matter if the job is done a particular way.
5. Managers are just as susceptible to Dunning-Kruger bias about their skill levels as anyone, usually because no-one argues when they say they will do things which bolsters their opinion of their skills.

How Can You Apply MRI to Your Project

There are four ways you can perform MRI in your projects:

1. **Let the team work**: Encourage the team to collaborate and find their solutions, only stepping in when necessary.
2. **Assess value**: Before introducing a new tool or technique, consider whether it adds value to the project and if the team can manage without it.
3. **Support, don't impose**: Offer support and guidance when needed, but avoid dictating how the team should work. For example, openly communicate the idea behind MRI so that they know you're not ignoring them, just letting them get on with their work.
4. **Evaluate and adjust**: Continuously assess the team's performance and make changes only when it contributes to project success. See the axiom, ***"# 27. The triple helix of Agile evolution."***.

Why do we need to practice MRI?

Adopting the interventionist managerial approach — the standard project managerial style - makes you a mandatory participant in every project process. This construct never works. Once you put your hands on something, the team will always expect you to be involved in that something.

Minimum Responsible Intervention is the opposite of what most Project Managers are taught — it's as if the concept of a PM is of someone who "directs" the activities of the project team and stakeholders.

The Bottom Line

Remember, a manager's first responsibility is to do no harm. If you intervene without an explicit value proposition, you risk reducing team efficacy and their ability to grow and learn. ***Minimum Responsible Intervention*** emphasises the importance of trust, collaboration, and empowering teams to leverage their natural human skills. By practising MRI, managers can foster a productive working environment, leading to more successful projects and team growth. Remember, as a project manager, sometimes the best thing you can do for your team is to step back and let them shine.

The Tags

#projectmanagement, #projectmanagementskills, #minimumresponsibleintervention, #self-managedteams, #prematureoptimisation, #managementinterference

9. The last resort custodian.

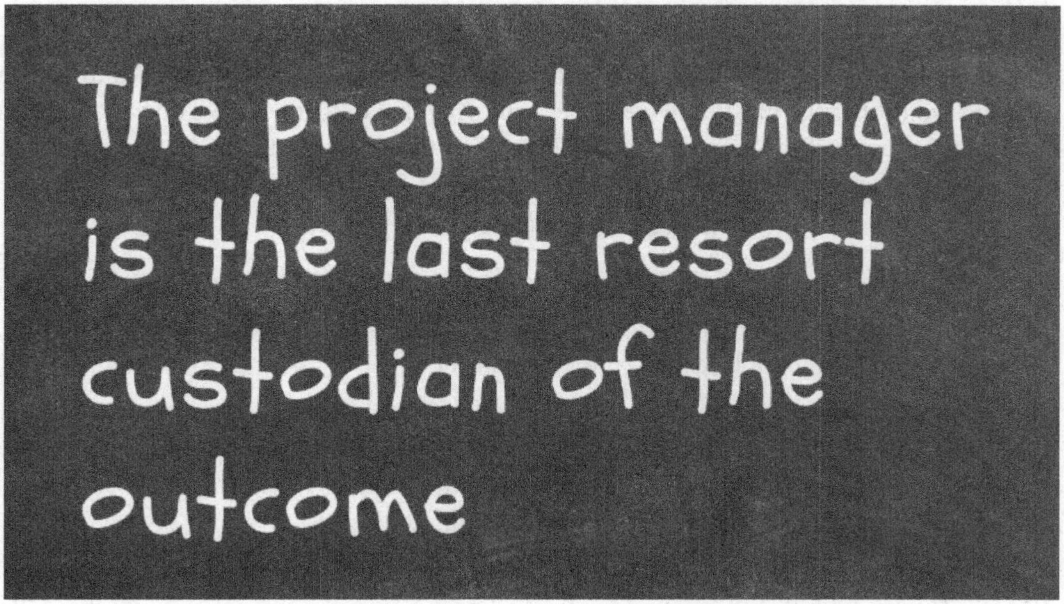

The Axiom

The project manager is the last resort custodian of the outcome.

The TL;DR

The role of the project manager is traditionally described as the "CEO of a Project". If that terminology isn't used explicitly, describing the role gives a similar tone and gravitas. But the actual role of a project manager is to enable the target outcome through the actions of others: the project team and other stakeholders. The PM's responsibility is to orchestrate the teams to deliver. A PM cannot deliver a project on their own. That is, of course, unless there is a failure of accountability or action by a team member or group. At that point, the PM must ensure the project completes and the outcome is enabled.

The Back Story

A project is a human endeavour created to enable an outcome - see the axiom "**# 6. What is a project?**".

If that is the definition of a project then the role of the Project Manager (PM) is to ensure that the project has the maximum chance of achieving that outcome unless other conditions apply, for example, if the project stakeholders decide to shut down the project.

Fulfilling the Project Manager Role

The role of a PM can be fulfilled in multiple ways. The traditional model of a PM is a single person who is designated to perform the role. This is the most common model you'll find, although the role may not be called "project manager".

You will find different perspectives on what the role of PM should do. One perspective is that they follow established project management practices. Another is that they are a facilitator for a self-organising team that decides for itself what processes it will follow. In such cases the PM may be given a different title or role description.

The role of PM can also be shared, as in the "**Decentralised Autonomous Organisation**" (DAO). The part of the PM may also be performed by someone who is not formally designated as the PM but is merely a good influencer.

How do we unify these varying and often contradictory requirements into an actionable strategy?

The Perfect Project Manager

For the answer, we look to a yarn written by Tom Peters on the nature of being a project manager in 1991 called "In Search of the Perfect Project Manager".

Tom was recognised as a thought leader in Management practice in the 1980s when he wrote In Search of Excellence, followed by many other books. Tom explored the nature of the Project Manager role in the early 1990s (notably well before Agile formalised itself) and was an early advocate of the benefits of projects as change agents in organisations — he promoted the concept that *"everything is a project"*.

I remember reading this article sometime in the mid-1990s, and I think it was around when I worked at Hewlett-Packard. It was one of the turning points in my career as it sought to define Project Management outside the bounds of traditional frameworks such as PMBOK and as an everyday business process.

Amongst other things, I decided that I could reach the goal of being this "Perfect Project Manager" and that it was a worthwhile objective to pursue.

This extract sets the context beautifully:

> *"But as "project" and "network" become the norm, "who's in charge?" becomes problematic. Everyone needs to learn to work in teams, "with" multiple, independent experts, often from multiple, independent companies; each will be dependent upon all the others voluntarily giving their best. The new lead actor/"boss"—the project manager—must learn to command and coach; that is, to deal with paradox. Here are eight dilemmas she or he must master"* — **Tom Peters** "Pursuing the Perfect Project Manager.

Balancing between Autocrat and Delegator

One of Peter's eight dilemmas is the tension between the project manager as an "Autocrat" and a "Delegator" —two ends of a continuum. In Peter's view, the project manager must *"Delegate unless there is no one else who can be right 'in the moment'"* but can switch instantly to the "Autocrat" behaviour when required.

In Peter's model, the "Autocrat" role is to be adopted only as a last resort - someone in the project must be decisive to ensure that the right things happen at the right time. Often all that is needed is to keep the panic at bay so that whoever can fix the problem can do their job. This person doesn't need to be the PM, but the PM needs to make sure that if nobody else does, that s/he does: to be the last resort: to make sure somebody in the team responds.

This ability to delegate yet be ready to ensure nothing gets missed is a prime capability for any project manager. In theory, a PM is the most expendable team member because the team's capabilities and activities cover everything necessary for project success.

As a PM, What do you do?

Try this exercise: look at what you are doing in your daily activities as a PM. Try keeping a daily journal. At the end of a week, go through it and put a line through the following types of activity:

1. *Activities that only service a concept of "project management"*: for example, writing reports, maintaining lists, cross-checking between documents.

2. *Activities you do to help other people do their jobs*: set up meetings, chase down people for task status, try to figure out why someone or a team is not meeting their committed timelines, escalate to more senior managers when you can't figure things out, etc. These activities are the responsibility of the task owners, not the project managers.
3. *Managing project artifacts*: for example, specifications, document signoff, and reviews of documentation.

All these tasks are things that each task or deliverable owner should be doing as a matter of their day-to-day responsibilities, and a project manager shouldn't be doing these things at all.

Everything a PM does can be done by someone else - Almost

Once you've completed the review, what is left on your list? What are the tasks that genuinely cannot be done by anyone other than the PM? You'll find that all of them can be done by someone else.

And yet we do. Why? There are two reasons:

1. *Make work*: project managers often see (or have been trained to see) this type of work as their job, or they don't know what else to do with 8 hours a day (or whatever utilisation they are assigned to the project).
2. *Laziness*: it's easy to hand off boring or mechanical jobs to other people — like having a personal assistant.
3. *Lack of time*: sometimes, how people are assigned to projects means they share the project with a day-to-day job and timeshare between them. Or they are given to other projects, and the available utilisation percentage is insufficient to cover this project's work.
4. *Lack of Capability*: people come in various shapes and sizes — everyone is different. Some people aren't wired to do some tasks that end up on a PM's slate.

Number 3 (Lack of time) happens mostly with senior managers, like your project sponsor. In theory, this person should be very active in the project because they are responsible for capturing the benefits. Your sponsor should be leaning into this project and ensuring that everything that needs to be done gets done.

You may not have removed these in the mistaken belief that these are PM accountabilities. Nothing is left if we eliminate all tasks related to responsibility for the outcome.

Suppose any tasks are left over in your list. In that case, they can be tackled only by someone with a deep understanding of project processes — someone with long experience who can characterise problems quickly and advise on solutions.

The last custodian of the outcome

So, if everything could be done by another team member or stakeholder what defines a PM? The answer is: the person or people who act as the "guarantors" of the outcome. The people who will always keep the outcome in mind and step in where necessary to ensure it is not lost.

When I use the word "outcome" I mean it in the context of the behaviour that is enabled for a customer or end-user. In other words the thing(s) they can do or value they can capture after the project is done.

Maintaining an outcome perspective is very difficult in project teams. It's all to easy - and common - for technology, technique and process to dominate the thought processes of the teams. So someone has to own it.

Whoever that person is (individual or composite) holds the role of Project Manager.

The Bottom Line

These are the tasks a PM should spend their time on, even if it appears they are doing very little. You could argue that a PM needs to be "hands-on" in multiple project activities to jump in and take control at any given time. I agree that there is some merit in that viewpoint. But unless this is handled carefully, the cost in compromised team structures is far greater than apparently "idle" PM neurons.

The Tags

#projectmanagementskills, #projectmanager, #enablement, #principlesofprojectsuccess, #abundance, #teambehaviour, #teams, #agency, #tompeters, #perfectprojectmanager

---

10. Shut the fuck up and listen!

The Axiom

Shut the fuck up, and listen!

The TL;DR

Project managers (PMs) usually talk too damned much. But you need to listen if you're going to be a successful PM—it's both a skill and a practise that you cannot succeed without. Other team members likely know more than you about topics important to the project. Other team members are probably closer to the problems or situations than you are. Whatever their situation—having more or less knowledge or experience than you—you must find that out quickly. If people in the team are generally quiet and not participative, then you need to start coaching or nudging them along the learning curve, so they improve. No project team benefits from non-participative team members—interaction is critical to successful teaming. And the best way to encourage that participation is to shut the fuck up.

The Back Story

PMs Like to Talk

As a “breed”, Project Managers (PMs) like to talk.

I’m not sure what it is, but most PMs think they need to be in the driver’s seat all the time: chair all the meetings, be the loudest voice in the room, drone out statuses, progress reports, or process instructions. Perhaps the personality type attracted to the PM role has this sense that their role in a project is to talk. Or maybe it’s just the nature of the position.

I know I suffer from this habit and must consciously work to stop myself. It’s natural to talk when I know what I’m about to say will be valuable — and probably the best comment or suggestion anyone could make. (that was a joke).

Correcting this habit is tough

Many of us do this unconsciously, and correcting unconscious habits is tough. I was in a management training stream on an assignment a while back. The course facilitator approached me in a break and said — very nicely — that my habit of always answering questions first inhibited some other folks and that I should think about whether I always needed to be first. She offered me a tip when I told her it was largely unconscious. (See the end of this axiom for ”The Tip”)

It’s not an original statement to say that managers generally must be good listeners; I’m not even sure where this originated. But Project Managers need to exercise this skill, especially temporary PMs (as in on contract or short-term assignment, who often know less about the project organisation than they do about the technology or domain).

But, everyone else in the project should be talking: they are the ones doing the work and know the conditions/situation “on the ground” in their areas of the organisation.

Enabling the PM’s Value

A PM’s most outstanding value in a project is to facilitate others in the team to deliver on their accountabilities. This value proposition applies whether in the actual deliverable or how it is executed. Raising concerns promptly, highlighting delays or blockages, and reporting accurate status are often the hardest things to get out of people on a project. Most people don’t feel able to voice the actual situation. Maybe they don’t know how to describe it, but most likely, they haven’t learned the skill of objectively raising a concern or issue that doesn’t sound like whingeing/whining.

For additional background on these concepts, check out the Axioms "" in "**# 8. Practice Minimal Responsible Intervention**", and "**# 9. The last resort custodian**".

A PM needs to have much input into a project, no doubt. But that input doesn't need to be talking.

Just listen.

The Bottom Line

For many people, the hardest thing to do is to allow silence in a discussion — they feel the need to fill it with something. This point is often made in courses on negotiation techniques that if you allow a space in the conversation, someone will feel the need to fill the gap and consequently lose some position in the negotiation. But for project managers, silence serves a different purpose — the need to let your team or other stakeholders participate.

The Tip

If you're in a situation where you are always (or mostly) the first person to talk, whether you are the PM, a team member, or a stakeholder, then try this tip.

1. Grab a sharp pencil or biro and put the sharp point on the ball of your thumb.
2. Listen carefully when whoever is talking sounds like they are about to ask a question or invite others to provide commentary or input to speak.
3. Press your thumb down gently — just enough to distract your attention from answering.
4. This will focus your attention momentarily and allow you to let someone else talk.

I tried this technique, and it worked really well. I let someone else talk first, perhaps more than one person. Then I could say what I was going to say, if someone else hadn't already covered it. Sometimes I would decide that what I was going to say wasn't that important after all.

Three things happened after I started using that technique:

1. I stopped answering first and let many people have their say.
2. Quite a few people asked me if I was okay — was I feeling sick, or was something troubling me?
3. My partner asked me why I got blue biro ink on my shirts and could I please stop.

The Tags

#listening, #projectmanagementskills, #communications, #communicationsskills, #interactions, #listeningskills, #birotechnique

---

11. The critical skill for a Project Manager.

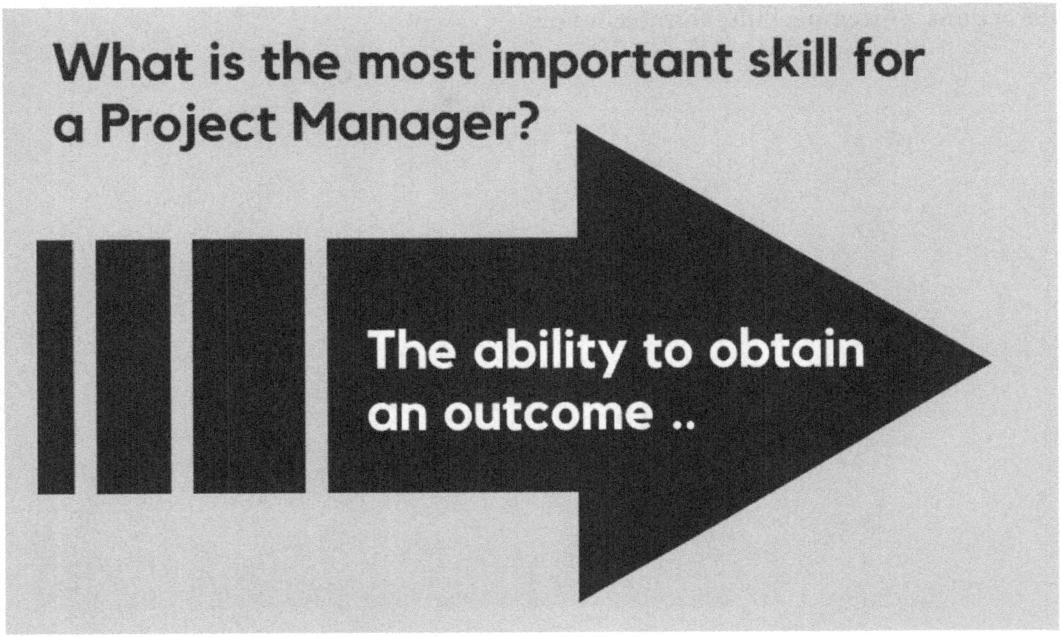

The Axiom

The critical skill for a Project Manager is the ability to obtain an outcome.

The TL;DR

Successful projects emerge from a long series of decision points at which stakeholders decide to move forward. These decisions may be implied and tacit as well as explicit and spoken. And the decision points range vastly in size and scope. These decisions result in outcomes that enable the project to proceed. Most decisions are not made spontaneously in any group activity; they require facilitation. At any of these decision points, one or more stakeholders might just as well have decided to pause, stop or go a different way, impacting your project's progress, direction, or even ultimate success. As a project manager, your primary job is to obtain these outcomes or to create or promote the environment that locks in these outcomes. Thus, the primary skill for a project manager is the ability to get these outcomes.

The Back Story

A successful project is the aggregate of many decisions, actions, and knowledge acquisitions over its life. The completion of each of these is an outcome of varying size in relation to the project's ultimate outcomes for its customer(s). Each completed step enables something in the downstream value chain.

Outputs, Outcomes and Enablement.

An outcome is the intended effect of a deliverable. A deliverable (an output) **enables** one or more outcomes. This is true at many levels of the project, from tiny deliverables exchanged between team members, up through the interim deliverables or components up to the final project outcomes.

As with the hierarchy of outputs, there is a hierarchy of outcomes and enablement within the project. Think of a project as a network of enablement in which team members hand-off deliverables that in turn enable other team members to perform their jobs.

A project is the aggregate of all the outcomes of a project throughout its life. As project managers, we must lock in outcomes at every level and stage of a project. By this process we lock in enablement and increase the effectiveness of our project activities.

Locking in outcomes drives a project to successful completion.

You'll find more about deliverables in the axiom **"# 90. Change your thinking about deliverables!?"** in **"Adam On: Projects (Volume 2)"**[7].

Don't ignore simple outcomes - they are the foundation for big outcomes.

Large and Complex outcomes are the project manager's normal work product. Most PMs have processes and techniques for dealing with those. What PMs ignore or simply treat differently are the simple and small outcomes.

Simple outcomes grow from the everyday interactions of your project team and stakeholders. What you might think of as regular and undifferentiated project activities. Examples could be:

1. A quick discussion in the hallway.
2. Getting the answer to a question.

---

[7] https://bjl.ink/aopv2

3. A meeting.
4. A design discussion.
5. A backlog review.

These interactions have three potential results:

- A locked-in outcome.
- An unstructured information exchange.
- A social touchpoint.

Interactions that result in locked-in outcomes have explicit value in our hierarchy of outcomes and web of enablement. Interactions that are an information exchange could be valuable or not depending on the quality of the information exchange. And those that are social touchpoints can have important team value but no direct effect on our project outcomes. Please refer to the axiom **"# 92. What are your hiring criteria?"** in **"Adam On: Projects (Volume 2)"**[8], for some background on the intrinsic value of interactions for project teams.

The more we can push our interactions up that value chain: from social touchpoints to information exchanges, and from information exchanges to locked-in outcomes, so we push our effectiveness in driving towards our final results. We add more to the accumulation of the project outcomes converging towards completion. Progressively, we build up to delivering all the project components, enabling the project outcomes and, ultimately, the planned impacts.

The more a team can build its simple interactions into explicit locked-in tiny outcomes, the more significant outcomes will build towards a whole project.

And so, in our five interaction examples above, how might they look at locked-in outcomes:

1. *A quick discussion in the hallway* becomes an **agreed understanding on some topic**.
2. *Getting the answer to a question* becomes a **validated fact**.
3. *A meeting* becomes a **set of recorded actions, issues and decisions**.
4. *A design discussion* becomes **a finalised design**.
5. *A backlog review* becomes a **prioritised and estimated backlog**.

A project manager must learn to see, hear and smell the *"outcome opportunities"* that present themselves to lock in even small outcomes from everyday interactions.

This ability is the most critical skill for a PM.

[8] https://bjl.ink/aopv2

How can you do this?

Here are five techniques for driving outcomes at every level

1. Prime your selective attention.
2. Never interact without an artifact.
3. Summarise key takeaways from every interaction.
4. Build an Outcome "Sales Funnel".
5. Always be Closing.

Prime your selective attention.

PMs can heighten their ability to recognise *"outcome opportunities"* by priming your cognitive resources - to put them *"on alert"*. If you train yourself in a particular thing: its form, function, component parts, and variations, you can prime yourself to be better at recognising those things automatically.

You are engaging your selective awareness so that it does not filter those patterns out of your perception: your brain is more likely to recognise that pattern in the noise of everyday project activities.

Never interact without an artifact.

You can improve the effectiveness of the tiny project interactions by always including something *"physical"*, or at least *"external"* as a discussion aid. This could be a diagram, a list of points, a specification document, or a virtual whiteboard. The possibilities are endless. This artifact will help ground the interaction on more concrete concepts, and to surface latent misunderstanding or gaps in shared knowledge.

For more information on this please refer to the axiom, **"# 79. Never interact without an artifact!"** in **"Adam On: Projects (Volume 2)"**[9], so that you have a framework for validating agreement and understanding (or otherwise).

Summarise key takeaways from every interaction.

Another method is straightforward but requires discipline always to remember to use: summarise the takeaways towards the end of each interaction.

[9] https://bjl.ink/aopv2

In simple interactions, it could just be a specific sentence or two to wrap up and confirm agreement.

In more significant interactions, like workshops or meetings, you interact verbally, but then document your understanding, and distribute it to interested stakeholders. The context will help you decide whether to write formal minutes with attendees, actions, decisions and similar content, even capturing what people said.

But I more frequently type out my *"Rough Notes of xxx discussion"* with very basic formatting, and then distribute via an informal collaboration platform (e.g. MS Teams or Confluence) with the comment: *"These are my rough notes, which may contain errors. If you want to change or delete anything, please give me a shout. Otherwise, I'll use them as is"*.

More significant outcomes usually have an established process governing the result's delivery. A software release cycle or a test process are other ways of locking in outcomes.

Build an Outcome "Sales Funnel".

A parallel for PM outcome locking resonated when I did some sales training many years ago. I think two aspects have good applicability for project managers: the Sales Funnel and The Close.

The sales funnel is a conceptual model describing a series of stages that a prospect follows between being unaware of the produce for sale and becoming a paying customer. It's a familiar concept. A salesperson develops a plan for each prospect that helps move them from stage to stage. Sometimes, this plan is formal and documented. Other times, it is tacit and instinctual. But regardless of how you define the sales plan, it is a framework that enables the salesperson to assess each interaction they have. They ask themselves, *"What will it take to get the prospect from (stage) A to (stage) B?"*. And afterwards, *"Did I help that prospect move from A to B?"*.

Each outcome has a lifecycle, no matter how tiny or fleeting. Build your "Sales Funnel" for each type of outcome and keep notes on the progress key outcomes are making through the lifecycle.

Always be Closing.

The final stage in the Sales Funnel is to turn the prospect into a paying customer. Navigating this last step is called "closing" the deal.

The 'art of closing' covers the many techniques, attitudes, and knowledge items salespeople use to obtain the last step in the sales process that locks in the sale. Some of these seem very manipulative to a non-salesperson, for example, a "tie-down" to get the prospect to answer a series of non-committal questions that accumulate towards a final sale. Another is called a "trial close", in which the salesperson will try out two alternatives, which implies they've already decided, for example, *"Would you want delivery in April or May?"*.

I'm not suggesting you start trying to "sell" your team or stakeholders, but knowing something about sales techniques will never hurt your ability to manage projects. But I strongly recommend you think of situations in projects in which the ability to move someone over the line would benefit everyone.

Tommy Hopkins wrote a great book called **"How to Master the Art of Selling"**, which I spent a lot of time reading, absorbing and practising. Although it's a bit old, it's still worth a read. Or google for books on sales techniques, emphasising "closing".

Selling is not for everyone. If you think managing projects to achieve a deadline is hard, you should try professional selling. No matter what your approach to sales might be, the entire operating tempo of the sales professional revolves around the sale event.

> *"Always be closing"* Blake (Alec Baldwin) from "Glengarry Glen Ross" by **David Mamet**

Just as a salesperson should always be closing, a Project Manager should always look for ways to structure an outcome.

The Bottom Line

A project professional should 'always be closing'. It's the process that helps validate understanding and commitment. It's where the rubber hits the road as far as agreement is concerned.

The Tags

#projectmanagementskills, #enablement, #value, #principlesofprojectsuccess, #closingthedeal, #outcomes, #decisionmaking, #decisions, #salestechniques, #davidmamet, #glengarryglenross, #tomhopkins, #salesfunnel

12. Be a Gowachin Project Manager

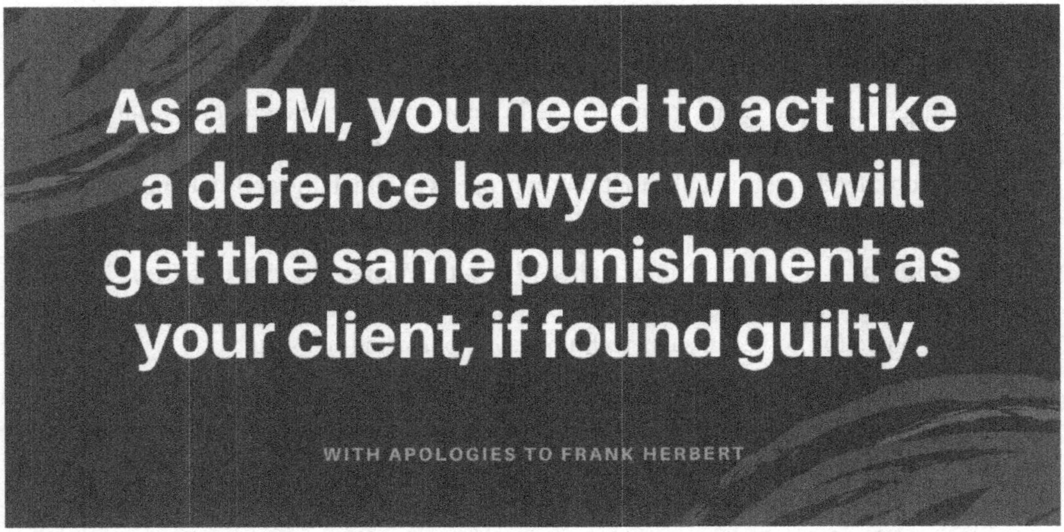

The Axiom

Act like a defence lawyer who will get the same punishment as their convicted client.

The TL;DR

In Frank Herbert's science fiction - he wrote the Dune books that are being released as movies - a fictional alien judicial system punishes the lawyer along with their convicted client. This is a powerful thought experiment or model for project managers as they go about their business: are my current actions and decisions the same as they would be if as PM they had to deal with the consequences of a failed project, as well as the sponsor? This thought experiment can help project managers take a broader perspective on the impact of their actions.

The Back Story

The world is full of relationships that appear symbiotic when things are going well, but which are, in fact, completely asymmetrical in terms of consequences when things turn bad. The classic meme is the surgeon who tells his unfortunate patient's relatives *"The operation was a success, but sadly the patient died"*. Project managers often seem to operate in the same mould, acting as if they can succeed even if the project is a disaster.

The Origin of this Axiom

One of my favourite movies for 2021 was Dune. Even though I wasn't aware that the movie covered only half of the first book, I still loved the way so many concepts from the books were rendered onto the big screen. Having read the Dune books in high-school, I've literally waited my whole adult life to see on the big screen the mental imagery the books stimulated.

Frank Herbert, the author of Dune, is one of my favourite science fiction writers. Herbert was a prolific science fiction writer who loved exploring socio-political-economic themes in great depth. Many times, he created whole societies within which to set his plots.

One fictional societies was the Gowachin. I won't go into too much detail, but they were - to human beings - a capricious, arbitrary, and somewhat cruel. The Gowachin system of justice was very contrarian to our thinking and the basis for this axiom (which is more a thought experiment).

There were many aspects of the Gowachin justice system, but the one used for this thought experiment was the standing of lawyers who were able to practice in the Gowachin courts. A defence lawyer representing a client was at the same level of jeopardy as the accused. The lawyer was subject to the same punishment as the defendant if convicted.

Literally "they" were guilty.

If you've ever been involved in a court case here on Earth, you may have noticed that the barristers say "we" a lot - giving at least the superficial sense of a team preparing to battle the enemy. Unfortunately, it is only superficial, and they are truly in the same category as surgeons: when there is a problem, it's the patient's problem.

What does this have to do with Project Management?

What has this got to do with project management? It is in the nature of who owns the outcome and what perspective a project manager should keep in mind when they are doing their jobs.

Instead, consider yourself as a defence lawyer and your sponsor as the defendant and you are operating under the Gowachin legal principles. Essentially, the sponsor is "on trial" for the satisfactory and successful completion of the project and on the value outcomes that will flow from the project's completion. They proposed the project, obtained the budget, and shepherded it through the approvals process.

In a human trial, whether the client is found guilty or not guilty, the defence lawyer gets to go home. In the analogy of bacon and eggs, the lawyer is the ultimate chicken and the client is the pig. But if the client is found guilty, the lawyer still gets to go home. They may lose some reputation or *"bragging rights"* by not securing a "not guilty" verdict, but that's pretty much it.

In projects, essentially the same thing happens. If the project is a failure, it is usually the sponsor who suffers that damage. The project manager may end up with some blowback, and even get fired - maybe for cause, or perhaps just as a scapegoat. But regardless of the outcome, the sponsor must live with the result. The project manager - unless they really were a stinker - goes on to manage another project. Situations like that can be explained away.

The Bottom Line

So, PMs, aim up! Look beyond "scope, schedule and budget". Think of the value that the project is supposed to enable. Instead of thinking about yourself as the lawyer who can breeze in and out of any case, think of yourself as a Gowachin lawyer. Would you do or say anything different if you were going to suffer the same? If the answer is "No" then fine, move on. But if the answer is "yes" then you need to think seriously about whether your position is correct.

The Tags

#projectmanagementmindsets, #projectmanagementskills, #enablement, #principlesofprojectsuccess

13. Projects are everywhere!

The Axiom

You can improve every human endeavour by viewing it through a project lens.

The TL;DR

The *"everything is a project"* mantra has been around since the 1990s with a mixed reception. The primary opponents of this perspective are the professional project management community, for whom the concept of a project is bound up with a particular set of criteria and the presence of a qualified project manager at its helm. However, the reality is that projects are everywhere, and most don't have project managers or even perceive themselves as projects. We can improve every human task or endeavour by viewing it through a project lens, even the most trivial and repetitive. All you need for a project to exist is the commitment to enable an outcome, as defined in the axiom "**# 6. What is a project?**".

The Back Story

"Everything is a project" is like the *"third rail"* topic of project management: step on it and you die! But I'm going to have a go.

The Conventional Narrative of projects

The conventional narrative about projects is very much founded on the concept of projects as a distinct form of management from the perspective of project managers. This narrative divides the world of business into *"Projects"* and *"Business as Usual"* ("**BAU**"), or routine operations, and every project has a project manager.

The narrative also holds that people naturally have a natural affinity for Projects or BAU based on their psychological makeup.

A false partitioning

Just as the New World was once arrogantly and preposterously divided in two parts, first by Pope Alexander VI and later by the Treaty of Tordesillas between Spain and Portugal, the "one-off" concept divides the world into two parts: a world of one-off projects and a world of repetitive "Business as Usual" containing repetitive operational tasks and processes.

This division into "Project" and "BAU" is as false as the global division created by Pope Alexander's Papal Bull in 1493.

A revised partitioning

My breakdown of the entire landscape of all *"goal-based human endeavours"*, looks like this:

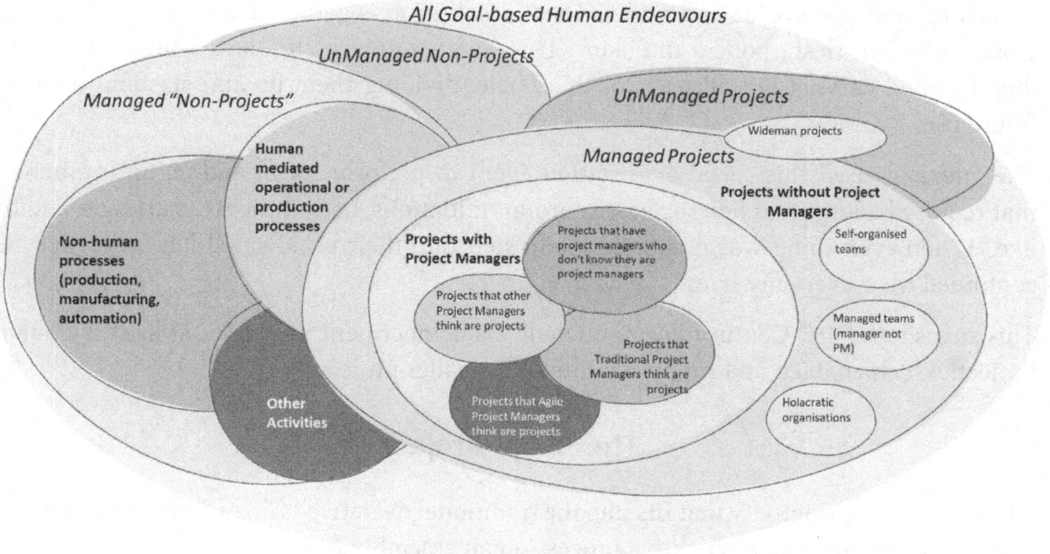

Figure 3. Breakdown of Goal-based Endeavours

Maybe my partitioning of this vast domain is not perfect, but it illustrates how vague some of these definitions have become. It's a complex world, and there are no easy definitions.

Projects in various forms have been around for tens of thousands of years, whether they were called *"projects"* or not. The history of project management focuses on monumental projects, like the Great Wall of China, the Pyramids of Egypt and the Panama Canal in recent times. Writers of historical project management draw from such massive projects many conclusions about the essence of project management. But significant, "nation-level" projects are outnumbered massively by the number of smaller projects at the local and individual levels.

Regardless of their size, some projects succeeded, and many failed, and humans devised various approaches to get them done. So, if projects succeeded before codified "project management" came into existence, how did that happen?

The social project

Here's an example: The people on Tierra del Fuego (before the arrival and influence of Europeans) lived in small family groups and kept to themselves. But sometimes, some unusual event would happen, say when a group found a beached whale carcass. In such circumstances, a different modality came into operation, and they activated pre-arranged signals to alert groups far and wide. These small groups gathered on site to harvest the whale: blubber, flesh, bones, and skin. This *"aggregation event"* lasted many days until they finished carving out all parts of the whale, dividing them up and stashing them for future use.

The Fuegians used this social aggregation event to perform social and cultural functions that required a large and heterogeneous group: initiations, betrothments, marriages and the like. When everything was done, the group split into their usual small family groups and continued their everyday lives.

This snapshot of 18th Century Fuegian whale dismemberment illustrates at least one major project, which enabled and supported multiple smaller projects.

The "BAU" Project

Lastly, let's take an activity that fits into the traditional narrative of "BAU": a human working in a factory performing a repetitive process on an assembly line.

This type of activity sits at the ground zero of a *"non-project"*. And yet, as we break it down, we see that each repetition can be viewed as a single end-to-end task. As we unwrap this cycle, we see the elements of a single goal-seeking endeavour.

Each cycle through the repetitive task has a beginning, a middle, and an end. If humans are not trying to improve how they perform each cycle, then they are not paying attention, and if they are not paying attention, then the process is getting worse through entropy.

As the second law of thermodynamics comes into play, we see a progressive degradation of performance. Perhaps this degradation is tiny, but it repeats with the cycles. Eventually, the process gets so *"out of whack"* that it triggers an alarm or someone notices, and there's a management intervention. That management intervention will reset how the process is performed to get it back into tolerance.

Given entropy and human variability, the only way to keep the process within acceptable tolerance is to be continually analysing how the process works and trying experiments to see how they can improve it. Even if unconsciously, if they have the right mindset, the operators of that process are continually trying different things to tweak the process. Maybe they want it faster, or better quality or whatever.

Within each cycle exists a project. It may be small and localised, and concern primarily only one person. The underlying ***principles*** of project management apply as much to this as they do to a mega-project.

The Bottom Line

Every goal-oriented human endeavour is a project, regardless of whether it fits the narrow specifications of ***"projectness"*** determined by modern professional practitioners. Projects are everywhere, and if projects are everywhere, there must be codified knowledge and project management skills that are essential and available outside codified project management practice. Whilst this view might not suit various vested interests, thinking this way puts us on the path to defining general rules that apply to all human endeavours. And what's the harm in that?

The Tags

#projects, #projectmanagers, #organicprojects, #axiom, #whatisaproject, #projectswithoutprojectmanagers, #maxwideman, #businessasusual, #bau

On Agency

Agency refers to the imperative for individuals and groups to act, choose, take responsibility, and reflectively make progress. It is the engine by which any project gains forward momentum, allowing team members to prosecute the project's objectives.

Through their Agency, people take responsibility for collaborating with other stakeholders, aligning their actions with the project's objectives, and adjusting their performance to converge on agreed quality.

Agency beats Autonomy as the driver for project success every day of the week, and twice on Sundays.

14. Proceed until apprehended!

The Axiom

Proceed until apprehended!

The TL;DR

The quote (see below) on which this axiom is based encapsulates projects for me and, therefore, is axiomatic. Projects exist as agents of change within their environment or context, so they operate largely independently of the norms within that environment. There may be guardrails of governance and oversight, but projects are based on action, and action requires independence. Projects also require individual and group Agency to prosecute the project's goals, adapt to changing circumstances, and continuously improve performance.

The Back Story

This quote jumped off the page at me from Bruce Harpham's interview with Micheal Lubrano, a Senior Program Manager at Google, in his excellent book of interviews with project managers about their lived experiences. I immediately appropriated for into my project management lexicon. I use it frequently, acknowledging the source, of course. This axiom defines the state of agency that PMs must always be in and encouraging in others.

The origin of this axiom

Lubrano was describing a project where he couldn't get a decision despite "doing the right thing" through approved processes:

> *"Even today, I see technical program managers have a similar problem. They often lack a sense of ownership for the problem. They think they need to ask permission. I have a personal motto:* **proceed until apprehended**. *This is a principle that I tell every single person on my team. It's a principle that I preach to everyone in the field. You are here to make decisions or facilitate the process to get a decision made. If you are not getting decisions made, you're not doing your job on projects and programs."* — **Michael Lubrano** quoted in 'Project Managers at Work' by **Bruce Harpham**. Apress. Kindle Edition.

On the surface, it seems to be the same sentiment as the corny saying, *"better to ask forgiveness than permission"*. Get something started and keep going until there's a reason to stop. Or *"just do it!"* in the Nike version.

More than "Just do it".

But I think it's much more than that.

This axiom captures the essence of someone who is in control and is confident to take responsibility for their actions. Such people both have self-belief in their ability to find the right action and are optimistic that they will find a solution to the problems that started the project. A project is an agent of change and needs to act. But management or bureaucratic rules can constrain the scope of change to the point of impairment or failure.

Operating within established norms will get you so far, but teams must at times deliver exceptional performance to act independently and decisively. Existing practices, procedures, and regulations are guardrails not roadblocks. Projects are based on action, and action requires independence.

Individual and group agency are essential for project success, because it drives the prosecution of goals, adaptation to change and performance improvement.

Projects require individual and group agency to prosecute the project's goals, adapt to changing circumstances, and continuously improve performance.

But what about Autonomy?

You may think, "Okay, but aren't you just talking about "Autonomy"?

Autonomy is a management concept that became popular after Daniel Pink's book **"Drive"** included it in the three factors he called **"Motivation 3.0"**, consisting of **"Purpose"**, **"Autonomy"**, and **"Mastery"**.

In this context, I interpret Autonomy as the need to direct one's life and work. However, there are two problems with using Autonomy as the "gold standard" for motivation.

Firstly, Autonomy is created by external parties, who control and limit the actions of a group or person. For example, a country that colonises another country or region and holds it by military or economic power. The ruling power can grant forms of autonomy to the ruled, allowing them more latitude in certain actions (e.g. voting or responsible government). The granted autonomy defines what they can do without seeking approval.

Being granted more autonomy allows a broader range of action within which a person or group can self-determine before they run up against the limits of their powers.

Secondly, since Autonomy is granted, it affects the predisposition to act. Knowing that there is a power structure that will enforce the limits of autonomy, people or groups may decide not to fully exercise their autonomy. By knowing the rules and the consequences of breaking them, they may choose not to approach their boundaries.

We see examples of this in the voting turnout rates in countries with voluntary voting laws. People have the autonomy to decide whether to vote and some people decide that their vote will change nothing and so they stay away.

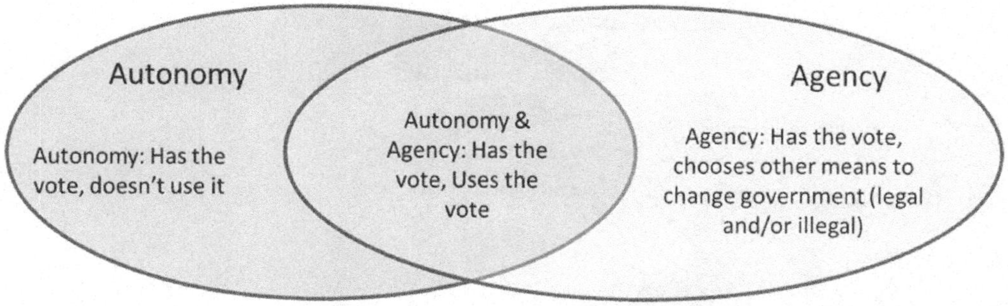

Figure 4. Autonomy vs Agency in Voting

Agency eats autonomy's lunch

Agency is the ability of people or groups to take action and be responsible for the results. Agency is superficially similar to autonomy, but is different in two important ways.

Firstly, agency is self-generated, not determined by an outside party. People with high agency are self-regulated, self-motivated and self-reflective.

Secondly, the concept of Agency does not include a definition of limits. People or groups with high Agency may recognise the existing rules or constraints and decide for themselves whether to work within them or to exceed them.

High Agency implies a willingness to act and self-determine the range of operation they have in a certain domain, e.g. an organisation or a project. They are aware of any externally-defined limits but decide for themselves what is necessary for them to achieve their goals.

Let's Look at the Detail

Let's look at the detail in the difference between Autonomy and Agency, illustrated in the diagram below. At the top of this diagram, we have an organisational or social structure at the top that delegates power or authority to sub-units, for example, a departmental manager, or project team.

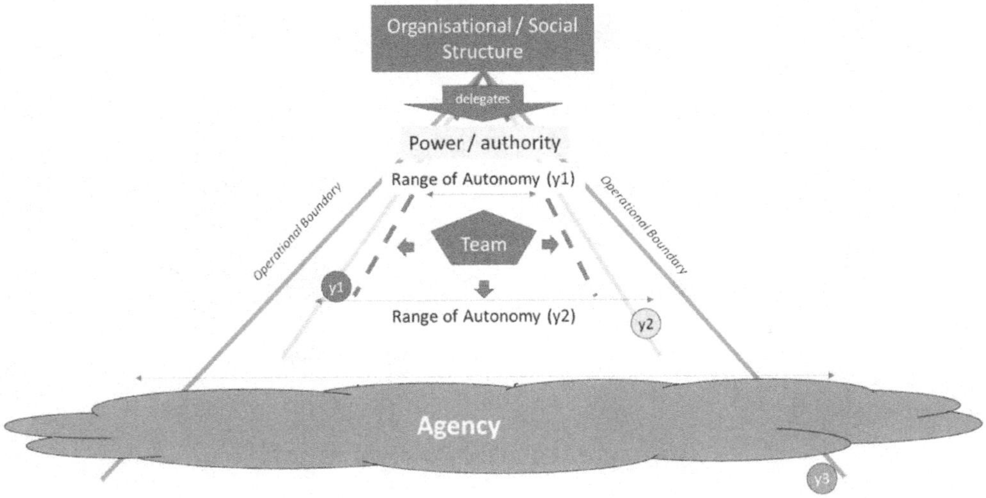

Figure 5. Autonomy vs Agency Detail

The team has a level of power/authority delegated to it by the "owning" structure, which gives the team a range of operation which has operational boundaries. Say the team has a "Range of Autonomy" at "Y1" in the diagram at some point in the project.

If the team operates within the range of autonomy given to it, then everything is fine, at least as far as the "owning" structure is concerned. To what extent the team exploits that range is up to the team and the context in which they operate.

The range of operation can be increased, but only by the owning structure. Let's say that the project team had its operational boundaries increased to "Y2", giving it a wider range of operations. That might feel like "independence" depending on how big the delta is between Y2 and Y1.

However, these two new boundaries still constrain the team.

With Agency, operational boundaries are set by the team or the individuals in the team. A high-agency team might recognise the operational boundaries but determine for itself where the limits on its behaviour.

The Bottom Line

Agency, not autonomy, is the key to project success. Without it, you will never come close to delivering on a project's potential, even if it completes with some sort of output. You must decide for yourself on your course of action — to wait is project suicide. So, Proceed until apprehended.

The Tags

#agency, #projectsuccess, #principlesofprojectsuccess; #autonomy, #agentsofchange, #guardrailsofgovernance, #quotation, #michaellubrano, #danielpink, #drive, #motivation3.0, #purpose, #autonomy, #mastery, #bruceharpham

15. First Action! Then see what happens.

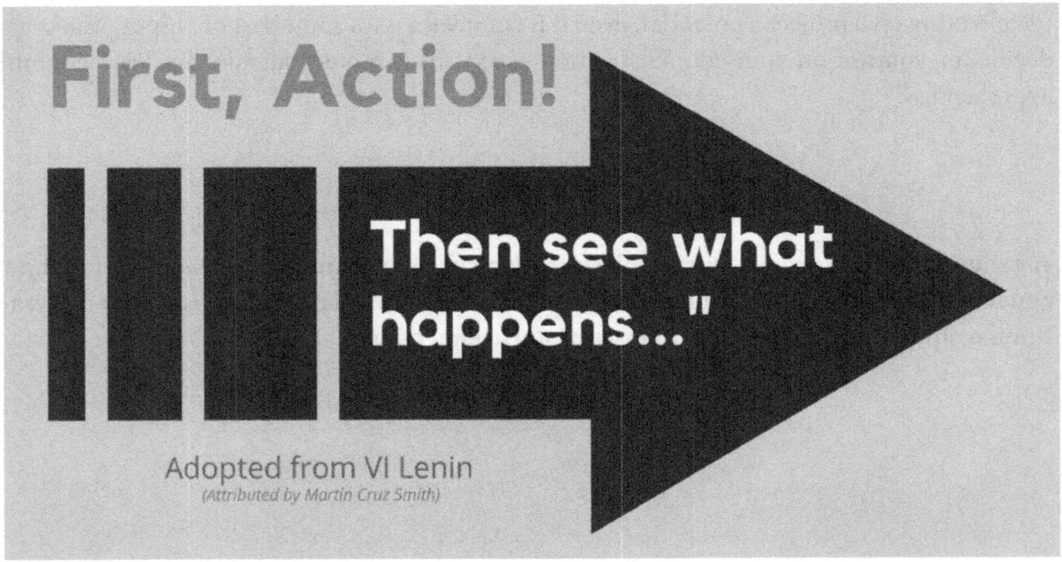

The Axiom

First Action! Then see what happens.

The TL;DR

Projects require action to survive and thrive. Action is a form of thinking; therefore, action will help you validate ideas and cull those that are unhelpful or nonadaptive. Action uncovers hidden issues and enables effective problem-solving.

The Back Story

Projects are action. Action is, in and of itself, a forcing function that crystallises gaps or latent issues and makes them visible.

This axiom is another appropriation, and it comes from a novel by Martin Cruz Smith. His famous character, Arkady Renko, claims it was a favourite and defining quote from V. I.

Lenin. I have no idea whether this is true, but it doesn't matter—it doesn't change the sentiment.

Projects are action!

Projects are action! This characteristic of projects is axiomatic. Projects are created to drive change and enable beneficial outcomes for their stakeholders.

And yet most projects, whether waterfall or agile or anything else, are tepid, timid instantiations of human behaviour.

Or maybe not

Partly this comes from the standardisation and normative prescriptions of branded methodologies and Bodies of Knowledge ("BOKs"). Over decades of evolution, the BOKs and branded methodologies have been refined, distilled and commodified. At least one contributor to this trend has been the focus on building a certification regime (aka business) that reduces the examination of skills and knowledge to a series of closed multiple-choice questions.

This results in a narrow and limited perspective in those PM's who come through the learning and development processes attached to the branded frameworks. It results in an endless emphasis on technique and method. This narrow perspective is manifested in the core practices and techniques of project management praxis — such as the "iron triangle" - as the ever-present touchstone for correct practice. Our lived experience becomes a never-ending cascade of information and process: issues, risks, budgets, schedules, change control, regimented reporting and progress exception handling, and competency scales.

Organisational Risk-aversion

Partly this comes from organisations. Everything that is put in place in a project environment is designed to try to guarantee that nothing bad will happen. That every project will succeed. Stakeholders want guarantees that things will work out.

See the axiom "**# 58. Everyone is fine with your risk management plan**", for more on risk aversion by organisations.

Action is a Forcing function

Action is a "forcing function" to drive the project through the noise, hesitation, bureaucracy, lethargy, confusion, lack of information, and other entropic factors that can bog down a project and cause confusion.

When I'm managing a project, if I ever come to a point where I'm in doubt about what I need to do, I think of what I can act on – what I can do that will help both move the project forward and clarify the circumstances.

Action is fundamental to our ability to 'think our way around' a project and its attendant opportunities and problems. There are strong indicators of the necessity for action in recent developments in neuroscience and how the brain works.

Thinking as a form of action

Jeff Hawkins, in his book "One Thousand Brains: A New Theory of Intelligence", proposes the theory that *"thinking is a form of moving"*, or in our context of project management, *"thinking is a form of action"*. Our brains learn by identifying the differences between predicted and observed states after movement.

Hawkins's theory is based on his view that there is a common algorithm for all thinking processes, from basic movements to higher-order knowledge such as law or project management.

The brain evolved to help an organism navigate its physical world by building models and adapting them to the observed changes as it moved. There are powerful features in the cortex called reference frames that are the basis for organising all types of knowledge. Our brains build a reference model of the world and predict what that world will be every time we move.

The necessity for action

This model is a compelling argument for the necessity of action – we learn by moving and comparing our prediction of what we thought we would find to our observations.

So, action is critical to our learning and thought patterns.

We can replicate this physical movement in our thoughts by activating a series of neural states that operate as if we were physically moving: we are "acting" out our thinking processes.

In this way, action is critical to all thinking and evolving ideas towards a goal.

One of the least-used actions in projects is validation through action: run an experiment, try something out, put something to the test or measure something. These are all forms of action.

Every idea in a project needs to be tested for value. All concepts need to be validated across multiple people to ensure alignment and to ensure they need to be carried forward and not abandoned.

The most extreme form of waste in a project is carrying forward concepts without actual viability or likelihood of delivery, which chews up cognitive bandwidth, time and energy.

The act of moving forward and doing something is sometimes the best validator.

Projects should "take no prisoners", or in other words, must not carry forward unvalidated or unviable ideas that absorb energy and focus.

The Bottom Line

Do something – then see what happens!

The Tags

#agency, #action, #projectsuccess, #principlesofprojectsuccess; #appropriation, #actionasthinking, #actionasvalidation, #neuroscience, #thinkingasmovement, #pmboks, #methodology

16. Every project has its own natural cadence.

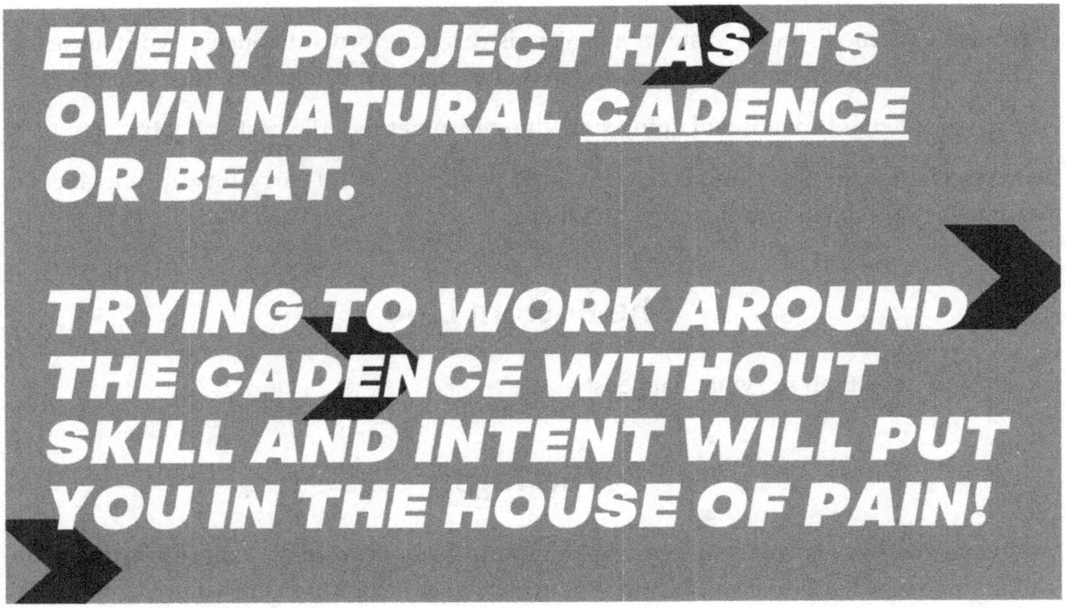

The Axiom

Every project has its own natural cadence that drives the pace of work, which cannot be easily changed.

The TL;DR

Every project has its own natural cadence or beat, and the project will make progress sustainably forever if work is performed at that natural cadence. Trying to change or work around the cadence without skill and intent will put you in the house of pain!

The Back Story

What is a project cadence? It's a critical concept for all project managers (PMs). It's the speed at which events occur in the project; it's the "beating heart" of each project.

The many cycles of human interaction

Think about the many cycles of human interaction in a project. They operate in many layers, from relatively slow to very fast, and from those involving the whole project community (teams and stakeholders) to those that involve only two people — for example, an emailed question and an answer response. The most significant interaction cycle in a project occurs when the sponsor initiates a project, followed by the project reporting the outcome of the completed project.

All cycles have a time dimension, for example, the cycle time between an initial email and the response. Other interaction cycle measures include how much notice people need for meeting invitations. Or how long they feel they need to review an artifact. All things being equal, these cycle times will be similar for people in different organisations or sub-groups of organisations: departments, branches, and offices.

The Messaging Cadence

There are many differences between individuals. Some people respond relatively instantly to a Slack message or email — ' instantly' in meaning responding as soon as they see it, say after a meeting. Some people respond out of hours, and others will respond the next business day. But overall, over all the people with whom you interact, you should be able to sense the average "SLA" on different types of interactions. These tend to be constant in a given organisation and cultural context.

So, let's take a project where multiple people need to respond to an event, say an email. That interaction isn't complete until the last person has responded. One person might be instant, another a couple of hours and the last a day or so. Over time you'll get the sense that there's no point trying to wrap something up in an hour because you'll always be waiting a day.

So, the "cadence" of the project starts to look more like a day.

The Meeting Cadence

Take another example — how long in advance it takes to set up a meeting. In some organisations, doing it in a day might be possible.

In other situations, you'll see that calendars are very cluttered, and getting a meeting together is tough quicker than a few days — possibly a week. Jammed calendars are very common when people are working on multiple projects or supporting "BAU" activities as well as one or more projects,

You'll feel how the cycle times work by looking at all the interactions.

Now, it's probable that the cycle times you're seeing are not unique, and it's more likely that all interactions of all initiatives operate on the same cadence.

The Bottom Line

The natural cadence of a project is the aggregate of cycle times across the people, processes and systems that make up the project's environment. Whether the PM feels it is too slow or fast, the cadence is hard to change. But slow cadence doesn't automatically mean slow throughput. Project managers (PMs) should invest time in working out how to leverage the natural cadence to match the throughput requirements of the project.

The Tags

#projectspeed, #projectcadence, #agency, #principlesofprojectsuccess, #interaction, #cadence, #velocity, #interaction, #interactioncycles

17. There are two contrary forces in the world!

The Axiom

In the long run, the forces of the bazaar will always overcome the forces of the cathedral.

The TL;DR

Eric Raymond—a visionary software guru who popularised the open-source software model, formulated the dichotomy of "The Cathedral and the Bazaar". He felt that the (software) world has two contrary forces: the Cathedral, representing conformity, ritual, and hereditary power, and the Bazaar, symbolising agency, adaptability, and individualism. In project management, as in software development, the Bazaar's collaborative and flexible approach ultimately triumphs over the Cathedral's rigidity. The bazaar's power is the main reason I still have hope for Agile. And Napoleon Bonaparte envisaged that the human spirit would always ultimately conquer the sword. In those two dichotomies we find the essence of project management.

The Back Story

This axiom is a mash-up of two concepts from two very different people:

- a riff on a quote from Napoleon Bonaparte; and
- a metaphor about open-source software versus established software companies.

Origin 1: Napoleon Bonapart

The first concept in this axiom comes from this quote:

> *"There are only two forces in the world, the sword and the spirit. In the long run the sword will always be conquered by the spirit." — **Napoleon Bonaparte**

It's an inspiring quote: it implies that people can overcome whatever boundaries or constraints are put in their way.

Some might think this an interesting thought from a man who at one time enslaved half of Europe and was busy working on the other half.

But Napoleon ignored one important thing - apart from ignoring the snow forecasts - the Napoleonic faith in the spirit of people ignores the fact that their hearts are not homogenous. People do things differently because they see the world differently and, often as not, one way is about as good as other ways. Not everything has to be done one way.

Origin 2: The Cathedral and the Bazaar

Which brings me to the source of the other metaphor: a seminal essay titled "The Cathedral and the Bazaar published in 1997 by Eric Raymond, which explored the differences between two contrasting approaches to software development and licensing. The essay was a powerful reflection on the hacker community and the principles of free and open-source software. Raymond's work highlighted the inherent strengths of decentralised, collaborative development methods and has since become a cornerstone in the open-source movement.

The Cathedral model, as described by Raymond, represents a centralised, top-down approach to software development, where a select few are responsible for decision-making. In this model, code is developed behind closed doors by a small team, with releases occurring infrequently, and contributions from outside the core team are often limited or discouraged. This approach can lead to slow progress and a highly protective attitude towards intellectual property. Raymond states in his essay, *"The Cathedral model has its place... but it is not well adapted to the all-important exploratory phase of the development cycle."*

In contrast, the Bazaar model embodies a decentralised, bottom-up approach where individuals can freely contribute ideas and solutions. This collaborative environment enables rapid innovation and adaptability. Raymond explains, *"Given a large enough beta-tester and co-developer base, almost every problem will be characterised quickly and the fix obvious to someone."* In the Bazaar model, developers work transparently and openly, releasing code early and often while inviting feedback and contributions from a broad community of users and fellow developers.

The Cathedral and the Bazaar of Project Management

We have a similar situation in professional project management. The "Cathedral" of project management is the professional association that formalises its catechism, builds its structures, rewards faithful adherents, and punishes the apostates. Their holy writ is guarded with zealous ambition and cannot be criticised.

The Agile Manifesto, created in 2001, embodies the Bazaar model, as it promotes a decentralised, flexible, and collaborative approach to software development. The core principles of the Agile Manifesto align with the Bazaar model's emphasis on adaptability, innovation, and individual agency.

The Bazaar is the messy but pragmatic lived experience of PMs as they figure out how to make their projects work.

The problem is that some of the ideas or trends originating in the Bazaar get so successful that the folks behind it decide they are going to check out of the market square and head on over to a vacant lot at the edge of the square and build themselves a Cathedral. When this happens it seems there are always folks who will blindly or even wilfully decide that what the Cathedral offers is what they need and launch headlong into memorising and repeating the catechism.

The Agile Manifesto most vividly exemplified the bazaar — the name echoes Martin Luther nailing his Ninety-five Theses (Luther's manifesto for the reformation of the church) to the door of his church.

But it didn't take long before folks decided that they needed some "Agile Cathedrals" and changed everything.

The Bottom Line

The Bazaar is the human spirit with the Agency to work out their ways of doing things after questioning the "accepted" processes and theories about some practices.

The Tags

#entropy, #churchandbazaar, #competingforces, #projectinfluences, #agency, #projectagency, #napoleonbonaparte, #ericraymond, #thecathedralandthebazaar, #cathedralmodel, #bazaarmodel, #agilemanifesto, #martinluther

On Enablement

We talk endlessly about projects "**delivering value**", but the reality is we cannot deliver "**value**", we can only deliver "**things**".

The concept of project "**Enablement**" holds that the value of a project the enhanced capabilities of end-users and stakeholders that enables them to "**capture value**" within their context, e.g. an organisation, a department, a school or whatever.

Thus, project managers need to think of *enabling value*, not delivering it.

18. Do you have a system-based objective?

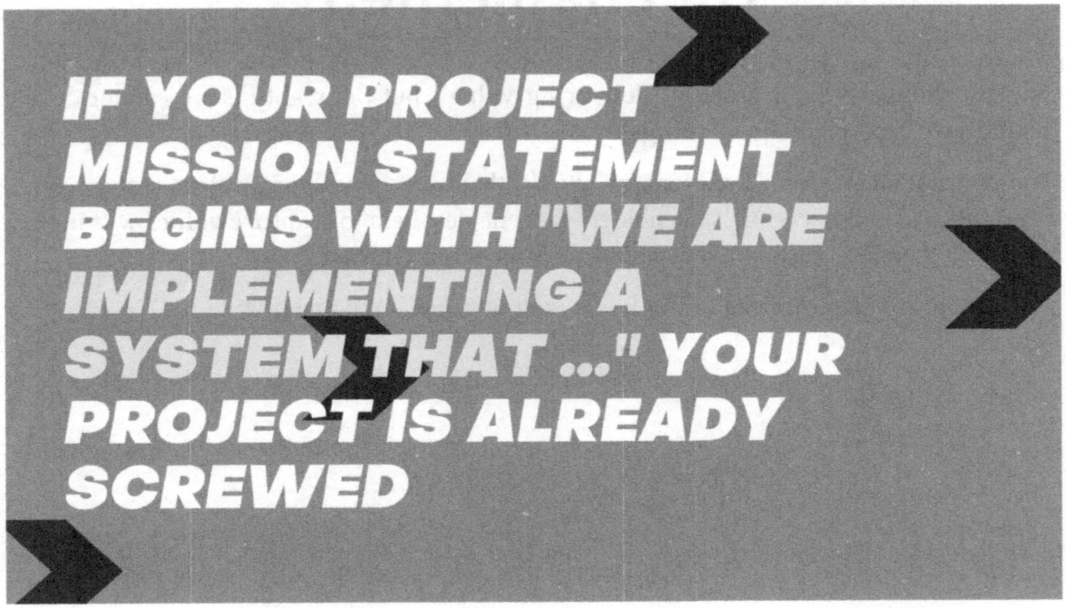

The Axiom

If you're not thinking of the entire end-to-end causal value chain, you're wasting your time and their money.

The TL;DR

A project manager must frame their project around a model of the entire end-to-end causal chain, from the tasks and resources to immediate outcomes and long-term impacts. If your project mission statement begins *with "we are implementing a system that ..."* your project is already screwed. Most project managers frame their projects in the context of what they will deliver — the components they hand over to a customer or end-user when the project is complete. But this project conceptualisation locks in the separation of value enabled by these deliverables and long-term benefits. If your project's "North Star" is not customer outcomes and long-term benefits, then you run a significant risk of a failed project.

The Back Story

The point of this axiom is that if the starting point for your project is to deliver a solution — or worse, a system — or even worse, a specifically named software package - then your project is in for a difficult time.

The Mission-statement based project

Mission statements are a little old-fashioned these days, but almost any Project Management Plan will have a purpose statement that describes what the project is intended to achieve. Even if you don't have a formal Mission Statement, there will be — at least one — unspoken project narrative in the minds of sponsors and key stakeholders about what the project is meant to achieve. If these expectations are tacit, you'll be lucky to have only one. But that's not the point of this axiom.

In the above cases, your project is founded in the solution space, and this frames the narrative of all concerned: you are looking at outputs, not outcomes.

This lack of a customer problem statement in a project briefing document indicates that the project mindset is a technical/deliverable one, not a value mindset.

The irresistible slide back to a "work" reference frame

The output reference frame triggers a cascading collapse of awareness: from value to deliverables, from deliverables to tasks, and from tasks to methodologies and work. This cascading collapse of awareness means that frame of decision-making changes multiple times and, each time, further away from the influence/guiding principles of customer value.

Issues or gaps created by this thinking cascade through the project as technical/deliverable decisions are made for technical/deliverable reasons, sometimes implicitly or unconsciously.

And, in case you think that this problem exists only for traditional, or predictive project approaches, taking on agile doesn't immunise you from this problem. Unless your backlog and reviews are done in the problem/outcome domain, you have just the same problems as I've described above.

Outcome-based project

Using best practice you start with a customer problem or customer value proposition. In this case, you're thinking of outcomes, not deliverables. In this case, you have a customer-enabled value focus.

A project manager needs to think constantly about the entire end-to-end causal chain, from the tasks and resources in their project to the immediate outcomes enabled by their solutions and the long-term impacts.

How can we ensure that our reference frame includes customer outcomes, giving us the end-to-end causal chain?

Enter, the Program Logic Model.

The Program Logic Model

A model that facilitates such thinking is the program logic model. As illustrated below, the Kellogg Foundation defines a generic program logic model.

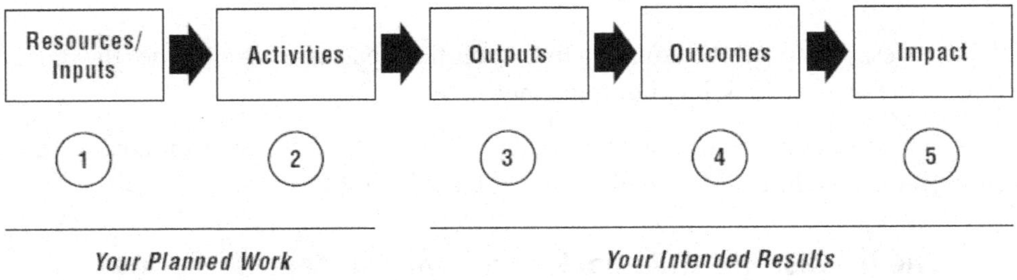

Figure 6. The Basic Logic Model (Kellog Foundation)

The program logic model above visualises how a project will achieve its intended results. It's more than just an abstract visualisation: the "logic" of the program logic design is that there is some level of certainty that each preceding step in the chain leads to the next one measurably.

Here's a further breakdown of the causal logic between each component:

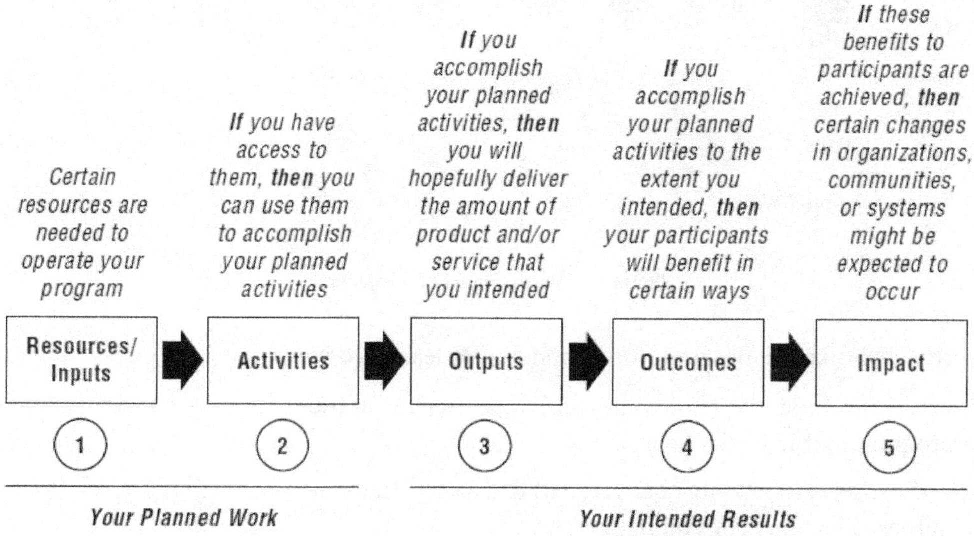

Figure 7. Reading a Logic Model (Kellog Foundation)

In my planning, I prefer to work from right to left, which changes the wording but focuses more on the intended long-term impacts and works backwards to each previous element of the logic chain.

Please see axiom "**# 34. If you can't define the enabled behaviour.**" for more about using the Program Logic Model to navigate around your project.

Breaking the causal link

Most Information Technology ("IT") projects are conceived and executed in the context of the red rectangle below: the project creates solution outputs, but outcomes and impacts are someone else's concern. Unfortunately, some projects are even worse, and no one seriously concerns themselves with intended results beyond the solution.

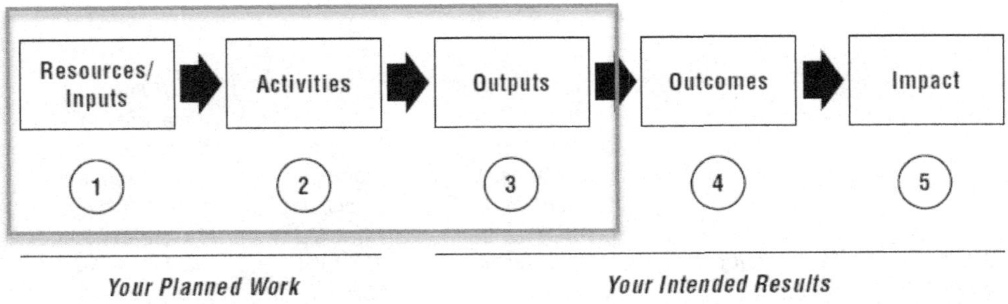

Figure 8. Focus of most IT Projects

Such projects broke the program logic model in at least two ways:

1. Minimal consideration of Outcomes and Impacts, even at the early stage conceptualisation of the program by the business; and

2. Lack of causal relationships between all the model elements means that the relationship between these elements is hypothetical.

Framing the project goal with only a solution-level context creates and promotes structural problems that endure for the entire project.

Please see axiom "**# 30. When tech folks talk to business folks what language do they speak?**" for an explanation of how the construction of requirements and user stories maps into the different stages of the Logic Model.

The Bottom Line

So, do yourself and your stakeholders a favour and be an outcome-mindset Project Manager. With a process/output mindset, it's easy to miss the critical drivers for implementation. Keep your focus, your language, and your planning, indeed all your activities anchored in the intended outcomes and impacts desired by the customer.

The Tags

#enablement, #principlesofprojectsuccess, #missionstatement, #projectmanagementapproach, #projectmanagementplan

19. Understanding the cost of delay.

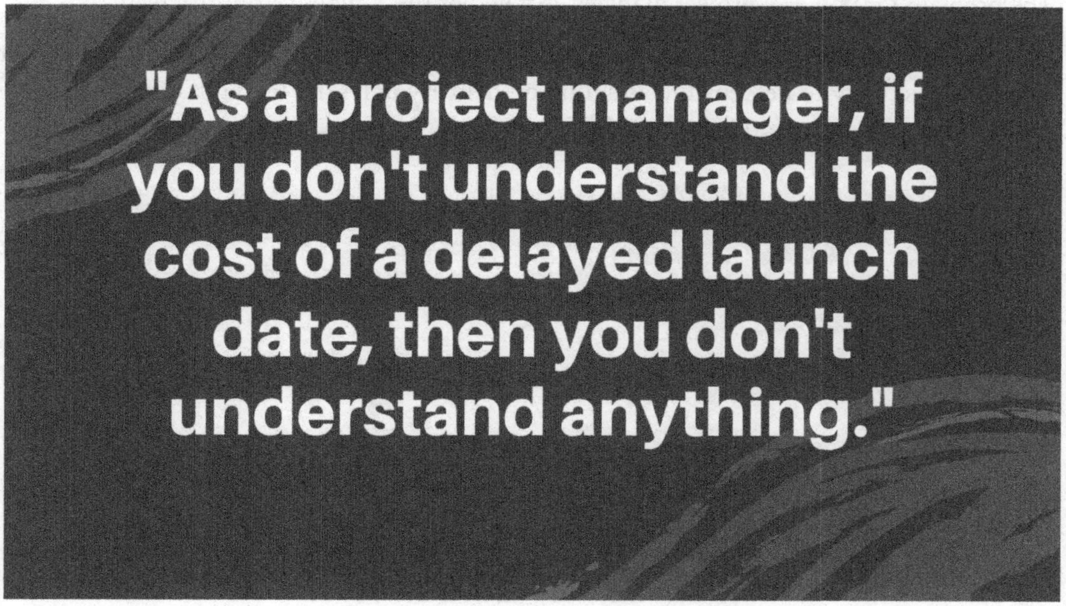

The Axiom

If you don't understand the cost of delay, then you don't understand anything.

The TL;DR

It is a rare environment in which a project does not have a target launch date. Enterprises and key stakeholders always have an expectation of when they want the capabilities available, even in agile settings. This expectation forms even if no one ever commits to these dates. If you don't understand these dynamics, and the costs of delay, then you don't understand your project.

The Back Story

It is extremely difficult to avoid having expectations set for your project's target delivery date. Even if you've never written a date in any document, and you're at the earliest stage of project initiation, your sponsor will know when they want your project to deliver, and when they want the benefits to flow.

The problem for you as a project manager is whether the timing is arbitrary or real.

I try to avoid having a target date enter the project discussions until as late as possible. At the very least, I try to defocus the attention on delivery dates, by taking them off the table for as long as I can, as in the example below.

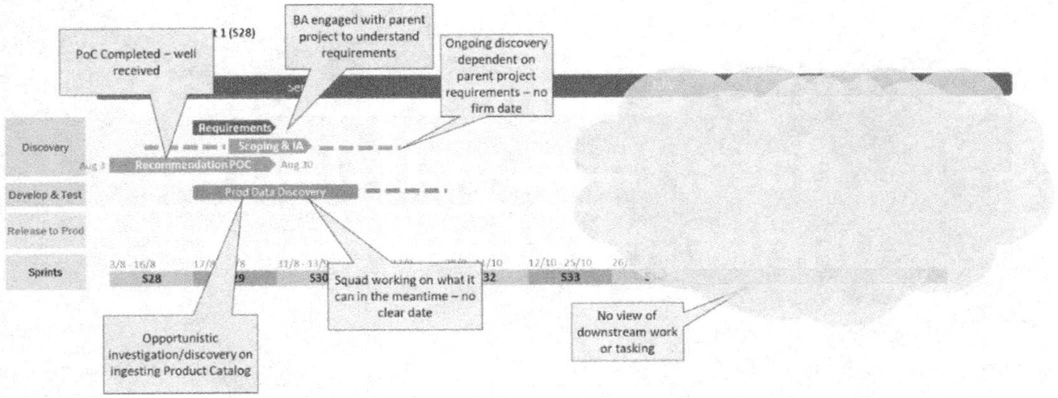

Figure 9. Defocusing Future Delivery Dates

I do this knowing that it won't prevent expectations from forming about the date or change the expectations that may already be set.

This matters because dates can mask the real factors in a delay.

What is a delay

Obviously, a *\delay* in project management is delivering your scope later than expected. But it is not always about dates — the date may be arbitrary or miscalculated. You must first understand delay in relation to key events. For example, you might have to deliver *"before HiTechCo releases their next version."* Or *"before that tax policy is rescinded."* I'm not saying this makes it any easier, but I am saying that there is a higher order dependency involved in many projects.

There are many valid drivers for date expectations, for example, market conditions, potential competitive position, or a regulatory deadline. These drivers don't control do-ability but they do shape solution or execution strategy.

Often a sponsor will give you a date, with little or no explanation. What explanation you get is usually one of the above, but often as not, these dates are arbitrary and aggressive. Or an executive has already pre- committed the date to their bosses.

This early-stage focus on dates is detrimental to a project team understanding the rationale for the project and the dynamics of the dependency network.

The critical objective at these early stages is to understand those dependencies and how they affect business value, not how they affect a sponsor's happiness (or lack of it) if s/he has to go back with a modified commitment.

Components in the cost of delay

There are four components of the cost of delay:

1. **Project holding costs**: sustaining the team for the duration of the delay.
2. **Deferred benefits**: deferring the date from which enabled value begins to accrue.
3. **Impaired team efficacy**: lost confidence, commitment, cohesion, and cadence in the team.
4. **Loss of trust**: missed dates imply that the team is somehow underperforming, and, in the absence of hard information, stakeholder speculation easily turns to the worst reasons, for example, lack of commitment or incompetence.

Most project managers will explore and understand the details of these project delays in the order above.

The accuracy of deferred benefits will usually be poor if it hasn't been explored up front. Unless there's a suitable business model available to the team, there's little to help the project manager determine whether they are real or fantasy.

And team impacts, such as loss of efficacy or trust, are considered only by the best project managers and sponsors. Often as not, they either ignore them or expect their teams will "suck it up" and keep going.

The critical issue in deferred benefit delays is that they might not only be deferred but are possibly lost forever. For example, how many customers might buy another company's product while your competitive offering is delayed?

Problems with a cost-based analysis of delay

Holding costs are relatively easy to calculate. The problem comes when trying to calculate the costs of deferred benefits.

Why is this a problem?

This focus on project costs is an excellent example of project manager myopia: a focus on the internal processes and deliverables of the project and little or no knowledge of the business value that the project is intended to enable.

The calculation of delayed business benefit requires (obviously) an understanding of how that value is captured and the metrics of value dimensions. Understanding business benefits is necessary for any successful project but is often only vaguely sketched, possibly fictional, or even non-existent.

Understanding the transformation from "as-is" to "to-be"

You cannot understand value without understanding the "as-is" problem to be solved and the functions or behaviour that are unlocked in the "to-be" environment after completing the project.

A straightforward value proposition, such as "reduce the cost of processing "N" documents by $20", is acceptable if there is some factual basis for the numbers. For the proposition to work, you need to:

1. Understand the direct causal relationship between the capabilities your project unlocks, and those metrics being achieved.
2. Know the current processing cost.
3. Have a reasonable basis for predicting the $20 reduction.
4. Understand how many documents are currently processed in a given time.

You might refine this proposition by understanding how the volume of "N" documents might change over time.

Although the above proposition may seem simple, even elementary, this information often hasn't been fleshed out in the project. Stakeholders often say the data is too hard to get, unreliable, or obvious.

Liquidated Cost of Delay

Now it is elementary to calculate the cost of delay: you add the deferred value capture to the increased project costs for the additional duration. Convert that number into a single rounded-up value per day or week.

You now have a single number that is easy to remember and communicate. Also, remember the two components separately: the cost of delayed benefits and the carrying costs due to duration.

The Bottom Line

Once you understand this simple benefit proposition, everything in the project flows. It becomes your "North star" because you can reconcile any problem, prioritisation, or decision to this core value. Without it, its small wonder projects get off track. Understanding the component values helps in different ways. For example, at best, benefit accrual is delayed at the same rate they are delayed. It is remembering this number helps when considering other aspects of the solution, like the total budget. Is the total cost far more significant than the benefits accrue? This concept might seem like it's obvious, but there are so many projects that sidestep this analysis or do it poorly. But if you can't calculate those numbers, it's possibly no surprise you're in a delayed situation anyway.

The Tags

#costofdelay, #value, #projectmanagementskills, #skills, #projectdelay, #enablement, #principlesofprojectsuccess, #axiom

20. Always be looking for the $1.95 solution.

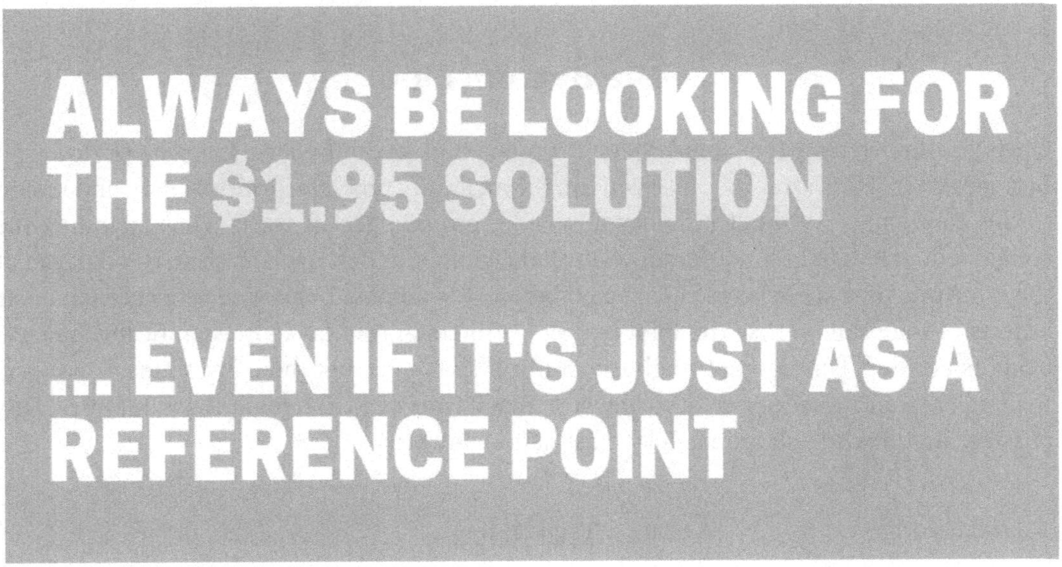

The Axiom

Always look for the $1.95 solution, even if it's just a reference point.

The TL;DR

It's relatively easy for projects to become over-scoped. It happens all the time. I doubt that any project is not over-scoped to some degree. I am constantly fighting to keep the scope small in my projects. There are many reasons for this, not the least of which is the "Fear of Missing Out" ("FOMO") on any given feature that might not have a natural home or clear value proposition and so gets loaded into a larger project. Paradoxically, obtaining approval for larger projects is often easier than for small ones. It's crucial to search for the '$1.95 solution,' representing smaller, more cost-effective approaches to project scope.

The Back Story

There seems to be a natural tendency of project teams and stakeholders to drive up the scope of projects. This imperative doesn't seem restricted to traditional predictive projects. It affects agile projects equally. The difference might be when these scope items drift into the project, not whether they will attempt to become part of the delivery.

Causes of project over-scoping

There are many causes for this, including:

Feature FOMO: the fear (or necessity) for features to be added into a larger project vehicle, whether they have an affinity for the project's goals or deliverables or not.

Optioning Up: the preference of many technology teams to introduce the latest and newest platforms and technology rather than use an existing (aka "old") component that may be perfectly serviceable but doesn't improve the overall value proposition for the team or individuals.

Process Overhead: the relative process overhead for small, stand-alone feature delivery is higher than for the same feature added to a larger project. Big projects have their own momentum and resource support, so it's simpler to "jump on the bandwagon" of big project governance.

Why would you want a smaller project?

Whilst there are clear drivers for adding features to projects, there are clear countervailing drivers.

The Agile Manifesto is clear on this point:

> *"Simplicity—the art of maximizing the amount of work not done—is essential."* — **[The Agile Manifesto, 10th Principle]**(https://agilemanifesto.org/principles.html)

The project overheads increase exponentially as the scope size grows linearly. This situation is the totally opposite impact of adding functionality to the project, pre-approval. I'm sure you've seen some of these analyses, for example, the additional communications overhead of adding people to a team. With each new feature, you can add multiple people to the team with all the other overheads.

So, if I add 2-3 features to a project's scope, the overhead for a project grows by about 4-9 times the additional scope. There are many reasons for this growth. And note that the example is not the maximum dissonance – the exponential increase in overhead is open-ended and unlimited.

We can see multiple drivers if we consider project complexity driven by solution and process complexity. Ultimately it all boils down to implementation cost. Everything can be reduced to money.

Implementation cost is a proxy for many project elements.

The primary elements include the solution architecture (and the non-functional requirements that drive the architecture), the component sourcing, design, and implementation method (custom development or "off the shelf" product), just three examples.

Secondary aspects of the solution include duration, component cost, number of people and their location.

Tertiary factors include the overheads: communications methods and complexity, stakeholder and project management, testing, and training.

Origin of this axiom

This axiom originates in a vague recollection of a book I read years ago. I think it was a book called "Structured Analysis" by Ed Yourdon, but I'm not sure. Wherever it came from, I've reproduced from memory the diagram below:

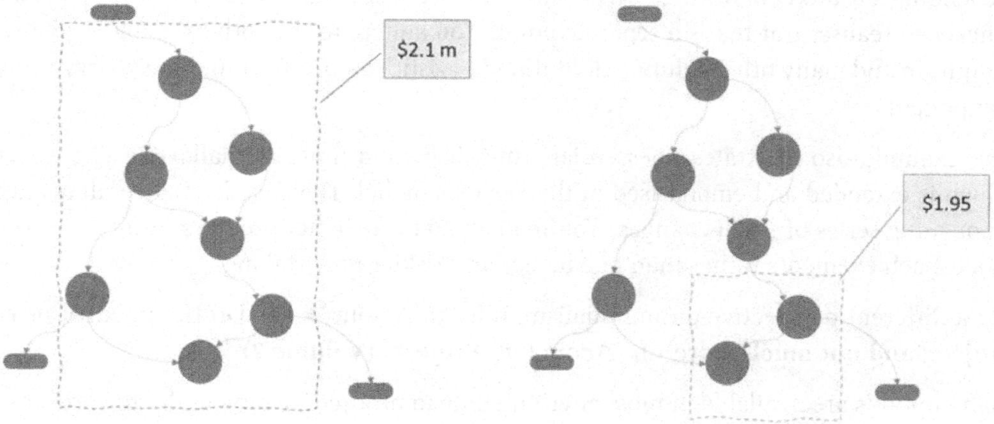

Figure 10. Comparison of alternate solution scope and cost

The diagram shows two versions of the same functional data flow diagram representing the scope of a proposed enhancement or component.

On the left, the solution scope (dotted rectangle) covers almost the full scope of the flow diagram. And on the right is the same functional flow diagram with a solution that implements a much smaller segment of the flow. In both cases, I show a notional cost to implement the scope. These are just illustrative values for a very rough 'order of magnitude' estimate, also known as a 'VROOM estimate,' of implementation cost.

The takeaway is that the price difference between the two solutions can be significantly bigger than the apparent scope differences.

These are fictional scenarios, and the "$1.95" is a bit dramatic, but it makes a point.

Drivers for cost differences

There are two drivers for this difference. Firstly, the cost is not uniformly distributed across all processes for a proposed solution. Equally, you can argue that risk is not uniformly distributed. And nor is the benefit.

Secondly, the non-linear compounding effects of multiple solution components kick in very quickly.

> " *"Perfection is achieved, not when there is nothing more to add, but when there is nothing left to take away."* " — **Antoine de St Exupéry**

Depending on the benefit, the "$1.95" cost might generate significantly more ROI and be quicker to realise. But that's a separate point. You adhere to the 10th Principle of the Agile Manifesto and many other solution definition heuristics by parsing out unnecessary solution components.

This example also illustrates an essential principle behind Agile's "small batch size" concept, which is extended and emphasised in the DevOps model. DevOps drives overall change in an ongoing series of small changes. You're likely to make better progress through a series of modest achievements rather than one bigger and riskier undertaking.

For a different perspective on minimalism, refer to Axiom "**# 75. Do the needful in your project, and not much more**" in "**Adam On: Projects (Volume 2)**"[1].

Many options are available in most environments to proceed incrementally towards an end solution, learning as you go and getting early benefits flowing.

The Bottom Line

So, you can see that this axiom has multiple applications and payoffs. It's always worth looking for the smaller version of a proposed solution — the $1.95 solution. Don't get locked into project size or scope until it has been validated that this approach is better than any available alternatives. Always question the construct of any given project and investigate whether there are cheaper or smaller options or if the overall objective can be implemented in smaller pieces.

The Tags

#requirements, #design, #solutionarchitecture, #solutionanalysis, #criticalsize, #solutionmapping, #projectbudget, #projectfunding, #fasterway, #projectschedule, #riskmanagement, #agilemanifesto, #fomo, #fearofmissingout, #structuredanalysis, #edyourdon, #smallbatchsize

---

[1]https://bjl.ink/aopv2

On Evolution

In a project sense, "**Evolution**" refers to the various ways in which knowledge and practice emulate natural biological evolution, as described by Charles Darwin and others.

Understanding the conceptual model of evolution, and having an evolutionary mindset when managing projects, helps resolve many practice issues and roadblocks. Having this mindset is fundamental to managing successful projects.

Applying the evolutionary cycle paradigm to your project helps simplify your approach, and de-noises the project environment. But also remember that natural evolution is painfully slow and inefficient and so must be adapted to the project world.

21. Everything in every project evolves!

The Axiom

Everything in every project evolves, regardless of its lifecycle, methodology or context.

The TL;DR

The principle of project evolution is that everything in a project progresses towards its end goal through a series of evolutionary steps, regardless of the approach or methodology employed. Evolution is unavoidable and unstoppable. As a project manager, it's critical that you recognise and leverage the evolutionary processes in your project. You need to understand how evolution works and how to leverage it to maximum benefit, no matter your lifecycle approach.

The Back Story

Evolution is a change process in which something transitions from one state to another in a series of steps. The "thing" could be an organism, a collection of organisms, an organisation, a concept or a system. Usually these steps are small and the change is gradual. In other cases there are "discontinuities" when a step is significantly bigger.

Evolution is part of the natural way people think and work together. Everything (ideas, needs, people, teams, and technology rendering of deliverables) evolves towards a future state.

Why is this?

A simplified generic evolutionary pattern

A simplified and generic pattern of evolution is shown below. The core of this pattern is a cycle of change to something, followed by a validation of fitness, in a fitness function. Depending on the parameters of the fitness function, the cycle continues or terminates.

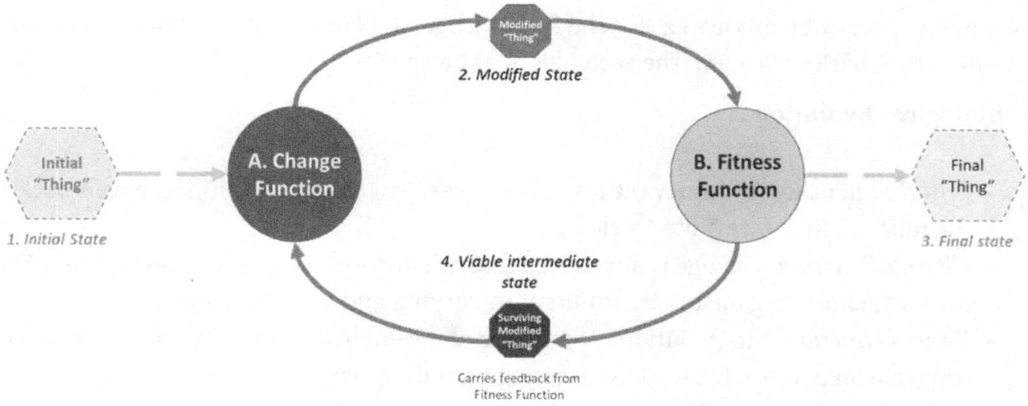

Figure 11. The Simplified Generic Pattern of Evolution

There are two main processes in a generic evolutionary pattern.

A. **Change Process** that applies change to something to produce a "changed thing".

B. **Fitness Function** that validates the "changed thing" against a set of criteria, for example, environmental conditions or stakeholder requirements.

The "thing" has multiple states in this process, as follows:

1. **Initial State** the way the "thing" was at the beginning of the process.
2. **Modified State** the "thing" after changes have been applied.
3. **Final State** the "thing" after 0 to n cycles through the process. At the most generic, there are either 3A Failed State, the "thing" has become non-viable and cannot transition through the change process again, or "Success State" which is the accepted final form of the "thing" after 1 to n change functions.
4. **Viable Intermediate State**: the "thing" that has successfully passed the Fitness Function but is not ready for one of the final states, i.e. it is still "viable" but not complete.

This simplified pattern of evolution can be applied to many scenarios. It is simple but incredibly powerful, so it's important to understand. The simple pattern can be extended with many additional details.

Let's look at two below.

Some Use Cases of the generic evolutionary pattern

Here are two very obvious use cases. The first is where it all began, in the study of biological evolution by Charles Darwin. The second looks at a specific type of project.

A. **Biological Evolution**

- *Initial State:* largely irrelevant for this use case - whenever evolution began back in the mists of time (see Note 1 below).
- *Change Function:* Change is introduced through meiosis or mutation and reproduction, after which the organisms are different in varying and unpredictable degrees.
- *Fitness Function:* the evolutionary pressure of the environment on the organism which triggers competition for resources during growth to reproduction.
- *Viable Intermediate:* all organisms that do not exit to the Final State.
- *Final state:* the organism exits the evolutionary cycle for some reason. Again, largely irrelevant (see Note 2 below).

Notes:

1. According to evolutionary theory, about 4.5 billion years ago, a few molecules in the primeval soup became self-replicating. But our real journey began with the creation of DNA-based genes in cellular organisms and the process of meiosis, which introduces genetic variation

2. If an organism fails to reproduce or a species dies out then it exits the cycle. There may be rare circumstances in which the organism is perfectly suited to its environment and undergoes no further change.
3. **Agile Project - Software Development**

- *Initial State:* whatever state the software is in on project inception - could be just an idea or an existing codebase for enhancement.
- *Change Function:* The cyclical planning and development tasks performed by the team.
- *Fitness Function:* the multiple validation stages, but primarily the feedback from the business stakeholders on whether the increment is moving in the required direction. Anything that is added that won't enable business stakeholders to capture value should be reworked or removed.
- *Viable Intermediate:* the codebase after the Fitness function moving into the next iteration of change and validation.
- *Final state:* once the business stakeholders agree there is value in deployment, or the initiative is killed.

How does this apply to traditional (predictive) lifecycle projects?

You can see how the generic evolutionary cycle applies to agile projects: it's baked into the concept of agile. But what about traditional, non-agile projects? Perhaps you're thinking "You're saying that everything evolves, but these projects are so structured and controlled. How does evolution affect these projects?"

So, let's consider how evolution occurs, and where the elements of the evolutionary pattern apply.

The "fitness function" is easy: at specific points, we review, assess, or test the results of our work and identify issues. We can do this in a project in a vast range of ways. And it is unavoidable: even if we omit all in-project testing, we will get automatic "live" validation of the project outputs, when we roll out the product to its users.

The "change process" is a combination of very explicit processes and more subtle processes that are nonetheless irresistible.

Two explicit sources of change in projects

One source is what we typically think about in a project as "change": a change in external circumstances or conditions or a change in business strategy. Traditionally, this type of change is dealt with by a "Change Request" that seeks to explicitly change the project specifications in some area.

We can generalise another source as "errors". For example, we omitted a stakeholder from our requirements gathering or made an error capturing requirements. Or there's a bug in the code found by testing. This source of change can be dealt with explicitly via a Change Request or a defect management process.

Thus we have two explicit two sources of change. Traditional project management gives us tools to manage these, such as the Change Request and Defect Management processes mentioned above.

But let's assume for a moment that we can omit or exclude all change events arising from these two sources. Would we still have changes in our projects?

The answer is an unequivocal yes.

Why is this?

The third source of change in projects

The third source of change is more complex and nuanced, because it derives from how we think and communicate information amongst ourselves. This type of change is "self-generated change", or change introduced by the human members of the team and its stakeholders. Since all projects involve humans, avoiding self-generated change in a project is impossible.

Within this type of change, there are five primary causes:

1. **Communication**: human communication has extraordinary bandwidth but is "noisy" and error-prone. Human communication is not mechanical and predictable encode/decode like as sending and receiving Morse code. We may start with an agreed and standard standard code book, but each person has the ability to both modify the code translation and introduce new codes in ways that are unkwnown to other participants. This means that each time we exchange information with other humans, the message is potentially modified.
2. **Perception**: our brains are much better at responding to a pattern we perceive through our senses (usually vision) than we are at originating information. Moreover, we cannot avoid responding to a pattern we see and mentally comparing it to what we expect to see and what we already know. Each time we go through the "sense-response" cycle, we potentially change the message.

3. **Translation**: when we think we don't use our senses directly. Instead, we operate on an internal representation of our world — a mental model. Mental models present two problems. Firstly, they contain less information than the actual thing they are modelling. Secondly, we build and maintain our model by translating between it and the information in the outside world. This translation generates differences and triggers the other two processes.
4. **Layering**: as we focus on a problem area for any length of time, our knowledge increases and advances as we learn new things and integrate them into our existing accumulated knowledge. Each time we interact with the project knowledge our perspective on the project baseline alters.
5. **Mindsets & Biases**: humans have a filtering mechanism that can both filter out or modify information in our perceived environment. So, even if you think you have an objective perspective on things, your internal knowledge network is highly personalised and opaque to others.

These five processes operate continually and largely unconsciously and rely on the interaction between us and our environment. More importantly, a project team relies on the interaction between team members and our project information. We go through constant cycles of validation and correction at multiple levels.

So even if you did operate in an environment where all other change was removed, our cognitive processes would still result in evolution in our projects.

Evolutionary patterns applied to projects

Ok, but how does this relate to projects?

The narrative of the "best" approaches to project implementation is usually framed as a grand battle of ideas between serialised ("Waterfall") and adaptive/iterative ("Agile"). Agile is set up to deal with all three sources of change, but most importantly, it is set up to facilitate and even stimulate the cognitive evolutionary cycles.

But the reality (and the joke) is that waterfall never existed, even though it has been slavishly followed. Even though there may have been grand attempts at imposing this structure (and the motivation for those attempts exists today), they could not quash the essence of the evolutionary process by which people think and work together.

Any project manager who worked under the heavy hand of a phase-gate approach knew they had to build in some form of iteration within that serialised structure. Everyone knew they would still be working on cleaning up things from previous stages, no matter the mandated processes. Some projects looked more like a hamburger than a waterfall because most phases stacked up one on the other.

In 1970, Winston Royce recommended this policy in his famous paper, "Managing the Development of Large Software Systems". For more, see the Axiom, **"# 97. What if there never was a 'Waterfall'?"** in **"Adam On: Projects (Volume 2)"**[1].

The Bottom Line

Evolution is a natural and inevitable process that occurs at multiple levels in projects. The evolutionary process can benefit the project and its stakeholders if understood and leveraged. But, if ignored or attempts are made to suppress the unstoppable evolutionary forces, extreme damage can be done.

The Tags

#principlesofprojectsuccess, #evolution, #projectlifecycle, #projectmethodology, #projectmanagementapproach, #waterfall, #biologicalevolution, #adaptiveprocesses, #changerequest, #changemanagementprocess, #defectmanagementprocess

---

[1] https://bjl.ink/aopv2

22. Is there purpose in your iteration?

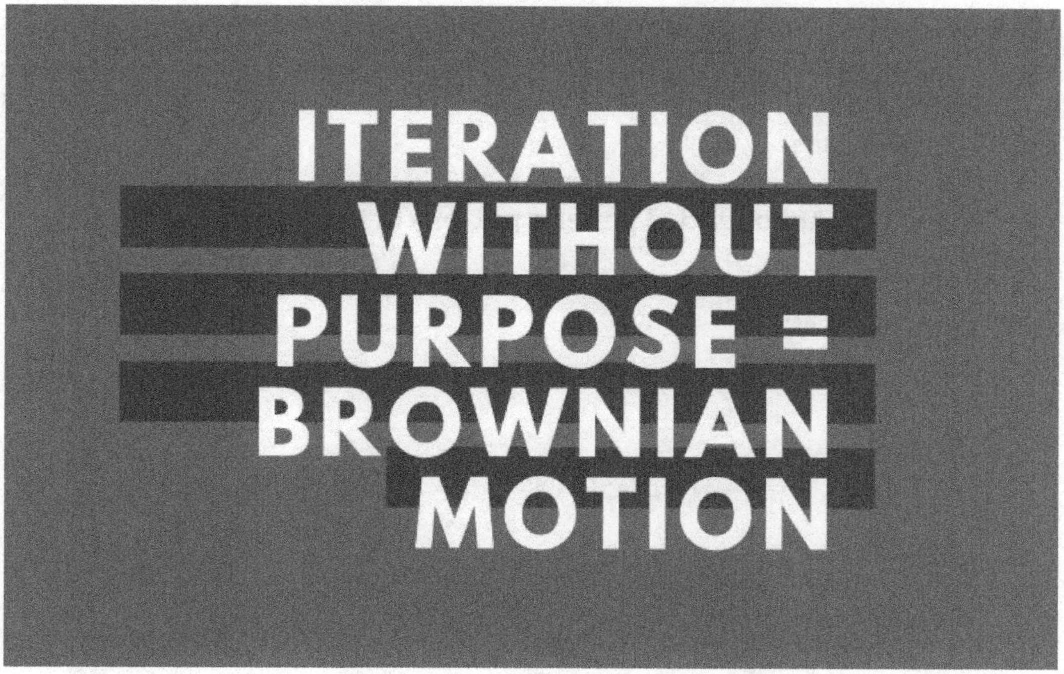

The Axiom

Iteration without purpose trends towards Brownian motion.

The TL;DR

It is possible to run purely empirical projects that rely only on fitness functions to drive the next step of the iterative cycle. This empirical process is even more random than natural (biological) evolution. But remember that biological evolution is extraordinarily inefficient and is measured in geological timeframes and millions of iterations. Projects can be open to new possibilities, but in most cases (the vast majority), we can be more directive about the axis of evolution. Our north star should always be customer value and solve customer problems. Pure empiricism (iterating without purpose) is Brownian motion.

The Back Story

The evolutionary processes in biological organisms show a pattern of cycles repeating over generations. But there are echoes of this pattern in all human endeavours.

The cycle of variation and validation that is the core of biological evolution is repeated in every goal-based human endeavour. The only things that change are the nature of the critical processes in the pattern.

An extended generic pattern of evolution

I presented a simplified and generic evolutionary pattern in the axiom "**# 21. Everything in every project evolves!**".

An extended version of this generic evolutionary pattern is illustrated in the diagram below.

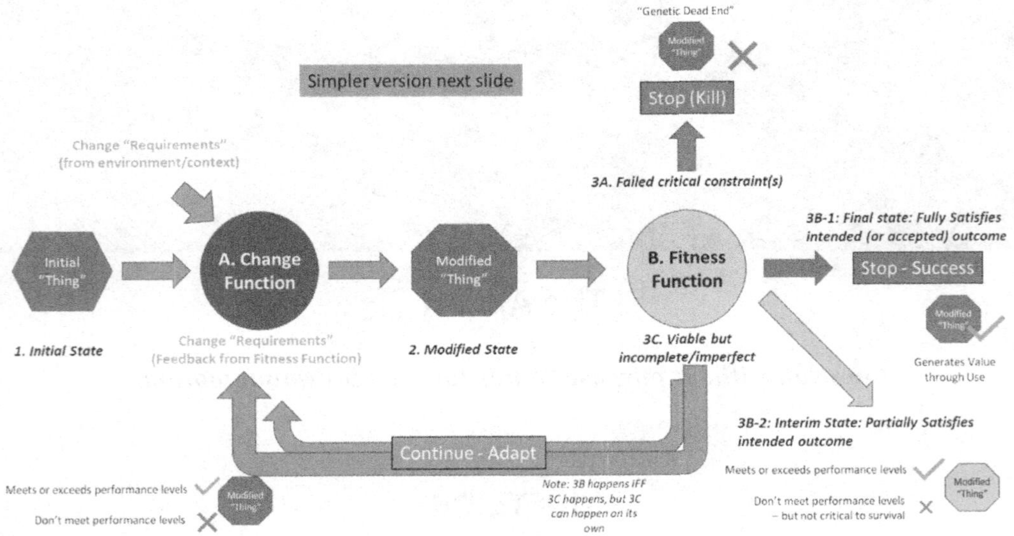

Figure 12. The Extended Generic Pattern of Evolution

Extending our discussion of the two functions in this cycle, in the context of agile software projects:

1. **Change Process** the variation on the software for the next iteration derives from multiple sources:

- the planning process, in which the current view of prioritised opportunities and problems is modulated by the feedback from stakeholders from the last validation process, e.g. the last sprint review. Frequently, experimentation is required to determine the optimum solution functionality.
- the build process, based on the plan, but also adjusting as build details emerge.
- technical validation of the built components.

2. **Fitness function** the determination of whether the variation elements are "adaptive" to the environmental circumstances. This validation is only performed in the business (aka "problem") space. Users and other stakeholders assesses the change(s) and determines that the variation (modified product) better positions them to capture value, or that the variation is sub-optimal.

The Fitness function has three output pathways:

a. **Stop/Kill**: the variant is not viable, and we're done. This could be just one or more components of the latest build, or a previous component that is now redundant. Or it could be determined that the whole product is non-viable, so the project is killed.

b. **Stop/Success**: the variant sufficiently meets the environmental conditions. There are two sub-cases to this output state. It could be a final state, in which all conditions are met, in which case the project terminates. Or it could be an interim state, which is viable in the environment but not meeting all conditions. In this case, the stakeholders determine whether to continue towards a more complete product, or to stop with partial fulfilment of the conditions.

c. **Continue**: the variant is viable but needs further modification. This happens in all cases where the project does not terminate. The product (codebase) feeds into the next change process iteration. In addition, information from the fitness test is fed back into the next iteration, which is another source of variation. Lastly, external factors can feed into the next variation process.

Note that a secondary pathway is available in this extension when we continue and adapt: a variant that partly meets our criteria can be released while we continue the process.

Also note that in biological evolution terms, the word "adaptive" refers to features or characteristics of the organism that help it survive and thrive under the environmental pressure. Hence its use in general purpose agile terminology.

How does this work in practice?

The two critical elements of this process are obviously the two functions. See below for how this applies to one Agile framework: Scrum.

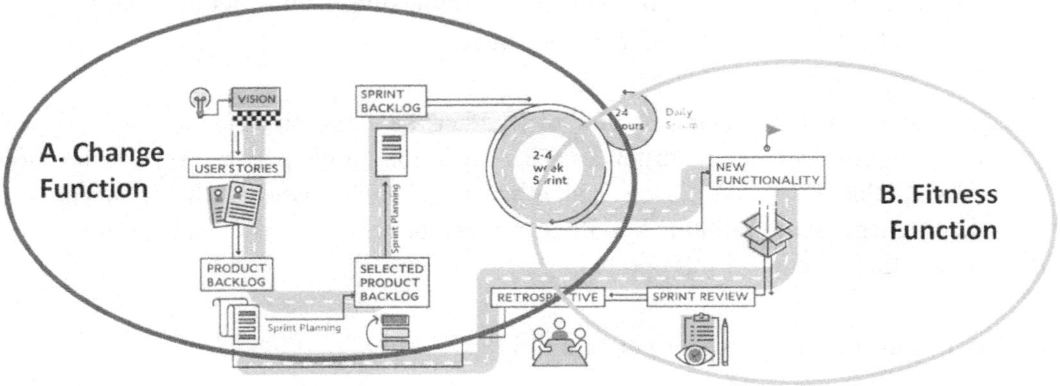

Figure 13. The Scrum Process Mapped to Adaptive Processes

Within the Scrum framework the "Fitness Function" is primarily the Sprint Review/Showcase, in which we present the results from the sprint to our stakeholders, who assess the latest changes against their problem space requirements. As shown above, there are other activities which contribute to the Fitness Function: the Sprint Retrospective, whilst generally about the team and their performance, applies Fitness Functions related to their team, which have a direct impact on their ability to perform the Fitness Function on the product/tech stack.

Similarly, the Daily Scrum involves acts of critical judgement about the way in which components are built.

Other methodologies handle the Fitness Function in different ways: for example, Kanban teams can still have a Customer Review periodically, or results can be validated with each ticket closure.

Still, it has — at least in theory — the same result: the project continues with another cycle, stops with a viable product version, or kills it as non-viable.

The problem with this theory is when the "Fitness Function" is applied vaguely or softly. Most showcases are simply that — an opportunity for the team to put on a "show" of what they've achieved. Feedback from stakeholders is often much like applause in a concert, pleasant to hear but not very effective overall.

Whilst the Change Process works in tandem with the Fitness Function in an iterative dialog of question and response, it is the Fitness Function that truly makes evolution work. Without it, anything can survive. The biological equivalent is when the environment into which offspring are born is very benign — many variations can survive and procreate that will inevitably die out if (when) the environment becomes more hostile. And more hostile it will become if only because growing numbers of organisms begin competing for the same resources or even degrading the environment.

When teams stop validating during the Fitness Function, then the product process stops evolving in its most important way. Once the team stops being ruthless about rejecting product characteristics, then anything will be passed through.

But because - as we saw in the axiom "**# 21. Everything in every project evolves!**". - change still occurs essentially randomly, this means that the evollutionary cycle is random.

Is evolution random?

Evolution is not random: but the degree to which the direction is clear depends on the intensity of the Fitness function.

On the other hand, Brownian motion is an example of a random process. It was coined in 1827 by Robert Brown, who observed the motion of pollen grains suspended in water. People had described this process on dust and coal particles back to 60 BC, but Brown got the nod for an eponymous law.

Since then, Brownian motion has been formalised into one type of the family of stochastic processes in mathematics and physics. Stochastic processes are random processes in which a series of changes occur in a measurement, variable or object where the relationship between one increment and the next is unpredictable. Over many iterations, patterns in aggregate changes can be detected, giving rise to different stochastic functions.

Random evolution in projects

What does this have to do with projects? Let me explain.

Every project changes through the underlying evolution of its concepts, understanding and intentions (see the axiom ***"# 21. Everything in every project evolves!"***). The main contributor to the nature of any given project is the relationship between evolution events and the overall pattern of that evolution over a series of steps (typically the entire project).

Projects with different lifecycle models handle evolution differently, but agile not only builds it into its fundamental concept but other methods are based on explicit iterations. The evolutionary cycle doesn't always align 100% with the iteration cycle, but the iteration cycle formalises when fitness functions can be applied.

Projects are ostensibly far more structured environments than untamed nature, where most evolution occurs. Projects, by definition, have an end goal that guides the project in a specific direction. The pathway may vary on the road to that goal, but the goal is relatively stable.

What happens to create a situation where iteration might become "Brownian Motion"? It's where our evolutionary process breaks down because we don't apply a fitness function that determines whether the result of the iteration is acceptable as an increment towards our end goal.

"Sloppy Evolution" compromised project progress

This results in "Sloppy Evolution", in which the team is executing an evolutionary model imperfectly. "Sloppy Evolution" is also described in the axiom "**# 107. What is the primary source of change in a project?**" in "**Adam On: Projects (Volume 2)**"[2].

I've seen many projects that operate in an iterative lifecycle, for example, Scrum, in which the sprints don't validate their outputs with the intended customers or key stakeholders. I'm sure you have seen this too. If we don't apply a "fitness test" to the sprint results, we cannot determine whether we're heading in the right direction. This approach is not even empirical because we don't use the evidence our senses provide us when we review, check, or assess a particular thing.

Even if you're not in an iterative lifecycle, you're still evolving, just not in neat increments. The incremental cycles occur within the framework of task execution, but they occur nonetheless. And fitness functions are required in predictive projects even more so than in adaptive.

The evolutionary fitness functions we apply in iterative development are designed to determine whether we are heading towards the agreed goal. Occasionally but equally well, the fitness test highlights problems with the plan. But either way, assessment and re-orientation are part of the process.

So, our iterations are random, in which case they are stochastic and will appear to observers as that particulate motion appeared to Mr Brown all those years ago.

[2] https://bjl.ink/aopv2

The Bottom Line

Iterations are not random. Even "throwing spaghetti at a wall" requires that someone checks whether it sticks. If the "Fitness Function" is not applied or applied in a gentle or indecisive manner, then we end up with "Brownian Motion".

The Tags

#evolution, #principlesofprojectsuccess, #iteration, #iterativeincrementaldevelopment, #incremental, #stochasticprocesses, #sloppyevolution, #empiricism, #brownianmotion, #fitnesstest, #robertbrown

On Abundance

The "**Abundance**" mindset, from a project perspective, is an evolution from that first popularised by Steven Covey, and which are now promoted by the spiritual guidance / lay psychology / self-help / personal growth coaching industries.

In a project context, "**Abundance**" refers to a positive outlook on the future: being confident that the project will find a solution and get the resources it needs to finish the job. It is an optimistic posture towards the future, even when current circumstances may be problematic.

Why is this important? Because optimists have "grit" - optimists endure - and get the job done.

23. Abundance is the soul of your project.

The Axiom

Abundance is the soul of your project - without it, you're just turning the dreary handle of process.

The TL;DR

Embracing the principle of abundance in project management fosters resilience, optimism, and grit. By cultivating an abundance mindset, project teams and stakeholders can confidently navigate challenges and uncertainties while focusing on achieving goals. This mindset, grounded in transformative optimism and pragmatic prospection, allows teams to persevere and adapt to change, ultimately driving project success.

The Back Story

Projects are challenging beasts, and achieving the stated goals can often be tricky.

We need a perspective on the future that enables project stakeholders to envision a beneficial outcome, even if all the elements are not in place and in the face of real or imagined problems.

Abundance in popular literature

In popular culture, abundance is a mindset in which people perceive their world, emotionally, physically, and spiritually, as having sufficient resources, such as time, money, power, and affection, to be generous with their energy, attention, and power.

Stephen Covey on abundance:

> *... Abundance results in sharing of prestige, of recognition, of profits, of decision making. It opens possibilities, options, alternatives, and creativity.“* — **Stephen R Covey** in The Seven Habits of Highly Effective People

The opposite of Abundance is the “Scarcity” mindset.

People with the “Scarcity” mindset perceive resources as limited and have a fear of missing out or being disadvantaged in the competition for resources.

Projects: a belief in a beneficial outcome

We need the project team and stakeholders to believe in the project’s ability to achieve its goals, even in the face of current or imagined problems.

Traditional projects approach this unknown future through planning and risk management. However, the common failure of predictive planning and risk management is to create a false sense of certainty through excessive detail.

Projects entail risk, and the success rates for projects are not great. Just to participate in a project, you need a level of optimism, openness to the future and a desire to collaborate with others to achieve that outcome that lies in the future.

What compels the project team to undertake and complete these endeavours? I propose that it is an abiding sense of abundance. It starts with our leaders, who can:

> *”... inspire energy, joy, productivity, and dedication in their subordinates stand out. Though research attempts to explain this phenomenon, no model fully captures the diverse behaviours exhibited by such leaders or the mental models driving those behaviours.”* — **Freebairn-Smith** (2009)

The concept of abundance has a long history, originating in ecology, evolutionary biology, and economics. In its original sense, abundance is about physical resources and their availability in the environment relative to demand. More recently, abundance has evolved in its definition and theory base, extending into Psychology, Organisational Behaviour, and Leadership.

We can view Abundance as having two parts in its view of the future:

1. **Optimism over Pessimism**
2. **Pragmatic prospection over prediction**

Let's dive into those two topics in the next two sections.

Optimism over Pessimism

The study of abundance and scarcity aligns closely with the study of optimism and pessimism.

From a project perspective, abundance both creates and results from optimism: we act confidently knowing that we will succeed in our endeavour to enable our "customer" in a way that captures the most value we can.

What is the source of a person's internal optimism? One argument suggests that our ability to control feelings without destroying them leads to an optimistic view (Vaughan, 2000)

Steve Jobs famously said, *"Real programmers ship"*. Similarly, Vaughan (2000) notes that *"optimists persevere"*.

Thus, optimism fosters grit and the capacity to persevere.

Are all forms of optimism helpful to projects? Probably not. Rossato (2004) describes four categories of optimism: blind, fatalistic, resilient, and transformative. From a project management perspective, we are interested in the transformative category. The "transformative" optimist hopes for the best possible outcomes and sees themselves as an intrinsic part of achieving them (Rossato 2004).

Pragmatic Prospection

Abundance is a mental posture towards the future: it is a form of "prospection":

> *"... prospective thinking as first and foremost a set of mental acts designed to guide future action for practical ends."* — **Baumeister** et al. (2016)

Prospection is not "prediction". Prediction aligns with planning: a formulation of what will happen, which means focusing on a specific future state, and is the basis of predictive project management.

Baumeister (2016) coined the term *"Pragmatic Prospection"*, which is more attuned to our concept of project abundance. Pragmatic prospection is about creating mental formulations of how our decisions can turn out and, therefore, involves multiple possible outcomes, including success and failure.

Thinking about the future often involves preparing for action to achieve desired outcomes.

There are two stages that make up "Pragmatic prospection":

1. Firstly, imagining what one wants to happen, which is thus initially optimistic.
2. Secondly, by mapping out the steps required to achieve the desired future state.

There is some evidence that after elaborating on the more pessimistic (realistic) plans, people return to their optimistic outlook (abundance), which maintains their energy to withstand inevitable disappointments and to persevere with the plan (Baumeister et al. 2016)

The Bottom Line

Project abundance, therefore, is a particular kind of optimism based on the process of mental contrasting. With abundance comes trust: we work based on our ability to operate in ways that don't require the preparation of defences against attacks or lean periods. As a project manager, whether we have an abundance or scarcity mindset determines how we position ourselves to take on and manage projects. Regardless of how much planning we do about the future state or monitoring during project execution, we never really know about project success until we get there.

The Tags

#planning, #agile, #projectplanning, #prediction, #plan-based, #predictive, #abundance, #stephenrcovey, #optimism, #pragmatism, #pragmaticprospection, #sevenhabitsofhighlyeffectivepeople, #mindset, #abundancemindset, #scarcitymind-set, #freebairn-smith

---

24. A project is a bridge.

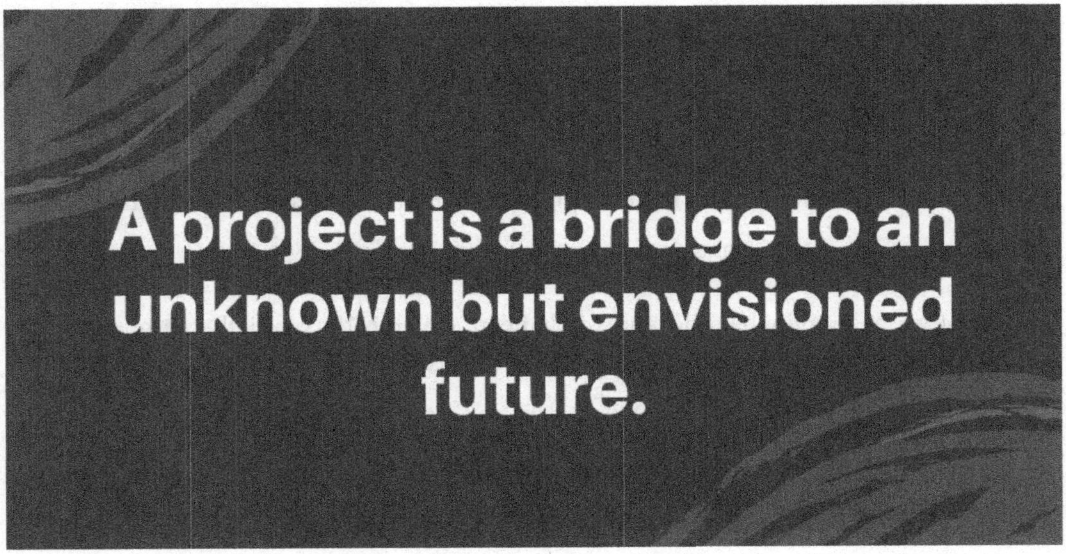

The Axiom

A project is a bridge to an unknown but envisioned future.

The TL;DR

A project is a bridge to an unknown but envisioned future. Known facts and assumptions support this bridge. The next section of the bridge is often being built as we walk over it. If both the ultimate future and the path to it are uncertain, we must position ourselves in the now to minimise wasted investment.

Too many project approaches give a perspective of "False Concreteness" to our plans, which sets invalid expectations about the likely future and usually wastes time and money.

Plenty of other opportunities will arise to waste time and money, so let's focus on managing those.

The Back Story

Most project approaches and mindsets try to write the future, either the ultimate deliverables or the project's pathway to get there. This practice consumes large amounts of energy and cognitive cycles. Of course, we need to plan at some level, but we also need to understand how unlikely it is that we'll be able to determine the future correctly.

The underlying theory of Project Management is Dead

In the paper **["The Underlying Theory of Project Management is Obsolete"]**(http://usir.salford.ac.uk/9400/1/2002_The_underlying_theory_of_project_management_is_obsolete.pdf), Lauri Koskela and Greg Howell (2002) argue that the traditional project management approach is outdated. Although targeted primarily at the construction industry, the analysis and recommendations echo much of the Agile Manifesto. Koskela and Howell argue that the traditional project management approach, which relies heavily on planning, control, and execution, is inadequate and outdated. They point out that this approach does not sufficiently address the complexities and uncertainties present in most projects, often leading to project failures, delays, and cost overruns.

Not much of this sounds new in 2023, but in 2002 it was among the few voices arguing for change. And frankly, little has changed in many parts of the project management industry besides adopting or aligning agile approaches.

Unknowable futures

Only a few years ago, I read a review of Koskela and Howell's paper by Hal Macomber, and the below extract caught my attention (my underlined emphasis):

> *"projects are distinctly human endeavors taking place in unknowable futures. Planning and plan execution are tied directly to both the people who are performing the project and the future that unfolds while they do that."* — **Hal Macomber** in "Notes on the Underlying Theory of Project Management is Obsolete" on his blog Reforming Project Management (link defunct — accessed by Internet Archive[1]).

The point here is that we can write a lot of plans and specifications and the like and set stakeholders' expectations about what the future will bring, but we never fully know where

[1]https://web.archive.org/web/20111008180447/http:/www.reformingprojectmanagement.com/lenses/project-management-theory/notes-on-the-underlying-theory-of-project-management-is-obsolete/

our projects will end up. We can't see the future, so our project management practices must reflect that reality.

We may think we can create a solid and immutable plan that ends where we want to go—-in the past, the definition of a successful project was considered to be following an immutable plan to its end.

Macomber's other critical perspective is that you cannot separate the people parts of a project from the non-people parts.

This perspective led to many project management changes and the Agile Manifesto. Koskela and Howell pre-dated the 2006 study called *"Rethinking Project Management"*, which called for numerous changes in how we thought about and managed projects.

Many of those changes recognised the human element in the project management process.

The Bottom Line

The "project as a bridge" concept is not new but is no less powerful. Incorporating the idea that the future is unknowable is somewhat new to project management but very apt, so I've adapted Macomber's comments to construct this axiom.

The Tags

#planning, #projectplanning, #abundance, #principlesofprojectsuccess, #laurikoskela, #greghowell, #underlyingprinciplesofprojectmanagement, #falseconcreteness, #agile-manifesto, #halmacomber, #rethinkingprojectmanagement

25. The Long Corridor.

The Axiom

A project is like a long corridor of untold locked doors.

The TL;DR

A project is a long corridor of many locked doors you must pass. Each door is a different material, strength, and lock. Your mission is to get through all the doors to the end; each is a challenge you must overcome. There's no point in getting frustrated at each blockage – it's just a job to be done. And don't let your hopes undermine you: don't become disappointed when you finally open one door, only to find another one. You never know how many, or which one will be the last!

The Back Story

This imaginary corridor of locked doors is just an analogy to help people maintain their resilience in the face of project frustrations.

There's nothing more frustrating than falling into the trap of thinking yourself close to the end of your troubles in a project. But I've seen people over the years bust a gut working on a problem and celebrate the win, only to find another one immediately. People hang their heads or take on a woeful tone of voice. Somehow, they convinced themselves that a problem fixed is the last one and that it will be smooth sailing from there.

Seemingly endless system integration issues

I started using this analogy during the testing phase of a large integration project — one of these "change the world" platforms we had to get out the door. The project was late and getting later.

This system comprised multiple applications built by different teams and many interfaces. Software quality was patchy: some components were not ready and had obviously seen little unit testing - in some cases, we were doing primary code debugging.

Every time we ran a transaction, we found a new bug - the developers would fix it, and we'd rerun the test. Sometimes it would work, and sometimes it wouldn't. Every time we got it working up to the last failure point, it would immediately fail at the next step.

We went on like this in a repeating cycle.

Occasionally, we'd rush through several steps at speed, and we'd execute a complete transaction. Momentarily we'd all feel a sense of relief and accomplishment. A few optimists would think we were done. But then, Bam! At the next interface, we found the next set of defects, and the next locked door.

I'd hear this same story repeatedly. By then we were running three or more defect meetings daily.

It was hell.

I had a dream - and stuck with it

I can't remember if it was a dream or a mental image formed during one of these meetings, but I can still see it in my head. It's like I was in an episode of "The Twilight Zone": I was facing a door and knew I had to get it open — I didn't know why, but I just had this compelling feeling that if I didn't get it open, something terrible would happen.

I'm shaking the handle and banging on the door, but it won't open. Suddenly, I somehow get it open, but I don't know how. Maybe I kicked it down or something. And behind the opened door, there's another door. Over and over — in my dream, I was bashing open doors and feeling the rising frustration and hope that the next one you open will be the last.

It wasn't the last project that involved this kind of situation. Pretty much every Systems Integration project is like this. I don't have objective evidence, but it feels like this situation has become worse over time. As projects use more virtualised components and platforms and solutions use more APIs and services, we find ourselves constantly in these situations.

So, the mental image of an apparently endless corridor of locked doors seems more valuable with every project.

The Bottom Line

You'll never know everything you must do on a project until you reach the end. It will be frustrating enough to get through without building hope or expecting it to end soon. It will be over when it is over. Keep going calmly and steadily; you'll get there in the end.

The Tags

#projectmanagermindsets, #analogy, #obstacles, #resilience, #patience, #determination, #grit, #optimism, #abundance, #problemsolving, #debugging, #integration, #testing

On Agile

The term "Agile" in a project context describes a lightweight approach that emphasises the satisfaction of customer value needs through rapid development using an iterative "inspect and adapt" cycle by small hyper-collaborative teams.

The reality is sometimes different.

Agile is a very noisy and contradictory marketplace these days, with many often conflicting perspectives on how to achieve "agility".

We need a different approach to agile, which unifies and brings practitioners together rather than fostering cliques and tribes.

26. Just because you want to do agile doesn't mean you can.

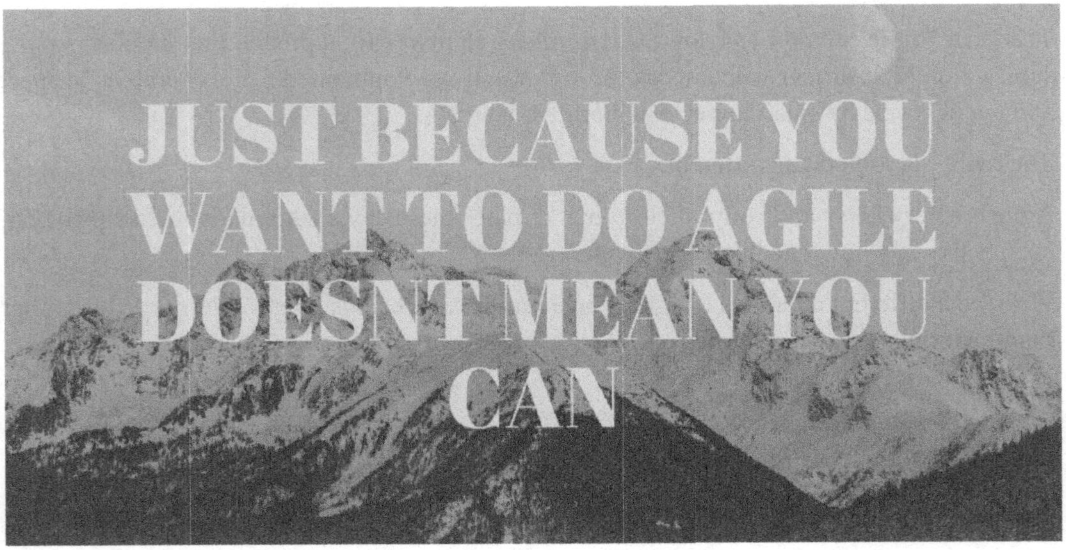

The Axiom

Just because you want to do agile doesn't mean you can or should do it.

The TL;DR

Agile transformations are widespread, with a growing number of people and organisations joining the movement. However, agile is often reduced to a buzzword rather than a practice, with many failing to establish the necessary conditions for its success. There are seven (7) critical enabling factors for Agile to flourish. Unfortunately, having all these factors fully developed in an agile practitioner (or team, or organisation) is rare. The intersection of these factors produces so few people who are "agile ready" or even "agile capable", making it a "Sad Venn Diagram of Agile Practice". Understanding and developing these factors is essential for a successful agile journey. It is unquestionable that agile—done well—can deliver many benefits. But success requires a deep understanding of factors far outside the norm for Information Technology ("IT") programs or any programs where agile is deployed.

The Back Story

Why do people want to do agile? And is everyone who "wants" to be an agile practitioner ready to be successful?

Just a heads up before we dive in: some factors that I outline apply to other lifecycle models too, just in different ways. I discuss them in terms of agile/adaptive practice because that's the focus of this axiom. I've included links to other axioms in which I discuss these factors in more detail.

Another heads up: this is a long axiom. I think it's a critical topic.

Everyone wants to do agile, maybe.

Sadly, many people — and organisations — want to do agile for spurious reasons: "It's better", say some, or "Everyone is doing it", say others. Others implement agile to achieve greater productivity from their IT programs: the same or more output with reduced costs and cycle times.

In the meantime, Agile has unquestionably become a brand — even a brand category. But for all the energy and resources spent on agile transformations, the 64 million dollar question is ***"Will everyone be successful?"***

The sad answer is ***"Not very many."***

There are many reasons for this, which I have covered in other axioms. But the main—and inescapable—reason that your agile journey most likely won't work is because you don't have the right enablers in place or even know they are pre-requisites for "being agile".

Even worse, perhaps you understand their necessity, but you think studying and practising agile techniques will bring those enablers into existence as a by-product.

So, what are these seven enablers for good Agile practice?

The project environment

The first enabler is the complexity of the project environment. Is the environment reasonably stable, or is it chaotic or something in between? And what do those words mean, anyway?

We can assess the environment's stability using **Cynefin domain analysis**. An alternative might be the "**Stacey Matrix**". Agile experts have used both frameworks for assessing the applicability of different approaches to projects.

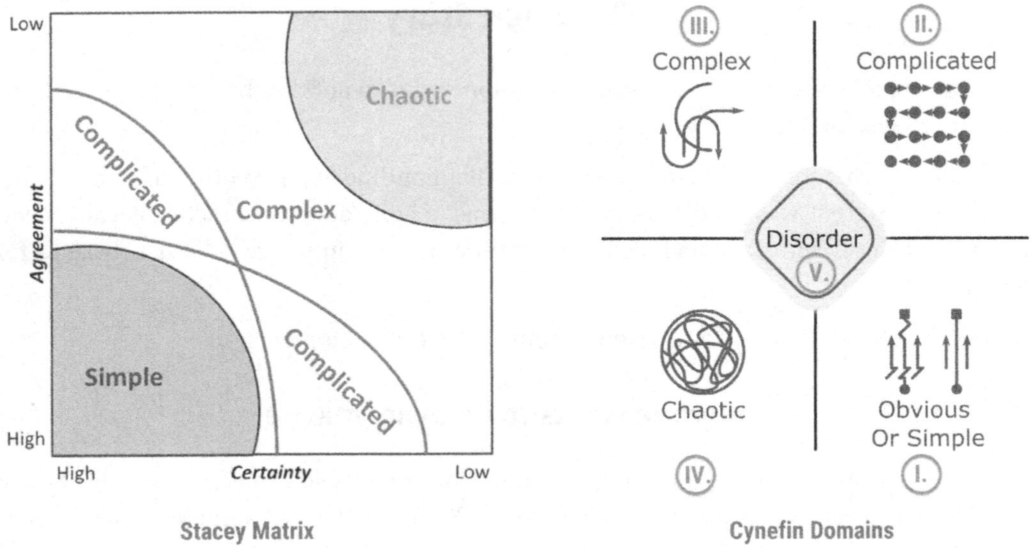

Figure 14. Cynefin and Stacey Matrix Frameworks

Many agile pundits have used both frameworks to differentiate where adaptive methods may be more successful and where predictive methods may be more successful.

Is your environment either "Complex" or "Chaotic", in which problems are ill-defined, and there is no clear cause-and-effect relationship? Or is there is no clear understanding of the problem or how to solve it?

For Cynefin, adaptive methods are more attuned to Domain III. Elements of the adaptive approach may help determine the context and navigating in other domains like IV and V. For the Stacey Matrix, adaptive methods are more useful in Complex and Complicated domains. I prefer the Cynefin framework because I think it has better diagnostic tools and helps map to a solution strategy.

Agile excels in domains that are not stable, where required information is both unknown and unknowable (at least timing-wise). Other project models may be better if everything is stable, predictable, and known. In such environments, it is easier to plan and estimate; and plans require less maintenance in a stable environment.

But there are no fixed rules: each team must decide for themselves how to approach a problem. If the team feels that they want to apply adaptive approaches to simple or predictable contexts, and it generates confidence and efficacy, then they should use what works for them. But we need to make these decisions objectively. We must be clear on the source of this complexity. Is our environment intrinsically complex, or are we making it so through our own behaviour, mindsets, and assumptions? We often make things seem more complicated than they are.

Also, keep in mind the trend towards two-speed agile: adaptive agile as it was originally intended, and predictive agile (or what I call "performative agile") that is designed to allow agile practices to operate in enterprise and at scale.

For more information on 2-speed agile, check out the axiom: ***"# 28. The saddest oxymoron of the 21st century"***. For more on team-caused complexity, please see the axiom ***"# 21. Everything in every project evolves!"***, and "**# 107. What is the primary source of change in a project?**" in "**Adam On: Projects (Volume 2)**"[1].

Organisational Culture

The second enabler is the degree to which the initiative's hosting organisation support and encourages agile behaviour.

We can use Westrum's "**Cultural Topologies**" model to assess the agile affinity of an organisation. Westrum was a safety researcher who identified that organisational culture could predict safety characteristics. Westrum believed that information flow indicated other aspects of culture. He developed his "**Three Cultures Model**" to predict how organisations might respond in difficult circumstances. The three culture types are "**Generative**", "**Bureaucratic**" and "**Pathological**".

A "**Generative**" culture type supports agile and is in perfect harmony with the principles and values of agile practice.

A "**Bureaucratic**" topology whose rules already support individual and team agency (see the fifth enabler below) might be also supportive or might be stuck in an immutable and static rule-set.

"**Pathological**" cultures cause problems with all project teams. Obviously one high-level category can cover a whole range of situations and be present in varying degrees, but mostly they are not nice places to work.

But "Pathological" cultures can be toxic to agile project teams and practices for one simple reason: these cultures affect the strength of the social forces that bind agile teams together. Teams following predictive lifecycle frameworks can also be impacted by "Pathological" cultures—everyone works better if team social forces are allowed free reign. But predictive approaches have other constructs that help form the project construct—explicit plans and process conformance—that don't suffer so much in Pathological environments.

[1] https://bjl.ink/aopv2

Unfortunately, "Pathological" cultures are all too common in our societies today. Agile transformations that don't address toxic cultures first are at a serious risk of failure.

You can read more about the social forces that bind teams together, in the axiom: ***"# 1. The source of project success."***.

Paradigm Zero

The third enabler relates to how people see reality and the existence of the knowledge required for projects.

To assess this, I use "**Paradigm Zero**", which is based on classical philosophical concepts but adapted to projects. Philosophers have pondered a fundamental dichotomy in thinking about reality and knowledge for two millennia, which I've now adapted and simplified for projects. I call it "Paradigm Zero" - a range from "Hard" at one extreme to "Soft" at the other.

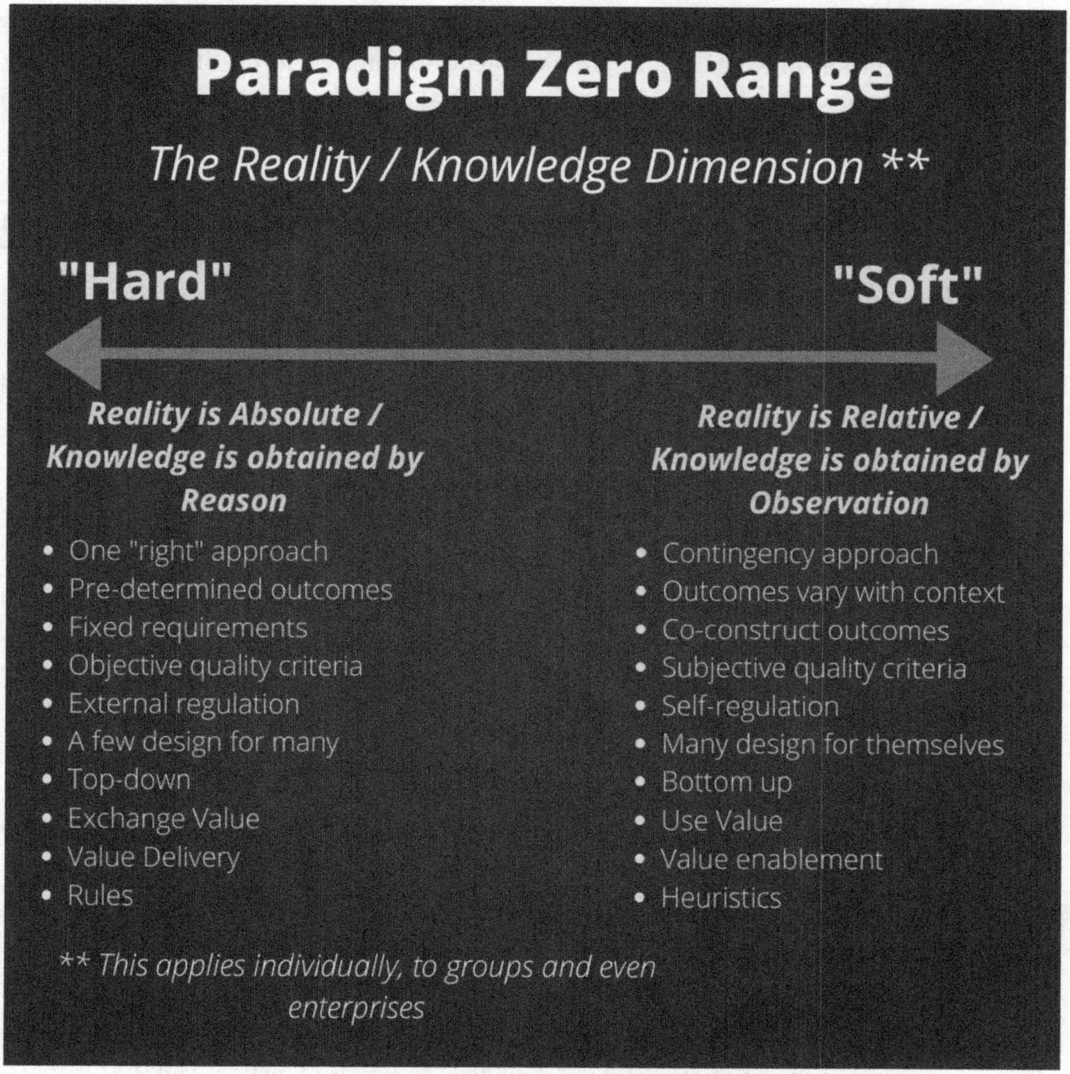

Figure 15. Paradigm Zero Attributes

I've highlighted some characteristics of Paradigm Zero extremes in the above diagram.

Please refer to the axiom "**# 113. What is your approach to documentation?**" in "**Adam On: Projects (Volume 2)**"[2], for more information about "Paradigm Zero" and how it affects behaviour in projects.

[2]https://bjl.ink/aopv2

This mindset distinction is important because it affects how people approach problem-solving and decision-making. "Hard" thinkers tend to think in terms of a single correct ("perfect") solution, whereas "Soft" thinkers can deal with multiple solutions and value context and co-creation.

It is much easier to see other people's points of view if you are open to co-constructed reality. This leads to an affinity for interactions, which leads to shared goals and values. It is much easier to instantiate and grow a Cross-functional team with "Soft" thinkers, whereas "\Hard" thinkers feel more protective about their roles and knowledge - they can feel they need to have ownership or dominance in a specialist role or solution domain.

This is not just an issue with agile projects, but it has much more impact on agile teams than traditional teams.

Emotional and Psychological Development

The fourth enabler relates to people's emotional and psychological development.

We can assess this using a scale developed by Robert Kegan, who divided emotional development into six stages, the first three of which occur in early childhood or in very immature adults. In the professional domain of project management, you will most likely interact with people in the last three stages.

For agile to work, in my opinion, people must be at Stage 4 or a very mature Stage 3. Otherwise, they will have difficulty dealing with the uncertainty of an evolutionary, adaptive mindset. They will be less able to relate to others in a way that *"puts themselves in the other person's shoes"*.

Kegan described Stage 4 as comprising only 35% of the general population, although it is unclear how that relates to the population of people who want to be agile, or even the population of people involved in projects.

Of course, we must deal with people as we find them. Kegan recognised that there may be dissonance between the emotional and psychological demands of task set and the attributes of employees. He recommended ways to deal with this, including the notion of "safe spaces" where people can develop.

For example, in **"Bureaucratic"** and **"Pathological"** organisations we are less likely to be able to choose team members freely: either they are assigned to teams in a resource pool approach, or the teams have little control over hiring processes. Please refer to the axiom **"# 92. What are your hiring criteria?"** in **"Adam On: Projects (Volume 2)"**[3], for thoughts on the impacts of such policies.

[3]https://bjl.ink/aopv2

Individual and Team Agency

The fifth enabler is the ability of people and teams to act and choose, to take responsibility and reflectively make progress.

This ability is called "Agency" and is the engine of any project. High levels of Agency fuel projects with energy and forward momentum, allowing team members to pursue the project's objectives actively. Its absence results in a project that loses its way.

Through their Agency, people take responsibility for collaborating with other stakeholders, align their actions with the project's objectives, and adjust their performance to converge on the agreed quality. High Agency is related to emotional development (see above) but is distinct.

I've unpacked Agency, and how it compares with "Autonomy" in the axiom, ***"# 14. Proceed until apprehended!"***.

Agile is highly dependent on the level of Agency in project teams. You might say that project environments have a requirement for high-agency people regardless of lifecycle, and this is correct. But as with other factors above, high agency in people is the result of other personal characteristics that are critical to agile, such as self-reflection and self-regulation.

Skills Profile

The sixth enabler is the team members' experience and skill level across various subjects.

I'm not just referring to project-specific skills, such as a particular coding language or skills in whatever technology stack supports the solution. Nor am I talking about the cross-functional skills that reduce dependency on outside teams. I also mean a range of skills in other domains, such as history and human psychology, skills in a hobby, a broad understanding of global cultures and societies, law, and humanities.

I'm not saying that, say, stamp-collecting skills or woodworking skills will necessarily help a project. I'm more interested in the curiosity about a subject and the motivation, prioritisation, and self-discipline that makes those hobbies work. And besides, who knows what another team member might be interested in when the team is "shooting the breeze". Google's Project Aristotle suggests that a team that talks about almost anything will be bound more tightly than a team that only ever talks about the project.

As with the other factors, skills profiles are relevant in other lifecycle models, too. But also, as with the others, agile teams are more susceptible to impairment in this area.

We can qualitatively assess and describe the range and depth of skills using shape analogies, such as T-Shaped, Pi-Shaped and "Comb-shaped".

Clearly, "Comb-shaped" skills profile—many skills with some depth to them— is the most appropriate for agile team members. But I like to think of the requirement as more extreme: it's not a "comb" but a long white picket fence.

Or even the seemingly endless **"Rabbit-proof Fence"**[4].

Value Alignment

The seventh enabler is how the people/teams in the project understand the value construct and the relationship between the project and the customer.

A key factor is customer empathy: the ability to sit inside a customer's head and understand what they do and how they create value for themselves.

Broad experience and mature emotional development enable this ability in part (see the relevant enablers above).

Customer empathy is a particular skill that requires people to suppress their focus on their team and the technologies they are working with and instead think like a customer. Many organisations and people pay lip service to this ability, but doing it is rare. Over my career, facilitating a value-focused view in a project team is one of the hardest tasks I've had to attempt and one that is extremely difficult to achieve in many teams.

Please refer to the axiom I've unpacked Agency, and how it compares with "Autonomy" in the axiom, ***"# 18. Do you have a system-based objective?"***. and **"# 86. Projects do not "deliver value"** in **"Adam On: Projects (Volume 2)"**[5], for more information about the different kinds of value.

This factor—or its lack in a project—is most highlighted most in the scenario where the IT team is agile, but the business stakeholders are not, in my opinion. This could be the result of other factors as well, such as the Organisational Culture or Cognitive Development. But I think this dissonance most plays out when trying to work with the business stakeholders to characterise outcome value.

I've talked to this topic in the axiom ***"# 52. Business people make lousy solutions architects."***.

What is missing?

What's missing from those seven enablers is expertise in agile concepts and methodologies. Unfortunately, processes and practices are where most organisations—and individuals—try

[4]https://en.wikipedia.org/wiki/Rabbit-proof_fence
[5]https://bjl.ink/aopv2

to start their agile journey.

This is the most fundamental - and fatal - error with most agile implementations: trying to "reverse engineer" these seven mandatory enablers by learning the agile jargon, rote-learning a methodology, or doing a certification. It just doesn't work.

If the enablers are present in the project's context or people the agile concepts and methodologies will not only make a lot of sense, but are probably not required for anything more than superficial alignment on terminology.

I've talked to this topic in the axiom ***"# 28. The saddest oxymoron of the 21st century"***.

What does this mean for you

What does all this mean? It's a bit sad. So, I call this my Sad Venn Diagram of Agile Practice.

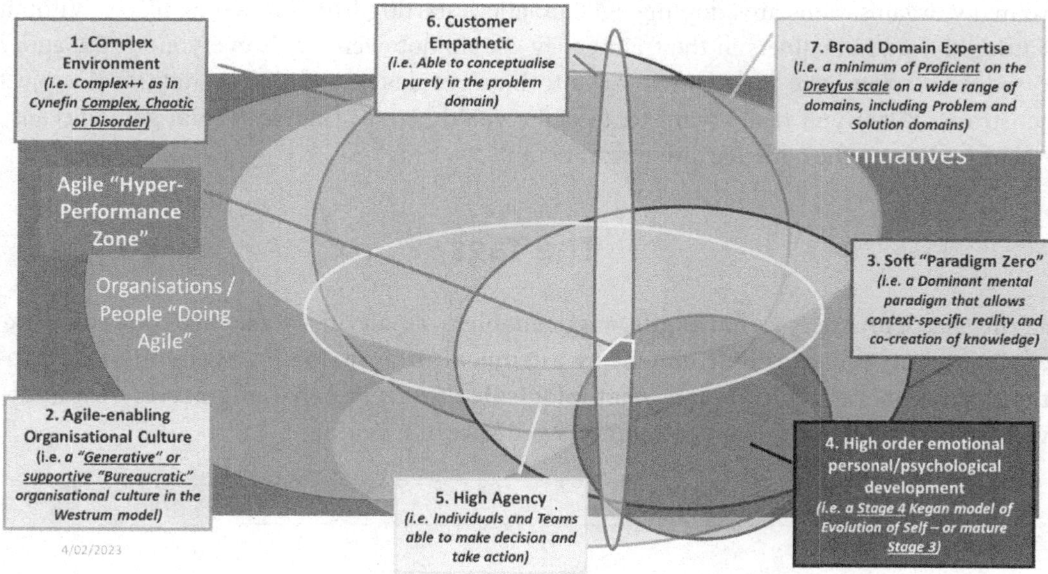

Figure 16. The Sad Venn Diagram of Agile Practice

That little red blob at the intersection of all those factors is the ecosystem within which Agile practice will thrive.

Now, don't lose hope!

The reality is that agile teams with all those enablers are scarce. The most important thing — and this goes to the heart of the agile mindset — is that these seven factors are at least visible to the participants: (aspiring) practitioners, coaches, and managers. Kegan describes ways organisations can help their employees' growth pathways, for example, by establishing "safe spaces".

You can practice agile at whatever level you and your team are and begin the evolutionary journey of improvement.

The evolutionary concepts can be leveraged to help times work their way up the skill level, as I outline in the axiom ***"# 27. The triple helix of Agile evolution."***, and also the axiom, **"# 69. Keep working the edge!"** in **"Adam On: Projects (Volume 2)"**[6], for more information about iterative growth, particularly at the personal level.

The Bottom Line

So many organisations are adopting agile practices starting from the wrong place. Without putting the seven enablers in the frame, they should not even try. Is everyone going agile? Who cares? You have many other ways to improve delivery within a traditional project construct. But if you really want to go agile, you'd better bring your total game because relying solely on the agile narrative won't cut it!

The Tags

#agile, #agilepractise, #whatisagile, #agileenablers, #cynefin, #staceymatrix, #complex-environment, #chaoticenvironment #westrumculturaltopologies, #generativeculture-type, #bureaucraticculturetype, #pathologicalculturetype, #paradigmzero, #kegandevelopmentmodel, #agency, #autonomy, #skillsprofile, #value

---

[6]https://bjl.ink/aopv2

27. The triple helix of Agile evolution.

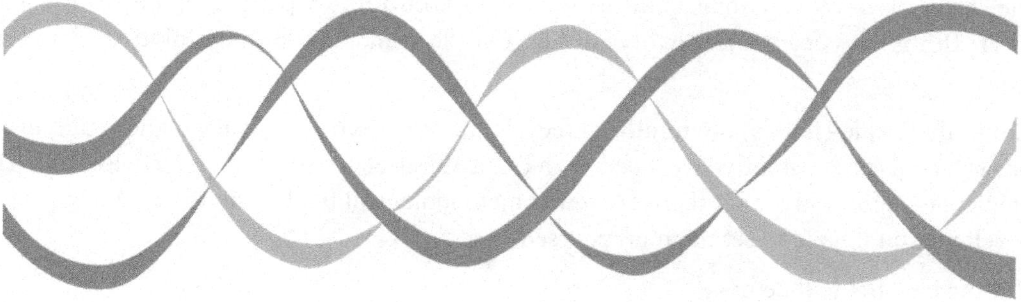

The Axiom

Successful agile endeavours must evolve along multiple distinct but related threads.

The TL;DR

Many agile projects concentrate on developing their product output and associated technology stack. But other elements of an agile endeavour must also evolve. If teams neglect to invest in and grow team efficacy and personal capability, they are not fully agile and run many risks. By incorporating these elements into the process and following the "Triple Helix of Agile Evolution," teams can reach a state of hyper-performance and drive holistic and beneficial agile endeavours.

The Back Story

Agile is based on "applied evolution", so we can start anywhere and iterate towards our goal: when we begin, we are where we are. We must work towards the goal of "hyper-performance" that Agile has promised since its inception.

If you're not clear on how critical the evolutionary mechanism is to the practice of Agile, then refer to the other axioms in the section **"On Evolution"**, in particular, the axiom, **"# 21. Everything in every project evolves!"** lays out the foundation of the evolutionary project cycle.

Could the Triple Helix apply to other lifecycle models? Sure, because we know that every project evolves constantly, we need to have a mindset that allows for evolution. The challenge you'll find is that there are fewer methodological hooks into the evolving project baseline. You'll have to set them up yourself.

But the benefits will be huge.

Why a Helix?

Firstly, why use a helix to represent iterative progress?

Think of a cycle (like the Scrum cycle) moving towards its goal. I think of that cycle rotating around the sprint before returning to the starting point each time. But the team moves forward along an axis of progress.

So, when anything rotating around an axis moves forward along the axis of rotation, a fixed point will trace a helix. For example, the tip of a plane's propeller will trace a helical shape as the aircraft flies forward.

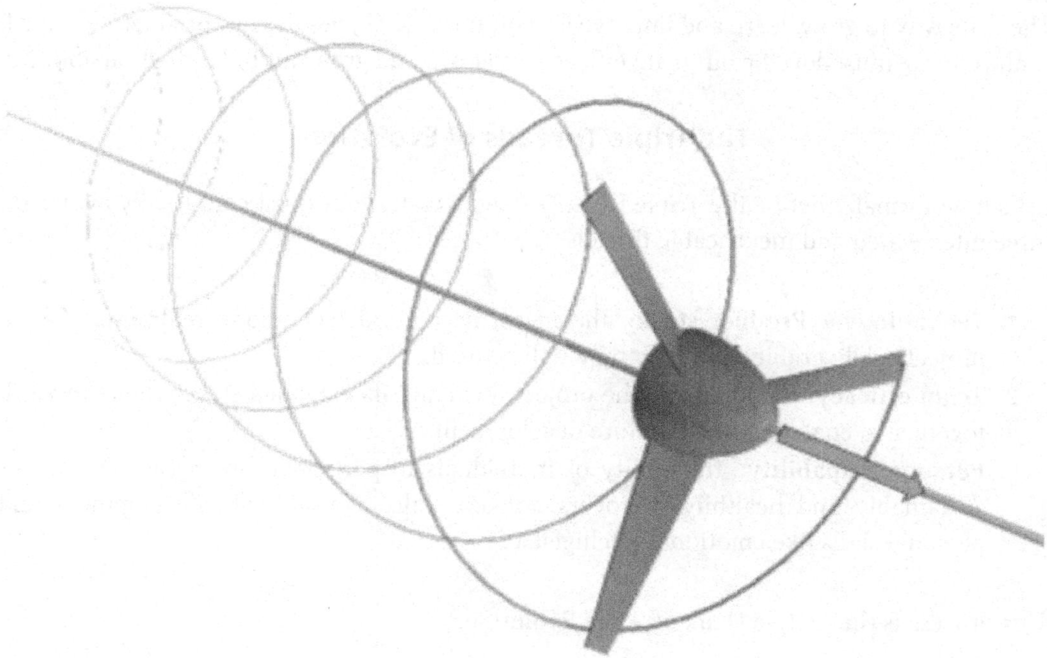

Figure 17. A rotating object moving along the axis of rotation

In the same way, an iterative development process drives forward along the axis of progress.

Why a Triple Helix?

Secondly, why "Triple"?

Simply because there are three distinct areas in a project that must evolve.

Agile teams' primary focus — in many cases, the only focus — is to evolve the product to *"satisfy our customer through early and continuous delivery"* (Agile Manifesto, first principle).

If we are doing evolutionary development at all, is most obvious in the *"working software"*, which is *"the primary measure of progress"* (Agile Manifesto, seventh Principle).

And yet, as we've seen in the axiom **"# 26. ust because you want to do agile doesn't mean you can"**, not all situations are equally ready to enable and facilitate agile at peak productivity. We often need to grow, learn, and improve at an organisational, team and individual level.

The agile way to grow, learn and improve is evolutionary. So, besides our product/tech stack evolution, we must develop our team efficacy and learn and grow our individual capabilities.

The Triple Threads of Evolution

Let's now formally define the Triple Helix. An agile endeavour must continually evolve on three interrelated and inextricable threads:

1. **Technology / Product stack**: the ideas, needs and technology realisation of the project's deliverables and how they will be used.
2. **Team efficacy**: the ability of the project team and its extended stakeholders to work together to enable product/feature development.
3. **Personal capability**: the ability of individuals to participate in threads #1 and #2 sustainably and healthily — covers domain skills like software development and personal skills like emotional intelligence.

This process is the "Triple Helix of Agile Evolution."

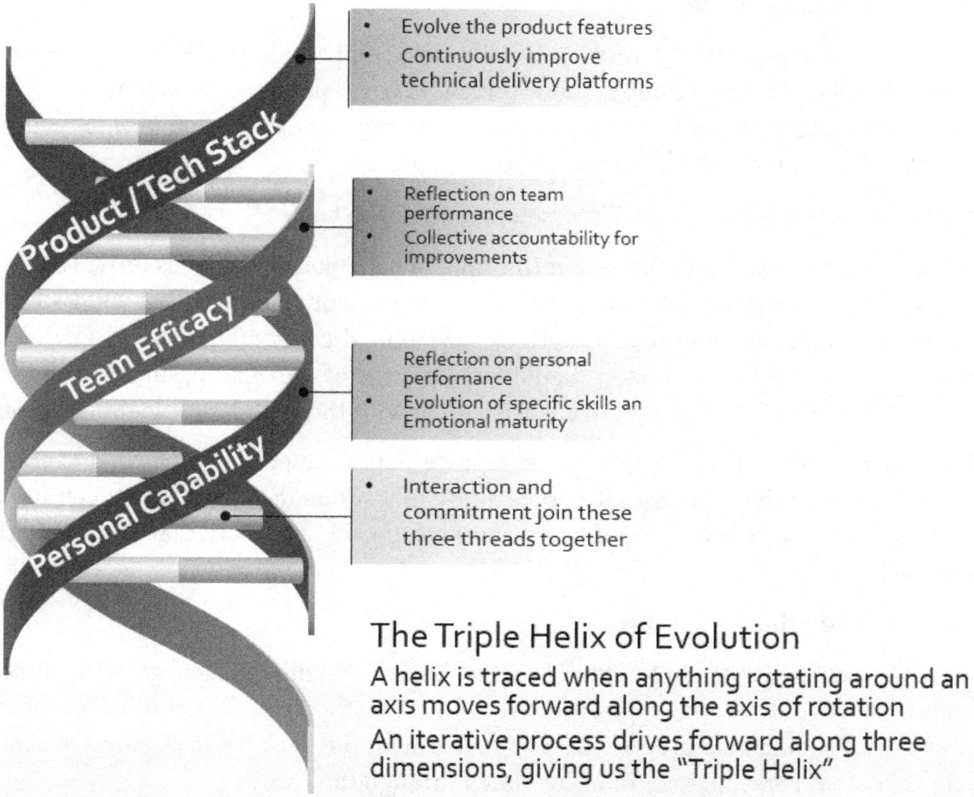

Figure 18. The Triple Helix of Agile Evolution

Every day, we improve our abilities on all three levels and reach the agile hyper-performance zone. The healthiest agile teams will ensure there is a focus on all three of these threads.

A Scrum framework Example

The Sprint Review

The Sprint Review, when the team presents the outputs of a sprint to stakeholders, is the "Fitness Function" in the evolutionary development paradigm. This process gives you immediate feedback on how the team is doing in its progress towards the ultimate goal. It can also identify misalignment in the goal framing, which allows for quick course correction.

The best reviews have a strong and positive interaction amongst all stakeholders to exercise that "Fitness Function", which basically says what to feed and what to starve.

The Sprint Retrospective

The "Sprint Retrospective" (**"retro"**), usually held after the Sprint Review, is intended to drive incremental and continuous improvement in our capabilities as a team. The manifesto says in the twelfth principle, *"At regular intervals, the team reflects on how to become more effective, then tunes and adjusts its behavior accordingly."*

The Sprint Retrospective is the Fitness Function for the team.

It should reinforce adaptive behaviour (the kind of behaviour that lets us thrive) and identify non-adaptive behaviour that needs correction. Non-adaptive behaviour includes how team members respond to gaps or blockages or sub-optimal contextual aspects. Of course, the team, through the Scrum Master, should look at ways of remediating those issues. But the team must also function as effectively as possible with those undesirable things in place.

If the retrospective becomes too focused on externalities, especially ones that cannot easily be changed, then the team loses the opportunity to work on things that are under its control. That includes, of course, progressively working on their collective ability to work with adversity.

Personal Growth

There is no explicit event or function in Scrum that deals with personal growth. Some teams may think it is outside the scope of the "retro" or even the team's accountbaility. Some may think that it should be a process that is handled with the person's line manager. And some may think that personal growth is facilitated through the "retros".

Because there is much variance in how teams, departments, and organisations approach personal growth, the "last resort" owner is each individual person, taking guidance from the principles behind the retrospectives.

The "Fitness Function" for personal growth is a period of self-reflection that mirrors the Sprint Retrospective but is focused on your performance. You should do it after the Sprint Retro whilst things are fresh in your mind. There are many personal growth tools available beyond the walls of each project. It might be journalling that appeals to you, or meditation, or mantras. You might decide to do a course or buy a book. Pick some ideas and try them out.

See also the axiom, "**# 69. Keep working the edge!**" in "**Adam On: Projects (Volume 2)**"[7], for more information about iterative growth, particularly at the personal level.

[7] https://bjl.ink/aopv2

The Bottom Line

We can only start a project, or our entire agile journey, wherever we are. Very few people are gifted with the ability to perform at the hyper-performance level of agile from the get-go. The seven agile enablers do not need to exist fully at the start of the agile journey.

Use the Triple Helix of Agile Evolution to drive holistic and beneficial agile endeavours.

The Tags

#agile, #agileevolution, #holisticteams, #agilepractise, #whatisagile, #agileenablers

28. The saddest oxymoron of the 21st century.

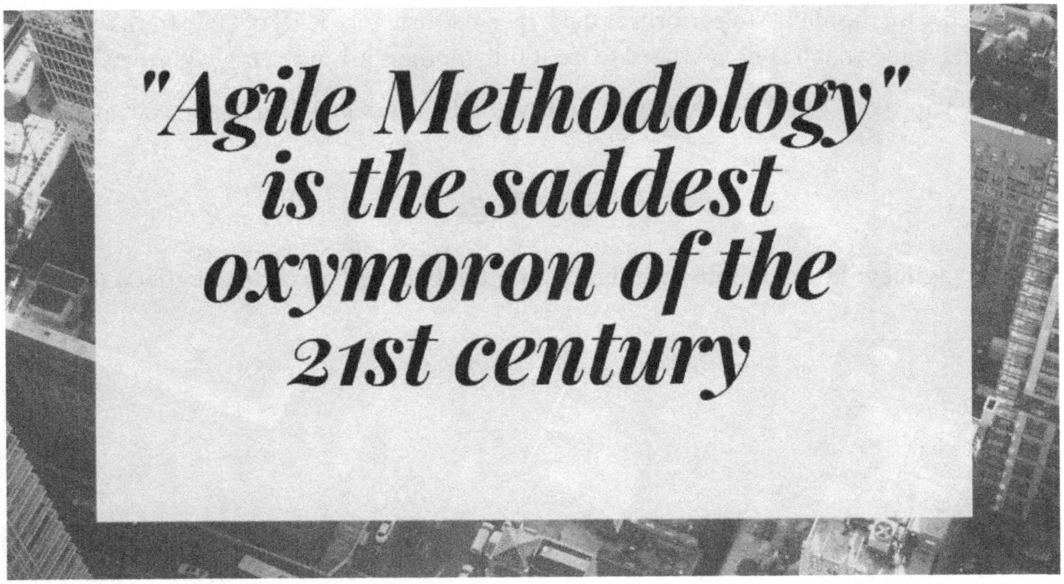

The Axiom

A team wanting to perform adaptive agile as it was intended must leverage every ounce of their courage and values to make it work.

The TL;DR

Most agile—at least as I've experienced it—practised today is not agile that we read about in the Agile Manifesto or (near) contemporaneous literature. It's not the kind of agile intended by the **"M17"** (see below), as far as I know. The adaptive agile that frees people from restrictive practices and enables the "hyper-productivity" that comes with tightly knit teams working with low process overhead, seems very rare. The majority of agile that I've experienced—both directly and indirectly—follow prescriptive methodologies or processes. Is this the end of the world? Probably not. Is it a problem that people cannot tell the two types of agile apart? Yes, I believe it is. A process-bound approach to agile can improve and operate at a certain level—you can get good productivity. But following that path creates a barrier to the ability to transition into the full hyper-productivity of adaptive agile. I don't really care what teams use, as long as they know what they are doing, and why they are doing it. The worst-case scenario is "schizophrenic agile", which causes harm to teams, projects, and organisations.

The Back Story

When it arrived, Agile stole all the attention in the domain of human goal-based endeavours. It held so much promise and generated so much enthusiasm - admittedly both for and against. But after so much promise, how did we end up, not right back where we started, but in a worse situation?

Let me present a light-hearted but pointed narrative of the history of agile, with some milestones that point to how we got here.

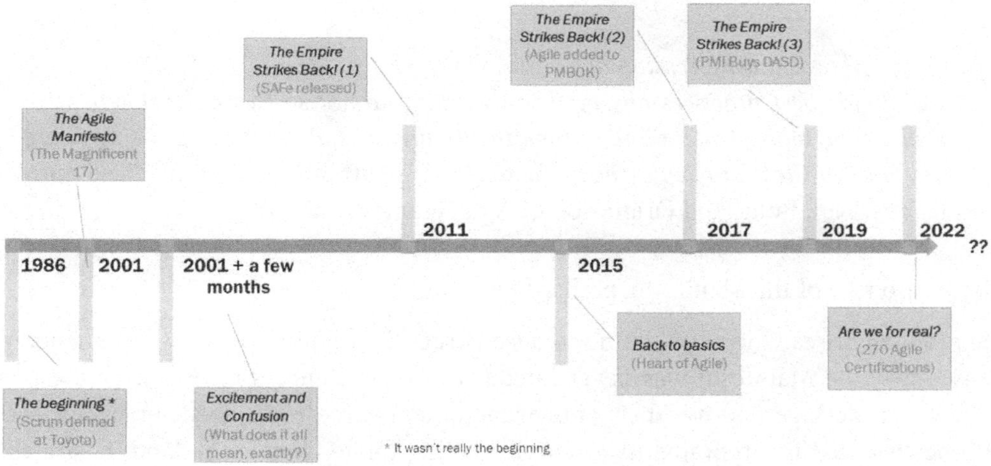

Figure 19. A Light-hearted View of Agile History

It all started with the Agile Manifesto - not!

The seventeen blokes - I call them *"The Magnificent 17"* (M17) - didn't "invent" agile at Snowbird in 2000. Agile didn't spawn overnight in a ski field.

The "**M17**" codified practices and ideas from multiple sources evolving for decades across society, business, and technology. They mainly drew from Western cultures but also included ideas rooted in Asian history and philosophy. Their sources encompassed business, philosophy, politics, and their experiments and practices in software development at different companies as they sought various ways to improve software development in line with these evolving ideas.

What the "**M17**" did was to agree on the contents of the Agile Manifesto, an achievement that should not be under-valued. They produced a short, elegant, manifestly wise, accurate, sometimes cryptic, and even slightly mystical text of some 250 words. The Manifesto possesses all the hallmarks of a document destined to go viral.

Implementing the manifesto - and our problems begin

Of course, the challenge since then was and still is how best to put the values and principles into practice. Jeff Sutherland, one of the M17, later referred to the Scrum methodology as a "compression algorithm for best practices".

> *"[Scrum] ... is a compression algorithm for worldwide best practices observed in over 50 years of software development ... it is simple to implement and automatically unpacks and encourages a software development team to deploy best practices ..."* — **Jeff Sutherland** in "The Scrum Papers: Nut, Bolts, and Origins of an Agile Framework" 2011

That is also true of the Manifesto, perhaps more so.

The problem arises when attempting to deconstruct the Manifesto into its components. In many ways, the Manifesto was never intended to be decompressed — one was supposed to "feel" its message and use their knowledge of software development practices to build a framework that incorporated its essence. Another quote from Sutherland illustrates this idea:

> *"... experience the quality without a name. This ... can only be spoken of as a set of core values the "speed of trust" the sources of "ba" often seen on Scrum teams."* — **Jeff Sutherland** in "The Scrum Papers: Nut, Bolts, and Origins of an Agile Framework" 2011

Other folks went in another direction: decompressing the Manifesto, building out the missing bits, and mixing it with other concepts where necessary or advantageous. We ended up with several fully integrated processes that could be taught and assessed with closed multiple-choice questions.

The Empire strikes back

I (half) jokingly call this "The Empire Strikes Back" because the established project management associations have most driven this development after having been at least partially sidelined in the 2000s post-Manifesto.

Agile can seem complex because it covers many concepts across the broad domain of achieving goals in human group endeavours. But, at its core, Agile is simple because it leverages the best of how humans think and work naturally together.

And this is where we have a dilemma.

With significant investment and market success in normative and prescriptive methodologies, such as SAFe and DASD, many organisations have adopted these approaches and are implementing them internally. It's uncommon to find advertisements for Agile roles that don't mention one of these frameworks, primarily SAFe.

I don't have anything against these types of predictive agile methodologies. I get what they are trying to achieve. What's important, however, is that that organisations adopting large-scale methodologies with the word "agile" in their brand names fully understand the transition they are making.

The contradiction is this: the more you focus on the normative process, the more you build forecasts and metrics and monitoring into your agile implementation, and the further away you get from the intent and benefits of the agile construct. And the more "ass-about-face" the understanding is of how agile works.

But this is inevitable when individuals, teams, and organisations focus more on form than meaning, a problem described in the axiom: **"# 68. Why do 'cargo cult' projects still happen?"** in **"Adam On: Projects (Volume 2)"**[8].

Who am I to denigrate organisations spending time and money on rolling out a methodology? It's not for me to criticise. The most common question in agile is, "Does what you are doing work?", "does it achieve what you want?" If the answer is yes — a genuine yes, not one that conceals a disaster — then go for it.

A stratified view of the agile practice landscape

But, outside of these local successes, I see a very stratified agile practice landscape, as illustrated in the chart below.

[8]https://bjl.ink/aopv2

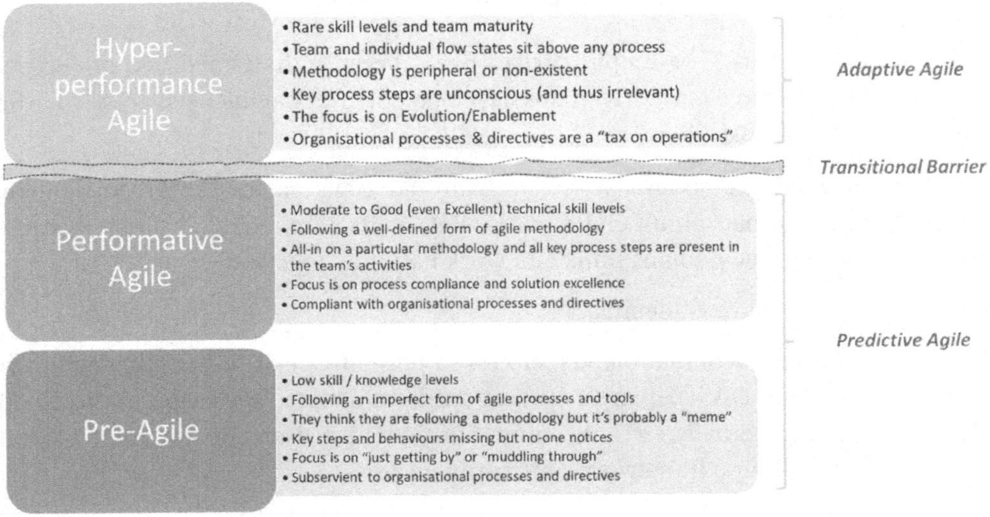

Figure 20. The Three Levels of Agile Performance

1. **"Pre-Agile"**, at the bottom, represents the least skilful execution of the agile model. There are several terms applied to this which are—unfortunately—quite pejorative, but they are used nonetheless. Terms such as **"Fake Agile"** or **"Cargo Cult Agile"** are used to describe the practices of people who don't understand what they are doing and are just loosely following the form.
2. **"Performative Agile"**, in the middle, are those folks who are invested in a well-defined agile process such as SAFe or DASD and attempt to practice the methods defined in that process faithfully. Obviously there is a range of skill levels across individuals and teams. But the key differentiator is a decision to follow a pre-defined process. In many—most—cases the formal definition of the methodology has been adapted or tailored to a particular organisation and most probably melded with organisational processes that fit its requirements for monitoring, control, audit and risk management, human resources practices and other elements of organisational management.
3. At the top, **"Hyper-performance Agile"** are those folks following the original intent of agile, which essentially is what I call *"people thinking and working naturally together"*. Hyper-performant agile is where teams "pop" in productivity and generate the returns Sutherland and others offered — orders of magnitude improvement in productivity.

So, I see this "two-speed" agile world, one of Hyper-performance Agile and one of "Predictive Agile" which is made up of the two layers "Pre-Agile" and "Performant Agile". To simplify,

I just call these two “Adaptive Agile” and “Predictive Agile”.

The Transitional Barrier from “Performative Agile”

The more people in the Performative Agile layer work on their agile processes, the less likely they will transition into the Hyper-performance layer. The more people focus on technique “purity” as they work their way up the credentials ladder, the less they will see the need to jump to hyper-performance level because their metrics tell them they are at the top of their game. The performative agile folks will hit the ceiling at the top of their tier and find it difficult to progress further.

One research paper (Rickards and Moger, 2000), identified this barrier when they were reviewing the Tuckman Ladder. They show two paths to hyper-performance, as illustrated in the diagram below.

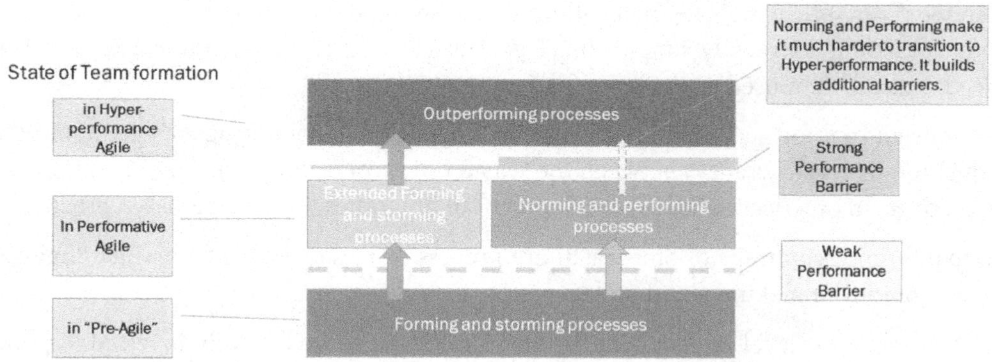

Figure 21. Mapping Revised Tuckman to Agile Performance (Adapted from Rickards and Moger 2000)

My adaptation of this to the world of agile considers the left-hand pathway as resulting from focusing on the seven agile enablers and how they work to grow team efficacy. The right-hand pathway, with the strong barrier to hyper-performance, being the result of focusing on agile process. I stress this is just my opinion.

For more detail on these seven agile enablers, refer to the axiom ***“# 26. Just because you want to do agile doesn’t mean you can”*** to understand what to focus on in the “Extended Forming and Storming Processes”.

For organisations following the right-hand pathway, individuals, teams, and organisations become ”captured” by a chosen methodology, sacrificing agility for optimisation and compliance. Individuals master the method to become qualified (achieving the initial compliance validation). The organisation establishes quality metrics to detect compliance and variation. This metrification stage is followed by the implementation of process instrumentation that facilitates data collection and analysis, and soon after, productivity expectations emerge.

Even if none of the above happens, it's hard for teams not to get caught up in their local monitoring: "We did 30 story points last sprint — how come we only did 20 this sprint?"

Shu-Ha-Ri

It's tempting to look at those three levels of agile performance, and say, *"that's just mapping skill level to Shu-Ha-Ri"*. I thought seriously about that perspective when writing this axiom. I looked at mapping this to Shu-Ha-Ri and to Kegan's Cognitive Development stages and more. But I just couldn't make it work.

Partly, I think this is because the Shu-Ha-Ri concept—and it is a beautiful concept–has been taken too far in its use in Agile. In a pattern that echoes the broader agile pattern I'm writing about, something extremely simple and elegant has been extended and modified and, if not proceduralised, then used as the basis for concrete strategies.

As a concept to inform at a high level how we might think about things it's great, but there are just too many differences between the way a dojo works with martial arts to the way a person or team practices software development or any other knowledge-based practice.

Too many representations of Shu-Ha-Ri are process or practice-oriented, which highlights the very point I'm making about agile.

But at the simplest level, if people in the Shu-Ha-Ri model are too fully invested in process and procedure, then letting go of this to make the transition from "Ha" to "Ri" will be more challenging because it requires a complete change of mindset. However difficult it might be for an individual practitioner working with a sensei to achieve that transition, it will be unimaginably more difficult if the individual is working in an organisation in which the practice focus is built into the organisation's bureaucratic infrastructure.

What does this mean for you?

At the end of the day, does it matter if you are doing performative agile or not?

I think I'm 50/50 on the answer to this.

On the one hand, it doesn't matter. The fundamental principle of good project work of any kind is that the team decides what their approach should be. I know this isn't always possible, in which case there are good and not-so-good outcomes from that decision point.

On the other hand, it worries me a lot for two reasons:

Firstly, if you can get into a team that practices Hyper-performance Agile, it's such an exhilarating experience that it's hard thereafter to accept anything else. Consider an analogy with air travel. Imagine you've travelled coach class all your life and your situation allows for nothing else (I think many of us are in that boat). If you travel first class—even just once—it makes the next coach flight suck! And the next, and so on.

Secondly, the risk of Performative agile is that everyone in the organisation— or even the department or team—are not aligned on the agile construct. There's nothing more frustrating than to hear one set of people talking in hyper-productive terms and even organising activities aimed towards that level of performance, but the reality that teams have to live with is bureaucratic layers of predictive planning, execution monitoring, and reporting.

I call this "schizophrenic agile" and it is probably the worst-case scenario.

Today, Agile methodologies vary in their adherence to the original intent. **"Predictive Agile"** focuses on normative processes and metrics, and **"Adaptive Agile"** practice facilitates natural human social processes.

I contend that only the latter approach leads to the significant productivity gains the agile approach has offered since its introduction. The essence of Agile lies in the compelling human social processes it harnesses rather than strictly following externally constructed methods or metrics.

The Bottom Line

The reality is that agile is governed by human social processes far more powerful (and more significant) than any externally constructed set of methods or metrics. Understanding and harnessing these processes can unlock the true potential of Agile, leading to unprecedented levels of productivity and innovation. Refer to the axiom ***"# 26. Just because you want to do agile doesn't mean you can"*** to understand where to start on this journey.

The Tags

#agile, #methodology, #fakeagile, #performantagile, #hyperperformanceagile, #cargocult, #socialprocesses, #realagile, #agilemanifesto, #jeffsutherland, #scrum, #compressionalgorithm, #safe, #dasd

On Requirements

Although the term "Requirements" is associated in more traditional methodologies, at its most generic it's about modeling the intended outcomes and impacts the project will enable.

Where, how and in what system we model these requirements may vary, but all projects of any methodology or lifecycle approach must be grounded in non-technical statements of intended value for the "customer".

29. Do your customers' answers confuse you?

On gathering requirements:

If your customers' answers confuse you ... ask better questions!

The Axiom

When gathering requirements, if your customers' answers confuse you, then ask better questions!

The TL;DR

The secret (not so much) to successful projects is to anchor everything the project does in the enabled value that your customer can achieve. Customers might not know what solution enables this value, but their lived experience is what connects you to what they are trying to achieve.

Your questions must focus on enablement, not the solution. Your questions must lead them to truths that they don't yet know exist. This can be scary.

The Back Story

A common perspective of gathering project requirements is like a detective asking questions of a witness to a crime. They saw what they saw and know what they know. The detective's role in this is to help them reconstruct a known incident.

The reality is often more like a psychotherapist helping a patient to expose knowledge that not only don't they know they have, but about which there may be deep trauma. It can be scary. Scary to the patient, because it opens up potentially unpleasant thoughts and feelings. Scary to the psychiatrist too - in some circumstances - because the information they dredge up may appear completely disconnected to the apparent problems.

The myth of faster carriages

An apocryphal quote by Henry Ford illustrates a solution category error:

> *"If I had asked people what they wanted, they would have said faster horses."*— attributed to **Henry Ford**, but no evidence to support this (citation)

Although there is no evidence that he said this, as a Project Manager or Business Analyst, I'm sure it resonates. You've heard a customer try to talk about solutions they want but misunderstand solution technology, design, or operation.

Jeff Sutherland formulated the Scrum approach to software development based on a concept that originated at Toyota in the 1980s. Sutherland underscored this issue as follows:

> *"The user will never know what they want until after the system is in production (maybe not even then)"* — **Jeff Sutherland** in The Origins of Scrum[1]

The point of these two quotes is fundamentally flawed: you don't ask users what they want.

Why do some projects gloss over requirements?

Most projects don't even gather comprehensive requirements about the solution, let alone customer enablement.

Why is that?

Just because you didn't ask doesn't mean the requirements disappear. Projects have a nasty way of reasserting their needs, usually at some inconvenient time.

The primary reason is that the management team responsible for initiating the project believes the problem and its solution are obvious, understood, and shared by all. To those managers, analysing this, especially writing it down, is a complete waste of time.

[1] https://www.scruminc.com/origins-of-scrum/

The second reason is that the managers who initiate the project believe they don't need to know, primarily because they think that an existing software application has already considered this in its design. They believe the application will be a "forcing function" to push stakeholders into a narrow range of options for solving the problem.

The third reason is a belief that the customers don't know what they want, and if asked, will "Rolls Royce" the solution by asking for a much bigger and more expensive solution than is needed.

The last reason is that the process is messy, the answers are vague, conflicting, or confusing, and it will take too long to gather information, analyse it and produce the desired result.

These reasons, or a combination, drive projects to jump straight into solution design or select a software supplier or technical architecture.

So, ask better questions

So, if requirements gathering is not easy, get better at doing it.

When I use the term "requirements", I'm using it very generally to refer to the foundational knowledge that a project must have to succeed:

1. A deep understanding of the problem to be solved.
2. A description of the changed behaviour that would solve the problem.

I am not referring to any specific practice, technique, or methodology. I'm not implying any formulation or timing.

First off, never ask customers what they want! Why? Because, as Henry Ford (maybe) discovered is that they will want some enhanced version of what they already have. Not only that, but what they want is in the future — it hasn't been created yet - and in the future **anything** is possible.

You might ask them what they want as an icebreaker, or because it is expected, but be careful what you do with this information.

You must find different pathways to the answer.

First and foremost you need to keep your questions out of the solution domain. Even if a user is an expert technologist, their role in the project is something else, and most users and business stakeholders are not expert technologists.

You must ask them what they want to *do*, or what they *cannot do now*. Ask them the behaviour they want to enable.

Or watch what they do. I'm sure you can figure out ways to observe your customers. Sometimes the best way to figure out the "as-is" process and the problems they face is to do a "ride-on" and follow them around. Whenever I've done a "ride-on" as a Project Manager I've found it very well worth the effort.

Projects need a deep understanding of the problem to be solved and a definition of the changed behaviour that would solve the problem. Generally, these two pieces of information are called "requirements". The process of capturing, editing, and supporting downstream users of these requirements is called *"requirements management".

This applies to all types of lifecycle models, from predictive to adaptive and everything in between. It doesn't matter whether you're attempting to capture all or most of the requirements in an up-front stage, or managing an iterative process through user stories. The concepts are the same.

Everything else in a project must serve this practice, including technology, tasks, deliverables, tools, techniques, and processes.

The Bottom Line

I've taken on many jobs to "rescue" projects in distress. The root cause is almost always due to the lack of requirements. Projects have a nasty way of reasserting their needs, usually at some inconvenient time. Any Business Analyst or User Experience Analyst worth their salt knows there are many ways to "ask questions" — read "elicit information", and only one is to ask questions.

The Tags

#requirementsmanagement, #requirementsgathering, #requirementselicitation, #enablement, #principlesofprojectsuccess, #fasterhorses, #henryford, #jeffsutherland, #toyota, #scrum

30. When tech folks talk to business folks what language do they speak?

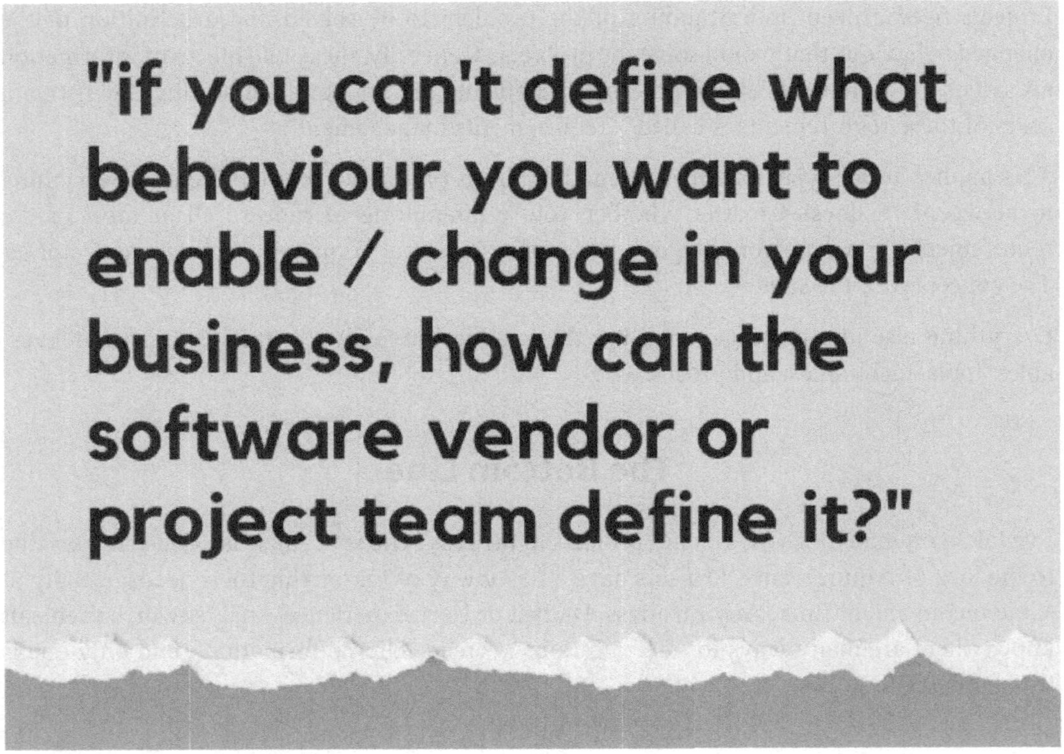

The Axiom

All your project conversations should be in the language of the business domain.

The TL;DR

If you don't have synergy between technology and business in your project, then just about everything will be much harder. The language we choose to collaborate is a key to this synergy. There must be synergy, but there also must be leadership. You must lead the project in the language of the business domain - ***"BizSpeak"*** - the ***"lingua franca"*** of project conversations. Project teams all too frequently default to ***"TechSpeak"***, the language of the technology domains, for reasons I'll outline below. Frankly, most teams find it very challenging to stay in BizSpeak consistently and thus forgo the transformative power of aligning project dialogue with business objectives. But if your project operates in TechSpeak, then you have significantly increased the difficulty of getting a good outcome. Read on and find out why.

The Back Story

This axiom is a corollary to the axiom "# 52. **Business people make lousy solutions architects.**", because it addresses a similar relationship between business and technology folks, but covers a unique problem in that relationship.

What is the "Lingua Franca" of your project?

A "lingua franca" is a bridge or common language shared by groups of people who do not share a native language or dialect. This makes communication possible between the groups.

In Australia, where I do much of my work, projects have a minimum of three distinct languages:

1. Australian Generic English
2. Problem / Business domain language
3. Tech Stack language

For brevity, I'll refer to these as "**OzSpeak**", "**BizSpeak**", and "**TechSpeak**".

"**BizSpeak**" is the precise and domain-specific terminology and semantics that is used to describe the business domain fully and accurately, which we also refer to as the "**problem domain**".

"**TechSpeak**" is the domain-specific language for the technology stack and context, which we often refer to as the "**solution domain**".

And of course, "**OzSpeak**" is Australian English dialect, a general-purpose language full of nuance, idiom, and unique words.

Each of these three languages have their own sub-dialects and other variations. For example, the TechSpeak language will have different variants for all the technologies and products that are within the project scope.

In most projects, my experience tells me that the Lingua Franca is TechSpeak. Although OzSpeak is the glue that holds the project together, TechSpeak is how most decisions are framed and goals defined. The TechSpeak project Lingua Franca is a simplified or abstracted version that is enough to describe outputs and deliverables.

Why does this happen?

When TechSpeak becomes the Lingua Franca for a project, stakeholders reframe their knowledge and experience from BizSpeak to TechSpeak.

In many cases, the business people actively participate in this reframing process. As I mentioned in the axiom "**# 52. Business people make lousy solutions architects**", business people tend to gravitate towards the solution domain when in project discussions.

For potentially a range of reasons, business folks are happy to shift their conversation to a language in which they are not expert.

One reason is that business stakeholders feel that their solution providers won't fully understand the details and nuances of the problem domain. Another reason might be that the desired business outcomes aren't well defined. Or that the solution is more "concrete" than the problem: the "thing" is definite, but the "problem" is likely to be fuzzy or poorly understood.

Also driving this reframing is that vendors have a strong vested interest in not being on the hook for customer outcomes. They have little or no direct control over how the organisation operates after their solutions are delivered, no matter how well the deliverables have been specified and constructed.

Lastly, again touched on in the axiom "**# 52. Business people make lousy solutions architects**", at least for IT solutions, computer skills are perceived as horizontal or generic skills, and, therefore, not a problematic domain for business teams to navigate.

Why is this a problem?

Because TechSpeak is the Lingua Franca of most projects, this means that project and contractual deliverables are expressed in technical terms that describe the characteristics and capabilities of equipment, software, people, and services.

Equally, project sub-specifications, such as enhancement or change requests, are defined as proposed changes to the technology. Most test cases and other validation steps are defined using software features and capabilities.

But the root cause problem with all this is that business folks will never equal — or likely to come even close — to understanding the technology in the same way the technology folks do. Despite a perception that "IT can't be that hard", IT solutions have become enormously more complicated over recent decades and at a rate of change that makes it hard even for IT professionals to keep up with changes and developments in their fields.

If business folks take their generic IT knowledge to an even moderately complex solution environment, it's like taking boxing gloves to a gunfight. You'll never win—"win" in the sense of fully understanding all the implications of a specification.

An example

This was nowhere more obvious to me than a rescue project I was managing before the Covid-19 pandemic. The business process was pretty mundane: not high-tech at all. For this example, it is irrelevant. The technology also was pretty straightforward.

But almost any system in the 21st century has complexities.

Because the original requirements were poorly defined it was inevitable that gaps would appear between the solution capabilities and business expectations. And, as those solution gaps emerged, we needed to raise Change Requests **("CRs")** with the vendor to get them to change their package.

Over the life of the project, we raised over 30 CRs. And every single one had problems. At least a third of them were cancelled before delivery when it became apparent that they would not meet the customer's needs. The rest all had problems after delivery. Either the CR didn't meet the desired business behaviour, or it had some unexpected detrimental impact on the business environment.

The root cause of these problems was that all the CR documents were written in TechSpeak. And because we were making changed deep in the bowels of the product, the TechSpeak was very technical - in most cases linguistically unrecognisable from the problem it was intended to solve.

Every time I tried to get the CRs phrased in business language instead of detailed software product tech-speak, the vendor dug in their heels. My business and management stakeholders objected to the time it was taking to lock in the CR and get it delivered. Ultimately, we submitted the CR, with assurances from the vendor of high-quality deliverables. And the same thing would happen when the change was delivered.

Sometimes - mostly - there wasn't much else that the vendor could do without major code changes in their underlying software. The problem was that only the vendor tech team really understood these limitations. And to be fair, sometimes even our direct vendor tech team didn't understand the implications and had a similar "language barrier" with their own core product development teams.

I'd have to say it was a major failing on my part that I could not prevent this from occurring. These issues could have been avoided if we had nailed down the business behaviour that was needed.

Ensure your problem statements are business problem statements

Many organisations find it hard to conceptualise and keep a focus on what behaviour has to change, and by how much. But the project sponsor must have some idea, even at a high level, of what they are trying to achieve.

We can define the behaviour we're enabling in scenarios, use cases, user stories or even old-fashioned business requirements and process diagrams.

Whatever technique we use, the aim is the same: imagining, creating, ideating or otherwise envisaging how user behaviour will produce long-term value for the organisation.

But the behaviour we define must actually be *user* behaviour and not a technical description of the enabler.

An example of this is how you write requirements. Let's take a simple example: User Stories.

Below is a high-level mapping of the traditional User Story pattern to the PLM. This illustrates four levels at which the elements of the user story are positioned.

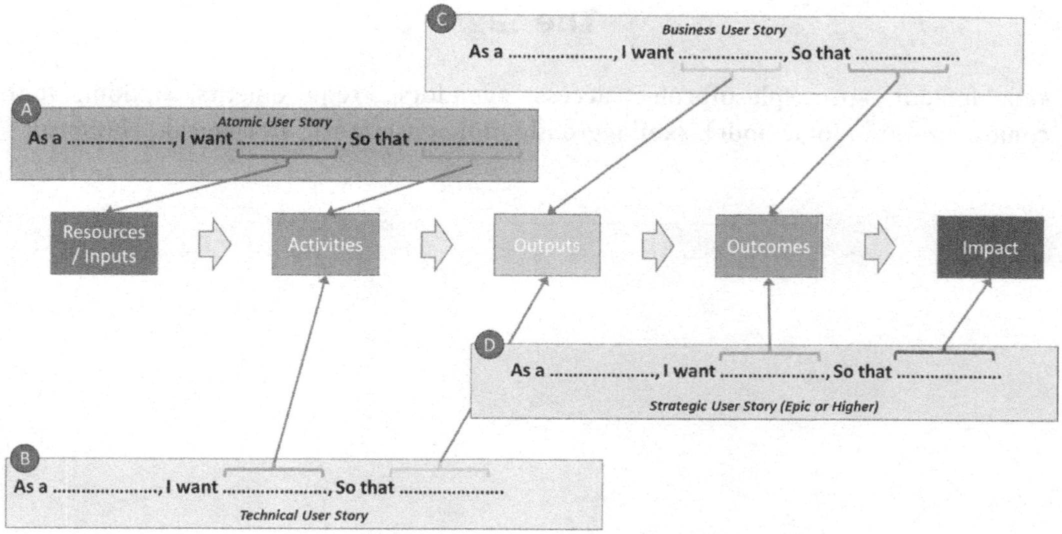

Figure 22. Mapping User Story Elements to the Program Logic Model

Note this diagram doesn't take into account the level of granularity at which we can express the user story. For example, the same pattern (A-D) could be expressed at a solution level, a functional level, or a feature or transaction level.

A high-quality outcome focused user story is shown in pattern "C" in the diagram. The enabler (output) is defined at its final state and is linked to the outcome desired (changed behaviour or capability).

A 'pure' user story is shown in Pattern "D". There is no reference to any solution at all. The language of this user story pattern only references organisational behaviour change and the results of this change.

Patterns "A" and "B" are totally bound into the solution.

The Bottom Line

Unless your project team can frame its objectives in business domain terms, you run the risk - the very high probability risk - of being a *"technology push"* project, resulting in the potential failure of the solution to enable the forecast value. Make *"BizSpeak"* the Lingua Franca of your project. It won't be easy, but it pays off big time.

The Tags

#enablement, #principlesofprojectsuccess, #vendors, #requirements, #axiom, #outcomes, #programlogicmodel, #kelloggfoundation, #userstory, #techspeak, #bizspeak

31. Non-functional requirements are a secret weapon.

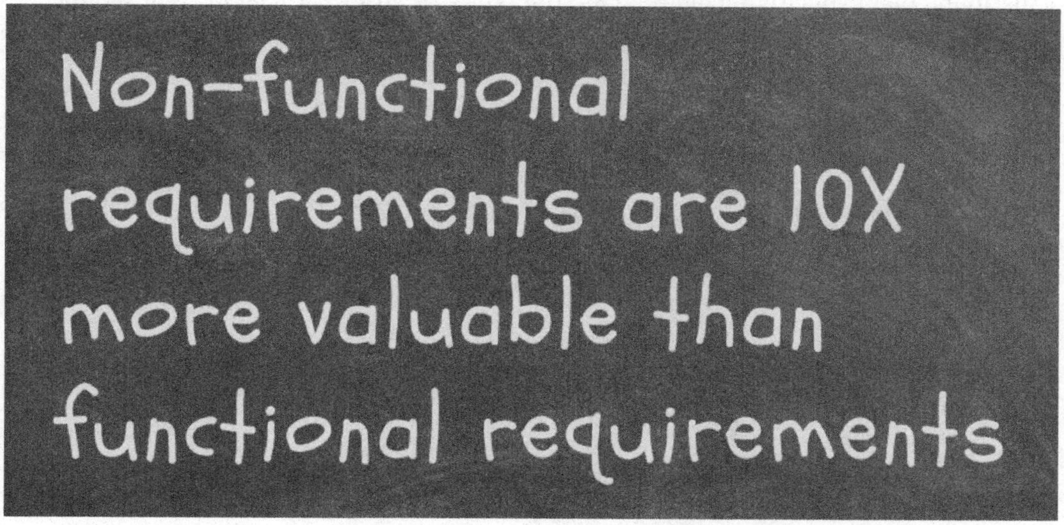

The Axiom

Non-functional requirements are ten times more valuable than functional requirements, at least.

The TL;DR

Non-functional requirements (NFRs) specify a measured quality or dimension the solution must meet, such as Responsiveness, e.g., "respond within 5 seconds of the user clicking the "Ok" button". Functional Requirements (FRs) specify what the solution should do, e.g., "accept a credit card for payment". NFRs are far more critical to the solution than any FR. More distressed and failed projects are caused by not understanding NFRs and how the solution will meet them than any failure to meet FRs. To say NFRs are ten times (10X) more valuable than FRs is a qualitative judgement based on my experience. But it might be underestimated.

The Back Story

Non-functional requirements (NFRs) are often seen as part of formally structured Predictive project lifecycles in which there is more likely to be a phase dedicated to requirements and a discipline that explicitly includes NFRs. But NFRs are just as crucial in Agile approaches but are often masked by the Agile process, which reduces documentation and emphasises conversation.

Most of the focus in most projects goes on Functional requirements (FRs) in describing what the solution will do.

Regardless of how requirements are managed, I believe that investing time in NFRs gives you a 10x better payoff towards project success than the time you spend on FRs.

Why are they crucial?

> *"Projects can implement any functional requirement if they relax the non-functional requirements sufficiently".* — **Tom Gilb** (exact reference unknown but confirmed by Tom)

Tom's statement indicates that NFRs have significant leverage over the solution. Let's look at why this is the case.

NFRs have a high "fan-out".

Non-functional characteristics typically affect more than one functional requirement. So the time you spend on the NFR pays off over many areas of the solution.

Whether it is security, performance, learnability, adaptability - any NFR - it is a rare system in which the non-functional capabities do not support more than one function. Let's take "responsiveness" as an example and let's define it as the time-lag between a user initiating some action and receiving a result. By this definition, "responsiveness" applies to every functional capability that involves a user interaction.

Meeting NFRs is what delights your users.

Users give scant and passing attention to functional aspects of a solution (unless they are missing).

Any delight a user might have in using a feature initially fades fast and that feature is just part of the system. But make that the feature hard to find or clunky to use those smiles quickly turn to frowns as the user experiences those issues day in and day out.

How quickly and successfully a user learns how to use a function is determined non-functionally.

Reduce that "responsiveness" interval and every user will see the results on every interaction.

NFRs drive solution architecture.

Most users and project stakeholders don't care about the solution architecture, until it punches them in the mouth. Everyone should care about what solution architecture can impact.

Don't confuse the concept of solution architecture with a traditional "Solution Architecture Document" and the processes that surround such documents.

The solution architecture is simply the whole-of-solution design that everyone in the team is working towards. How the architecture is recorded is unrelated to the architecture itself.

There are two parts to this Non-functional requirements narrative.

1. Can the system change?
2. Will the system end up in the media?

Let's unpack these in more detail below.

Can the system change?

One perspective on solution architecture is the:

> *"parts that are hard to change later"* – **Neal Ford et al.** in "Building Evolutionary Architectures".

Anticipating change requirements upfront allows you to deal with change and avoid technical debt. Technical debt is primarily driven by the inability to change fast enough to meet changing demains. It is also very easy for teams to "sleepwalk" into Technical debt if you don't have clear guardrails in the form of non-functional measurement criteria.

Agile claims to be better suited to handle change, but there's very little in any methodology that sets projects up to deal with the impact of change. Just because agile projects *"welcome change"* doesn't automatically mean that change is impact or cost-free.

Will the system end up in the media?

We've all read news about major online system launches that crashed soon afterwards. These post-launch system issues directly result from a complete and utter failure to assess the NFRs correctly or develop the solution to perform at the necessary levels.

It's amazing to me that every year during peak demand events, such as "Black Friday" sales, organisations will promote the hell out of an online sale, only to fall victim of the attention when the system fails to perform to the demand which the company itself stimulated. And this happens time and time again. Somebody isn't paying attention; and in particular they are not considering the non-functional aspects of the solution.

Sponsor: *"that's an awesome looking order page you've got there, team. I love that you can look up your order history on the fly and it has AI to suggest up-sells to products in the cart already."*

(Nobody): *"Yeah, awesome! But will it work with 100k people hitting it in the first minute?"*

The NFR ecosystem

NFRs define a solution "ecosystem" within which the system needs to perform, but it does not have to fulfil every requirement on day 1.

Neal Ford et al. describe the aspects of the architecture that enable change as the "-ilities" because many of them end with that. For example "Flexibility", "Adaptability", "Expandability" etc

accessibility	accountability	accuracy	adaptability	administrability
affordability	agility	auditability	autonomy	availability
compatibility	composability	configurability	correctness	credibility
customizability	debugability	degradability	determinability	demonstrability
dependability	deployability	discoverability	distributability	durability
effectiveness	efficiency	usability	extensibility	failure transparency
fault tolerance	fidelity	flexibility	inspectability	installability
integrity	interoperability	learnability	maintainability	manageability
mobility	modifiability	modularity	operability	orthogonality
portability	precision	predictability	process capabilities	producibility
provability	recoverability	relevance	reliability	repeatability
reproducibility	resilience	responsiveness	reusability	robustness

Figure 23. Partial list of '-ilities' (Source 'Building Evolutionary Architectures' - Table 1-1)

Approximately 30 years earlier Tom Gilb pionerred the same concept but in a far more structured and managable way in what he called "attribute specifications". Gilb defined how NFRs could be written to enable progressive refinement and understanding. Gilb also represented his NFRs in a hierarchy, which gave significantly more semantic meaning and validation compared with the flat list provided in Neal Ford et al. in their book.

Whatever method you use to define your "-ilities" you end up defining the solution ecosystem through the aggregate set of non-functional constraints.

A personal experience

In one of bigger projects as a direct "hands on" Project Manager we were building a new email platform for a major Internet Service Provider ("ISP") which would support all the

ISPs many millions of customers. The email replacement was the first part of rebuilding the entire ISP computing and network infrastructure because the previous email platform, largely designed in-house, had blown up about a year earlier when the customer numbers reached a level of demand that found a flaw in the underlying architecture. Customers, both individual and business were without email service for days or weeks, which brought daily news reports of how this ISP was killing businesses.

We went to a global software company that specialised in large-scale email platforms for the replacement, and their teams had a well-oiled delivery process that included very clear documentation of NFRs.

Our engineering team chose to run performance tests on the newly built platform to determine the system's behaviour at full design maximums: volumes of users and mail that we weren't going to reach for 5 years. The system performed beautifully up to about 80% of capacity and then started to develop instability. There was a flaw in the solution somewhere that wasn't visible in the architecture or in normal functional testing.

I won't bore you with the details of what the problem was or how we solved it; my point is that we had a one-time opportunity to do an exhaustive test and we took it. But the test would have been useless with the wrong NFRs. Fortunately, we had good ones.

The Bottom Line

A deep understanding of the NFRs in your project forces you to address architectural agility in your solution.

Increasing the focus on NFRs in your project gives you a perspective on your solution architecture that enables you to identify constraints to change. What works in the final product should work in the development cycle.

The Tags

#requirementsmanagement, #functionalrequirements, #non-functionalrequirements, #requirementsanalysis, #requirements, #requirementsmodeling, #tomgilb, #agile

32. A false separation.

It might seem like you can separate Functional requirements from Non-functional requirements ... but it just *seems* that way.

They are endlessly and critically interconnected.

The Axiom

You cannot separate Functional requirements from Non-functional requirements; they are endlessly and critically interconnected.

The TL;DR

Although it may appear possible to separate Functional and Non-functional requirements, they are inherently interconnected and cannot be truly separated. Functional Requirements (FRs) and Non-functional Requirements (NFRs) are endlessly and critically interconnected.

The Back Story

According to the Requirements engineering narrative, there are two kinds of statements that capture details of a project's expected beneficial outcome. The first kind of statement focuses on the functional value of the solution, while the second kind of statement addresses the quality or value aspects.

The usual terms for these two types of requirements are *"Functional Requirements"* (FRs) and *"Non-functional Requirements"* (NFRs), respectively.

NFR to NR Relationships

The relationships between FRs and NFRs can be many-to-many (n:n) in nature.

- A single FR would be very unusual if it had only one NFR related to it, so from a cardinality perspective it is 1 FR to "n" NFRs, where "n" can be 1 to the total number of NFRs.
- Conversely NFRs can affect multiple FRs, so that means 1 NFR can relate to "n" FRs.

Reconciling multiple NFRs across multiple FRs is a non-trivial process without specialised software or lots of people's time. Efforts at traceability in most projects these days are seen as too great to be worth the trouble, but this is short-sighted and shows a lack of understanding about how projects work: just because you can't be bothered understanding the relationships between FRs and NFRs doesn't mean they aren't related.

It's typical to separate FRs from NFRs

It is common practice to separate statements of functional value (what the solution should enable) from the quality/value statements (how the solution implements these capabilities).

In older Requirements Management frameworks, FRs and NFRs are in two sections of the Requirements document, if not in two separate documents.

Agile frameworks have multiple options, but they all involve separating the NFR from the FR. If the NFR specifically relates to just on FR User Story, then it can be written on the back of the User Story card if those are used. Alternatively, the NFR is recorded somewhere in the digital version of the card. If the NFR relates to a functional area or system component, separate cards are created to record the details.

But this is pointless - even destructive

FRs are meaningless without a thorough understanding of the constraints they must meet. And they are even more meaningless unless *all* the constraints, or at least the material constraints, are known and considered in the solution design.

It's also not uncommon for projects to give scant coverage of NFRs or even omit them completely. In traditional project frameworks, one or more "Requirements Documents" enumerate the FRs and NFRs.

In Agile frameworks, the User Story is the usual way to express FRs. It's not the only option but the most used (and misused).

In the basic definition of a User Story, there is no specific place to record NFRs. User Story experts like Mike Cohn suggest several ways to handle NFRs in User Stories, but in my experience, it is pretty rare.

The result is that all (or almost all) the focus is on FRs, one of the project teams' most common focus errors.

Figure 24. NFRs are where most of the problems occur

The misdirected project focus is one serious problem, but even when NFRs have some direction, there is an additional problem – separation.

The Bottom Line

Projects are at risk of neglecting Non-functional requirements (NFRs) when they are treated separately from Functional requirements (FRs). This leads to a lack of focus on NFRs and likely issues in the project.

The Tags

#requirementsmanagement, #functionalrequirements, #non-functionalrequirements, #requirementsanalysis, #requirements, #requirementsmodeling

On Software Packages

Software packages, whether implemented "on-premises" using customer owned infrastructure, or as "Software-as-a-Service" cloud-based or hosted solutions, are an important and much-used solution strategy. The premise of a software package is that pre-built software is high-quality and addresses the common needs of customers in a specific functional or industrial domain.

Software package implementation is necessarily a three-stage process:

1. First, you need to understand enough about your problem to define the selection criteria.
2. Second, you need to go through a selection process to pick a package.
3. Third, you need to implement the package.

These top-level stages all have to be executed. There's no way around them. And each stage has potentially sub-stages or sub-tasks, depending on the circumstances.

There are many ways to work through those three stages. You can short-cut them, you can overlap them in different ways and you can vary who does the work. For example you might try to get the software vendors to do much of the work. You could conceivably change the order in some situations.

But you can't avoid the overall structure. In many ways it is no different to any purchasing process. But the nuances of software mean that there are different opportunities and risks in this process for software packages.

There are smart ways to optimise this process - and there are dumb ones. The axioms in this section all refer back to this immutable three-stage process works, different ways organisations follow it or attempt to hack it.

33. Why did you buy that software package?

The Axiom

You'd better have a better rationale for buying that software package than because you read about it in a consultant's market report.

The TL;DR

The risks of selecting software are generally pretty high. Buying a package is an enormous commitment. So, whoever decides to make that investment better be on solid ground. Sadly, there are many reasons why managers decide to buy software, and many of the reasons are not only bad but tragic. There's nothing worse for a project team than to work through all the technical, social, political, and other issues in a project, only to find that the core product won't support the business outcomes. If this axiom doesn't serve as a cautionary tale, urging against impulsive, uninformed decisions, then you've got bigger problems than I can help you with.

The Back Story

Over many projects, I've heard many reasons for buying software. And I've seen many software selection processes unfold, most of which are pretty bad. Reading about it in a third-party consultant's market analysis report is probably the worst reason.

Setting the scene: a project rescue.

Some years back, I took over a project as a rescue: the project team had been trying to integrate the various components and failing for some time. There were many reasons behind this situation. Firstly, the internal IT team had designed a network integration that was far too complex and costly for the project objectives. It also proved to be beyond their capability to implement. It was too complex for them to make it work.

When I arrived, the IT implementation team and vendor teams were blaming each other and had become completely alienated.

They were actively not cooperating with defect identification and triage. Including the two vendors, we had five separate teams, and relations were terrible.

Initially, I couldn't even get the two teams to sit down together to run through the multiple lists of defects - they were maintaining their own lists!

An unfortunate discovery.

Project Management 101: the first task was to get the various teams working together. At the very least, we needed one list of defects that everyone treated as authoritative. This took weeks, but we finally triaged them all, got rid of the fixed, the irrelevant and the political defects.

The next task was to resolve the integration issues in the platform. The main blocker was the ego of the internal team who designed the solution. It was no simple task to get them to admit that the residual issues were in the design, and then - once fixed - to work co-operatively with the key vendors to debug their respective configurations until we had the integration working.

At this point, we had put out all the fires and got rid of most of the noise. In that clarity was the unfortunate discovery that the underlying product was - to use a technical term - *"crap"*. Not only did it have a poor user experience (UX) and limited functionality, but the whole value proposition was marginal for the target market.

The project team couldn't do much about that, but after all the work we'd done to get the lousy product working, it left us with a depressingly limited feeling of success.

The product is launched ... and immediately tanks.

Despite this, our business stakeholders were desperate to launch the product to market. So, having fixed the underlying technical issues, we ran through the product launch process, and finally everything was in-market.

Unsurprisingly, take-up was poor, and those customers who bought into the sales pitch reported low success rates. Reviews were negative. The mood was bleak.

Even worse, because of the existing contracts and the complex network implementation, the cost of modifying this solution was very high. This was the compounding effect of late delivery of a gold-plated solution - no-one wanted to invest anything more in what looked like a loser of a product.

Market analysis wasn't my responsibility, but my view was that the problem wasn't the product quality - the problem was that there was no real market for the product. If there was it would be at a price point way below what the organisation was seeking.

Finding out why the product tanked.

The division's executives asked me to dig into the project's history and find out how we ended up in this situation. But, I couldn't find any formal product requirements or market analysis that might shed light on the genesis of the situation. The project records were also in a very poor state. I talked to all the original stakeholders and managers but still couldn't get a handle on the project's origins and early decision-making.

Finally, we ended up in a make-or-break meeting of the divisional VP, directors, and the key project team members: the decision was whether we would kill the project or continue with recommended enhancements. I summarised my research into the project's background and repeated my finding that no one could tell me why we ended up with this product set.

The VP turned to the manager responsible for this product and said,

> *"You owned this from the start. How come we don't know why we bought this software?"*

The response was:

> *"All right. Ok. I'll admit it. I bought this product because I read about it in [consultant report]. It was in the high-performing section of their analysis chart.".*

Are you kidding me?

But wait, there's more.

I was shocked at this admission, especially after talking to this person multiple times and not hearing this beforehand.

But I was even more appalled at the VP's response:

> *"Well, ok then. Good enough. Let's move on."*

I have nothing against consulting agencies that review products and market trends, and I've used them many times. And I've used their positioning matrices to identify organisations to talk to about participating in procurement activities like Request for Information (RFI).

But purchasing software based on this?

Apart from the [consultant report] I'm not sure wheter there were vendor meetings or functionality reviews or any other validation or investigation before the procurement decision.

And there we were, in a pickle, and no one in management thought this was a problem.

The Bottom Line

I've seen the same thing in many projects: companies doing "seat of the pants" or "gut feel" evaluations of product capability without any evaluation criteria or formal requirements. And all of these projects have run into problems. By all means use market reports for initial discovery. But don't stop there. Don't use that as a buying criterion.

The Tags

#procurement, #requirementsmanagement, #requirementsfail, #productconsultants, #productratings, #consultingreports

---

34. If you can’t define the enabled behaviour.

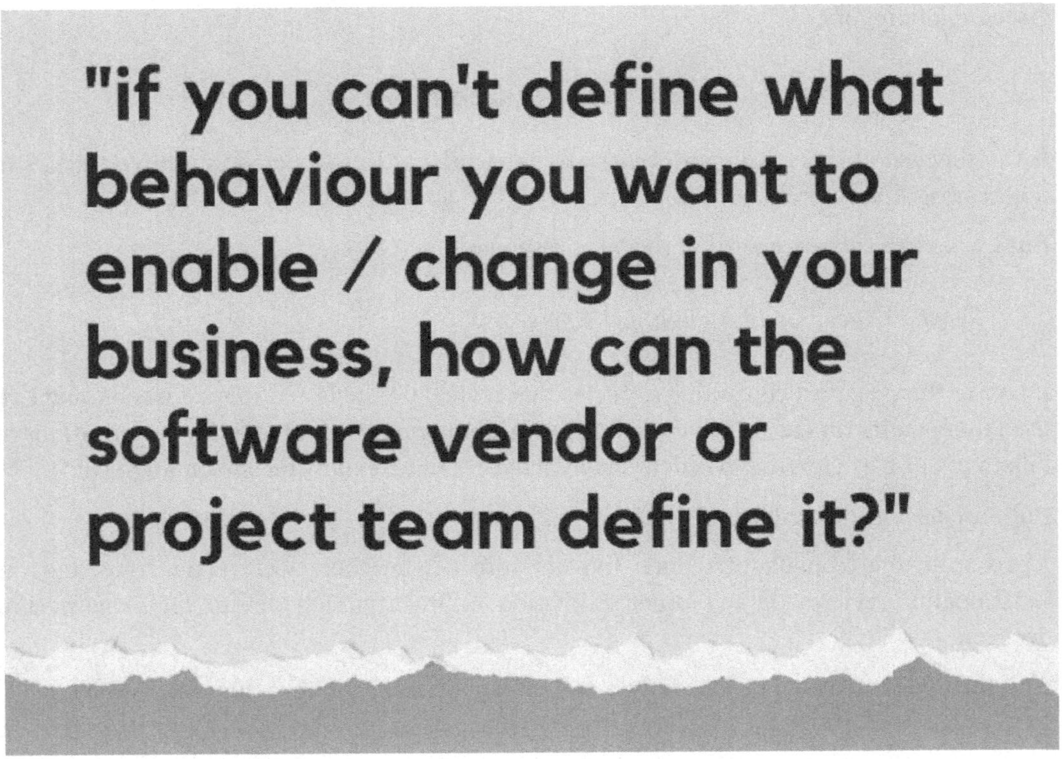

The Axiom

Using a software package implementation as a forcing function to define requirements is a fool’s game. you can’t remove the need for analysis, you can only change when it is done and how much it hurts.

The TL;DR

If you (as a sponsor, product owner, or critical user) can’t define what behaviour you want to enable in your business, how can the software vendor or project team define it? An organisation only captures value from a project after it delivers a solution that enables changed behaviour. The worst project strategy is to use a software package and/or the package implementation process to flush out what this behaviour should be. But sadly, this approach is common, dysfunctional, and rarely succeeds.

The Back Story

What happens when a project bypasses or de-prioritises outcome formulation but uses a software package as a "forcing function" to drive change?

Remember that this issue is lifecycle independent - I'm not advocating any approach. For example, this axiom is emphatically not advocating for an up-front requirements analysis phase in a project.

This axiom is primarily concerned with the domain in which analysis is done. There are some key timing elements with packaged software that are unavoidable.

The scenario

This problematic but common scenario breaks down into three elements:

1. An organisation wants to solve a business problem.
2. The stakeholders do not believe it is a worthwhile investment to identify the business changes they need to make to solve these problems. They think it too costly, time-consuming, or simply unnecessary.
3. They believe that the software package itself can be a template for both business problems and technical solutions.

I frequently hear key managers say:

> *"We know what the problem is. We're experienced managers in [the business domain]. We don't need to spend the time writing documents that no-one will ever read. We need to get on implementing a solution."*

In some projects, they purchase the software before setting up the project team.

Sometimes, they buy it before almost everything else: please see the axiom "**# 33. Why did you buy that software package?**".

One other impact of this mindset is that business stakeholders become solution architects for the implementation. Please see the axiom "**# 52. Business people make lousy solutions architects.**".

Why is this so problematic?

Customers take these unhelpful pathways based on many false assumptions.

Assumption 1: The software product/business boundary forces requirements discovery "for free".

This assumption is based on an expectation that one of three things will happen during implementation, either at a solution or sub-function level:

1. The software perfectly integrates with the company's desired automated processes.
2. Some minor manual workaround or process change can bridge the small gaps between software and automation.
3. Customisation or a larger process change can resolve any other gap.

But it doesn't work that way.

In most cases, the vendor wants to follow their defined process that includes many assumptions. The largest assumption is that the customer understands the change that they want to enable.

The vendor's quoted implementation cost is likely predicated on a "fill-in-the-blanks" software configuration process, to which immediate and specific choices or inputs are required. There is little time for research, experimentation, or decision-making.

Most business teams will resist change forced on them without adequate communication and preparation. No team will welcome additional manual work to compensate for functional gaps. The size and impact of a process change could vary significantly between the business and implementation perspectives.

Assumption 2: The vendor aspires to be responsible for business outcomes.

Does the vendor want to acknowledge that they deliver your business outcomes, or do they want to be accountable only for delivering their package? Of course, there are many different vendors and vendor business models, but always the core of their value proposition is implementing and customising a package.

The reality is this:

1. All vendor teams modulate all their activities around the software package. Every dialog you have with them is in the language of implementation.

2. The vendor's livelihoods depend on a deep understanding of the software package and their relationship with the software developer (if they are separate companies).

The vendor will calculate risk very differently between the software package domain and your business domain.

And if the business outcome responsibility isn't written clearly into the contract - if it's just a tacit agreement - then you won't get much out of that at all.

For more on tacit contractual agreements and what they are worth, please see the axiom **"# 100. The secret to managing vendor negotiations."** in **"Adam On: Projects (Volume 2)"**[1].

Assumption 3: You'll have access to "world-class" business functional experts.

I frequently hear key managers say:

> *"These folks are worldwide experts in this area! They've worked with people all over the world and seen it all. They know how to solve my problems using their software."*

The second assumption is that you have access to "world-class experts" in your business problem who can do what you decided not to do: primary business analysis and process change. And not only that, but you are expecting them to perform this analysis on the fly. You may not even have access to "world class experts" in the software package unless you are careful with the contract.

Not that you cannot buy generalised business consulting services from your software vendor. It's just that they are likely to be very expensive and still likely to work within guardrails set by the software solution.

Why agile can't fully solve this problem

In principle, agile lifecycle models can inspect and adapt their way to a successful outcome. In many cases, this approach is superior to a broad-brush requirements analysis process or business process modelling exercise.

But some problems that need to be solved to make this work, especially with software packages.

[1] https://bjl.ink/aopv2

The first problem to solve is adding deep vendor software knowledge to your cross-functional team ("CFT"). This will be challenging after you've picked the software, but even more so beforehand.

In each of the main implementation stages of a software package, the CFT has different skill requirements. Such people are not likely available from a vendor or even an integrator during the pre-selection stages of a software project. And even during software implementation, people with deep package knowledge are likely very scarce. You'll find that good software people are scheduled very tightly into the vendor's implementation process and so it's harder to keep them "on tap" for just those moments when you need their deep-domain knowledge.

The second problem is where are you modelling the problem? If you plan to model the problem/solution space in the software package, this implies that you have already made the buying commitment. Even if you have a low-cost sandbox environment, you're still potentially investing in knowledge acquisition. If you're modelling requirements somewhere else, this reduces some benefits of agile. It's not a showstopper, but it needs to be considered.

The flex-point for your approach is when you make a commitment to a particular product.

What can I do to solve these problems?

We've outlined (some) of the problems with this approach. What are the solutions?

Define the landscape with the Program Logic Model

In terms of value streams, this scenario happens when the organisation wants to bypass the definition of "Outcomes" and "Impacts" and jump directly to the solution ("Outputs").

So let's unpack this perspective a little and provide some structure around the debate.

The Program Logic Model (PLM) construct defines the terminology of **"outcomes"** and **"impacts"**. See below for the Kellogg Foundation generic PLM:

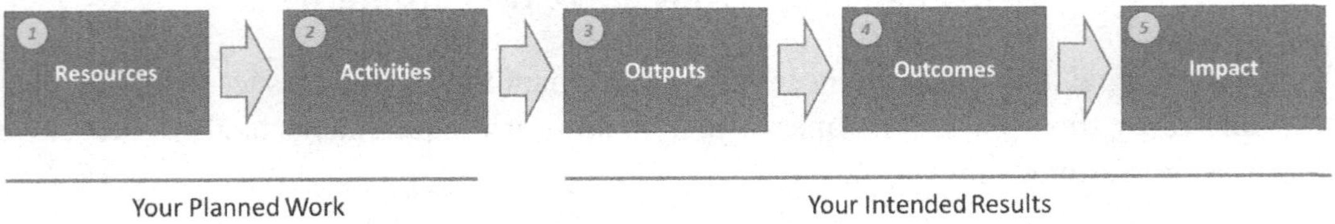

Figure 25. The Program Logic Model (PLM)

The "intended results" of the Kellogg PLM include the project outputs made available to a customer context at the handoff point, as shown below.

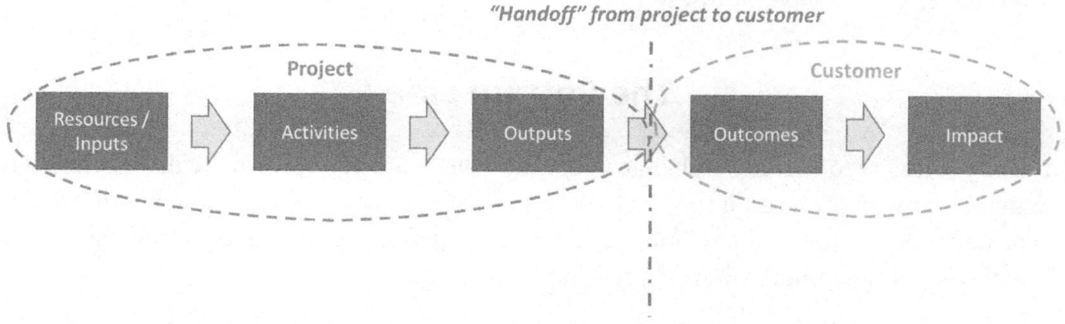

Figure 26. Typical Project Handoff to Customer

The PLM is an important reference model that will help you to *"think your way around a project"*. Please see the axiom "**# 18. Do you have a system-based objective?**", for more on applying the PLM to projects.

Take responsibility for business problem and solution definition

Understanding the landscape is a first step. Now we need to work out who is responsible for each element. It should be pretty obvious that the vendor is speaking to the deliverables. But who is speaking for the outcomes and impacts? The business folks in your team, or the vendor or someone else?

Who are the business experts in your business? If you're looking for "world-class" expertise, your organisation has more than enough people who are "world-class" experts in your organisational processes.

You just have to ask them.

Don't rely on a software vendor for authoritative advice on your business problem. Some vendors may do both, but don't rely on it.

Ultimately the responsibility for clearly articulating the required behaviour change falls to the users or their domain representatives. The business user thus requires expertise in both the general domain and the specific customer operation, skills in communication, and the time to "get your head around it". A Business Analyst may help, but it's the same problem type.

Organisations must adequately resource projects with skilled business users who articulate how business value will be unlocked. This requirement holds regardless of the project lifecycle approach you use.

Anything else is a recipe for disaster.

The Bottom Line

You buy software to enable the change you want; you do not buy software to drive behaviour change. Many projects run into severe problems because they expect their software vendor to provide some "magic" that eliminates the need to define requirements or understand the "as-is" state of the organisation. There is no such "magic".

The Tags

#enablement, #principlesofprojectsuccess, #vendors, #requirements, #axiom, #outcomes, #programlogicmodel, #kelloggfoundation, #inspectandadapt, #iteration, #asisstate, #tobestate, #agile

On Project Debt

You may be familiar with the term "Technical Debt", but there are other debts that your project can incur, often without the project manager knowing about them.

The meaning of "Technical Debt" has evolved since it was first coined in 1975, and now has "spalled" to the point of being unhelpful in a project context. That doesn't stop teams and their stakeholders talking about it.

It's not the job of a Project Manager to understand the intricacies of the term or the sort out the definitional debates. It is the job of a PM to understand the nature of TechDebt and the different perspectives so they can help the team navigate through that dissonance, and do the needful.

35. Where did you borrow your TechDebt?

The Axiom

You borrowed TechDebt from the worst kind of loan shark; it only gets repaid with sweat, tears or blood!

The TL;DR

Regardless of your definition of Technical Debt (TechDebt)—and there are many—they all maintain, at some level, the metaphor of financial debt, even if it's vague. But in this metaphor they often miss the impact of the debt interest and repayment schedule, which renders the metaphor fairly toothless and benign. TechDebt is an instance of a psychological phenomenon called "**Akrasia**", in which people make decisions that compromise their long-term interests to satisfy short-term desires. Akrasia is by far the most powerful model of TechDebt precisely because there are so many different perspectives. It even covers the related concept of Organisational Debt ("OrgDebt"). We can draw from the prevention and treatment strategies for Akrasia in thinking about how we approach TechDebt or OrgDebt. This sidesteps many of the complications that arise because of all the different perspectives. This is where the idea of borrowing from a Loan Shark helps us.

The Back Story

When Ward Cunningham coined the metaphor "Technical Debt" in 1992, he positioned it as a legitimate technical strategy: a mechanism to gain a jump in progress at a manageable cost over time. The 'debt' metaphor was a deliberate comparison of businesses borrowing money to buy a piece of equipment that generated value. The debt enabled the company to bring forward that value stream to start much earlier than if the organisation had to wait until it had the free cash to buy it.

> *"I coined the term technical debt to describe a software development strategy by which skillful and alert teams could create excellent software in a competitive environment. Through careful attention to accumulating insufficiencies one could engage customers and learn what is both valuable and possible together without losing control of the product itself. I was drawing an analogy between the debt financing of a growing company and the incremental intellectual investment in a growing program. I used the idea of debt metaphorically, a metaphor that has been lost on pretty much everyone."* — **Ward Cunningham** in "Done is Dead"[1]

A Term with Many Definitions

These days, the TechDebt plot isn't so simple, and there are now many definitions of the term TechDebt. The definition has expanded in many directions to mean any other kinds of software development problems. In essence, TechDebt now seems to include any remediation that costs money. In 2015, Steve Blank expanded the concept to "Organisational Debt".

Each definition has its history, terminology, and taxonomy – often more than one. This is a project management book, so I won't enumerate the details, but you'll be able to find them easily on Google.

[1]https://web.archive.org/web/20160202195443/http:/forage.ward.fed.wiki.org/view/done-is-dead

This leads us to a situation where the definition is far less effective, along the lines I described in in the axiom “**# 5. The Power of the Dog**”.

Rehabilitating a bad practice

The problem with broader definitions of TechDebt is that they include both good and bad practice which cannot be differentiated without complex analysis. And the deeper taxonomies and rationale are not aligned.

> *"A mess is not a technical debt. A mess is just a mess. Technical debt decisions are made based on real project constraints. They are risky, but they can be beneficial. The decision to make a mess is never rational, is always based on laziness and unprofessionalism, and has no chance of paying of in the future. A mess is always a loss."* — **Uncle Bob Martin**

Using the term “TechDebt at the top level tends to rehabilitate bad software practice by including it with good. As Ron Jeffries says,

> *"the term ‘technical debt’, as used, is too mild to properly describe some pretty bad behavior.’* — **Ron Jeffries**[2].

However, regardless of how fuzzy the definition has become, the common theme is a perception that something is rotten in Denmark that will—at some point in the future—inhibit or prevent the modification or evolution of the software.

There’s also a viewpoint, again elegantly expressed by Ron Jeffries, that TechDebt is an indicator of poor quality in the development process more broadly.

> *"I believe that teams generally slack on quality due to feeling pressure, and either do not make a conscious decision to do so, or rationalise the decision based on the notion that they can make up the time. I believe that any such decision is most likely to be wrong."* - **Ron Jeffries**[3]

So, regardless of the TechDebt typology, preventing it or increasing the commitment to remediating it sounds like a good thing.

---

[2]https://web.archive.org/web/20151111011323/http:/ronjeffries.com/articles/015-11/tech-debt/
[3]https://web.archive.org/web/20151111011323/http:/ronjeffries.com/articles/015-11/tech-debt/

TechDebt is a form of Akrasia

TechDebt is an instance of behaviour in which people make decisions that compromise their long-term interests to satisfy short-term desires. Why do people make these choices? It's a form of akrasia, which is:

> *"a lack of self-control or the state of acting against one's better judgment."* – **Akrasia**[4] (Wikipedia)

Akrasia comprises two components of decision-making:

1. How we decided on the course of action.
2. How the decision-makers behave after the decision, particularly how they deal with any post-decision commitments.

There are many strategies for overcoming akrasia.

For the first part of Akrasia, the decision-making process, psychologists recommend a range of strategies, including:

1. **Education**: ensuring that decision-makers fully understand the components and implications of making the decision.
2. **Visualisation**: thinking about the post-decision situation and in particular imagining the consequences of not fulfilling the commitments – both explicit and implied – that come from making the decision.

For the second part of Akrasia, post commitment behviour, one recommented strategy is called a "commitment device, " which is a technique that locks someone into future actions.

A trivial example of a commitment device might be someone wanting to lose weight. They use a "commitment device" such as giving a friend a $500 cheque made out to a charity, with instructions to send the cheque to the charity if the person doesn't complete a set of actions, such as reporting their weight each week and achieving certain loss milestones.

Before we look at examples of Akrasia strategies for TechDebt, let's quickly map out their foundation, which is based on the notion of TechDebt being modelled on a financial strategy.

[4] https://en.wikipedia.org/wiki/Akrasia

Digging into the "Debt" Metaphor

The TechDebt metaphor uses "debt" in an abstract and benign sense modelled on financial debt. But financial debt comes in many forms, some of which are not benign or friendly. To consider this, let's expand the debt metaphor into three common debt models in business and personal life. These are:

1. **Term Loan**: Term loans are specific sums borrowed for a set purpose, traditionally obtained in-person but now primarily online, and often with a rigorous approval process. Repayment is typically structured, and some loans allow early settlement to save on interest.
2. **Revolving Credit Line**: Revolving Credit Facilities, e.g., a Credit Card, offer a flexible spending limit without a fixed repayment end date. Due to easier initial approvals, they often carry higher interest rates to offset increased default risks.
3. **Street Loan**: a loan provided by unregulated "Loan Sharks", is a simple verbal agreement with exorbitant interest rates. Weekly payments (the "nut") cover only interest, which the borrower must pay until they repay the full loan amount. Non-compliance can cause violent repercussions, making debt clearance challenging without a significant financial windfall.

You may know some - or all - of the information about these three forms of debt. And we've all seen Loan Sharks in the movies. But I wanted to establish a baseline description so we can use the terms reliably.

The question for you is what type of finance model is your project or team using? I'm guessing that most teams think they are using a nice, friendly, low-impact Term Loan.

TechDebt-specific strategies for Akrasia

For TechDebt, a "commitment device" that covers both pre- and post-decision elements is to think of any TechDebt as a Street Loan.

Before the decision: the decision-makers can ensure they understand the parameters of the transaction and explicitly understand that they are entering into a decision with a very high-interest rate - think of 1000s of per cent a year. This exaggerates, of course, but you need something to balance the benign and sunny bias inherent in Akrasia.

After the decision: whenever there's a temptation to postpone remediation, try visualising the "blood, sweat and tears" that will be spilled when trying to repay compounding interest rates may seem extreme, but it looks more balanced once you understand the actual costs of TechDebt. I'm sure Ron Jeffries would approve.

The Bottom Line

Cunningham thought that TechDebt, like financial debt, could gain a short-term advantage, but was balanced against an explicit commitment to pay it back. So, the next time you think about incurring TechDebt, don't think about it as if you were taking out a personal loan from a friendly, law-abiding bank at a low-interest rate. Imagine the raw terror of trying to come up with 10x your original loan in the face of meaty thugs holding axe handles. Then make your decision.

The Tags

#technicaldebt, #techdebt, #requirementsmanagement, #functionalrequirements, #non-functionalrequirements, #decisionmaking, #wardcunningham, #ronjeffries, #akrasia, #commitmentdevice

36. The root cause of technical debt.

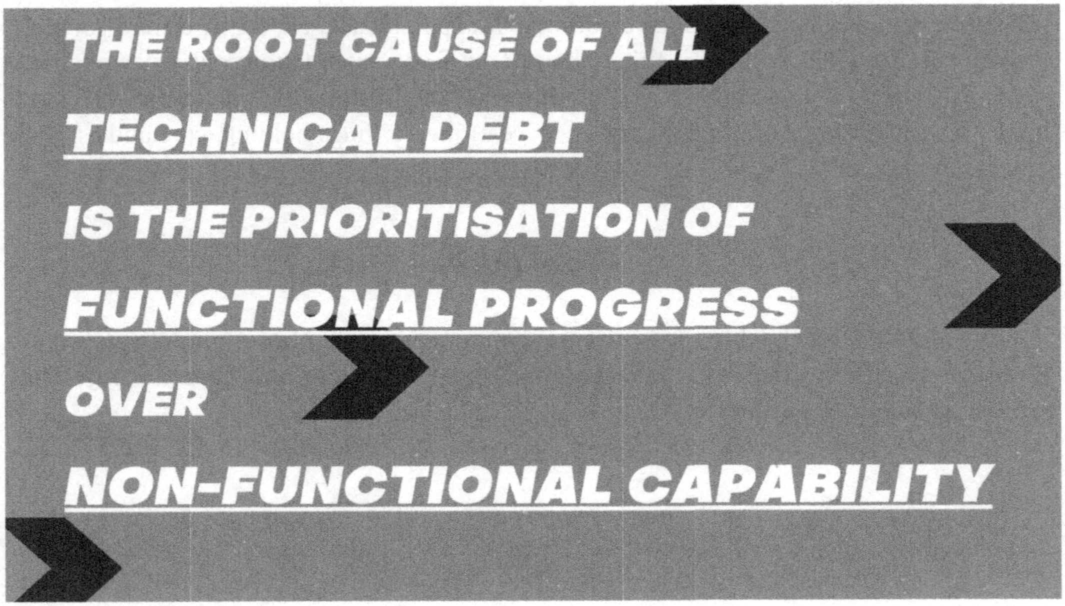

The Axiom

The root cause of all technical debt is the prioritisation of functional progress over non-functional capability

The TL;DR

"Technical Debt" ("TechDebt") appears to have many definitions, at least some of which deny its value as a development strategy. Knowing the type and source of TechDebt is vital to a Project Manager only in terms of the gains that can be made by allowing these issues into production traded off against the limitations that this introduces to the solution under development.

The Back Story

It's hard to figure out whether "Technical Debt" ("TechDebt") is consistently understood and treated in project teams these days.

Many impaired projects can be trace their impairments back to decisions or compromises made before or during project ideation, often before the project team is onboarded, or to decisions made (or not maid) in the business domain.

TechDebt: A single root cause

But all these reasons collapse into one single root cause: ***the failure to maintain the non-functional characteristics of a codebase in line with the user's desired functional capabilities.***

Non-functional requirements (NFRs) are critical to the quality of a software solution. They define the system's properties that are not related to specific functionalities but are still essential to its overall performance. These properties include reliability, scalability, maintainability, security, and usability. When NFRs are not adequately considered, the resulting code may not meet the user's expectations, leading to significant technical debt.

Please refer to the axiom **# 31. Non-functional requirements are a secret weapon.** for more information on "NFRs".

Why do NFRs Cause TechDebt?

The failure to address NFRs can result from various factors, including time constraints, lack of understanding of the requirements, or organisational culture. When a project team focuses solely on delivering functionality, they may disregard the system's non-functional requirements, leading to inefficient, difficult-to-maintain code and often vulnerability to bugs and other issues.

Over time, this code becomes increasingly difficult to modify, leading to technical debt build-up, ultimately affecting the system's overall quality and performance. Therefore, project managers must be aware of the importance of NFRs and ensure that the project team is also familiar with and committed to addressing these requirements throughout the development process.

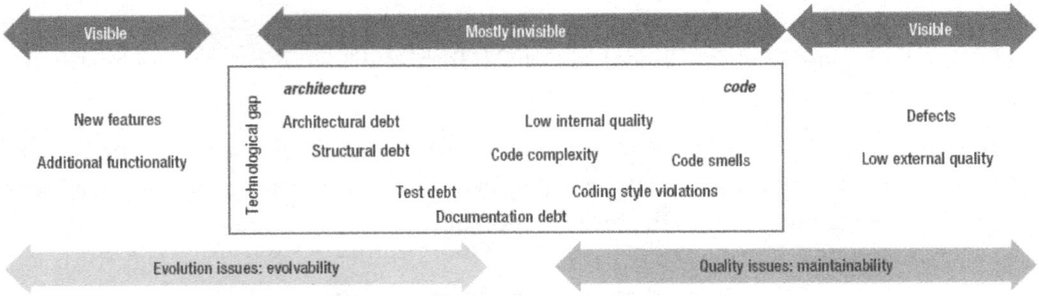

Figure 27. Technical Debt Landscape (Krutchten 2012)

Krutchten et al., 2012 proposed a landscape for TechDebt in the above diagram, which shows the two main categories of NFRs that are impacted by TechDebt: *"Evolvability"* and *"Maintainability"*. Whilst this provides some structure to an area that has become very unstructured, these two NFRs are symptoms, not root causes. It is these two NFRs that create "friction" when teams want to make changes to code that had existing TechDebt.

But the root cause for TechDebt can originate from compromising any of the vast number of NFR categories. These compromises can happen at anytime. For example:

> *"we don't need to scale this version up beyond 1k users." "we don't need to cater for older O/S versions right now."*

And so on. The decisions (if the TechDebt is intentional) are all about NFR capabilities.

The Bottom Line

A project manager (PM) must be involved in decisions around TechDebt and, therefore, have sufficient knowledge to participate in discussions and understand the impacts. A PM must support the developers by tracking TechDebt decisions and defending them from potential downstream criticism when effects surface and the bill must be paid.

The worst failure of project management is to allow the team to downplay or ignore servicing non-functional requirements ("NFRs").

This is the primary reason for TechDebt, incurred deliberately or otherwise.

The Tags

#technicaldebt, #requirementsmanagement, #functionalrequirements, #nonfunctionalrequirements, #nfr, #decisionmaking, #axiom

---

37. There’s a bigger problem in your project than TechDebt!

The Axiom

Business debt is incurred by making expedient compromises when defining and mapping the problem to frame it as a project. Prioritise OrgDebt over TechDebt in managing your projects.

The TL;DR

“Technical Debt” (“TechDebt”) describes a legitimate but often misused code strategy. But there’s a much bigger problem that might be lurking in your project — it’s called “Business Debt” (“BizDebt”). BizDebt is incurred when project stakeholders make decisions early in the project’s life to frame the initiative for entry into an organisation’s portfolio governance and onboarding processes. BizDebt occurs at the intersection of TechDebt and Organisational Debt (“OrgDebt”).

The Back Story

The root cause of many impaired projects occurs before or during project ideation. Decisions or compromises are made upstream before the project team is onboarded, or in the management domain during project execution.

Before we dive into project-specific BizDebt, let's first look at a broader problem, of which project BizDebt is a sub-class. Let's look at "Organisational Debt".

What is Organisational Debt

Steve Blank coined the term "Organisational Debt" in 2015, and gave it the following characteristics:

- Arises from suboptimal organisational structures or processes due to expedient past decisions,
- Accumulation of outdated policies, norms, or roles as the external environment evolves,
- Results from actions or decisions skipped or delayed to ensure optimal operation.

Similar to how financial or technical debt accumulates over time, organisational debt can also compound, leading to inefficiencies, strained relationships, and possible decline in employee morale.

Organisational debt, if left unchecked, can have far-reaching repercussions on a company's growth trajectory and internal harmony. By understanding its intricacies, maintaining open dialogues, and fostering a culture of continuous improvement, organisations can navigate their challenges and set themselves on a path of sustainable growth and success.

Now, since we're in a book about Project Management, let's look at the project-specific types of Organisational Debt: BizTechDebt and BizPro

Business Technical Debt ("BizTechDebt")

"BizTechDebt" is TechDebt created by board level or executive decision or omission. For example, a decision might be made to reduce operating costs to levels that don't support defined service levels in the long run or that increase the impact (and possibly the probability) of significant system outages during peak usage.

A common term for this is "sweat the assets", which is, unfortunately, a term that makes it sound clever. This strategy results in actions such as delaying licence upgrade renewals or maintenance contract service levels, cutting back on training or replacing people when others resign.

Another term used is "efficiency dividend", which pushes arbitrary macro savings onto division managers, who then work out who gets what cuts in their budgets.

Business Project Debt ("BizProjDebt")

"BizProjDebt" covers project impairments caused by executive decisions or poor practice in how the project is scoped or set up. For example, you are defining a significant, vague project goal or setting an aggressive, arbitrary launch date. The worst kind of "BizProjDebt" results from pushing through a pet idea for a product or system: one which hasn't been validated in the target market or user group or perhaps includes a platform selected well before the goal is understood.

These decisions and trade-offs conceal essential information that is necessary for a project to have a good chance of success. These early ideation activities involve a high-level and fundamental mapping between the problem and solution spaces. Once that mapping is locked in, it becomes concealed from later team members.

Even when the project concept is provided to the project team, sometime later, surfacing this mapping is problematic and flawed. For example, numerous people may be involved in those early sessions, but it's unlikely they will all be involved in the handover. Project teams play a game of question and answer to unearth the rationale for decisions or to understand why alternatives were eliminated.

Concealing the mapping between problem and solution spaces

Concealing the mapping between problem space and solution space leads to much bigger problems. I call this "BizDebt" as compared with "TechDebt". BizDebt enters a project when decisions are made about the value, scope, or implementation of a solution before the technical teams are engaged in the project. BizDebt is far more sinister and challenging to detect in a project before problems occur. BizDebt also requires project teams to play "Twenty Questions" about these decisions, omissions, and other harmful aspects.

Preventing the creation of BizDebt is very simple: involve the project team (or at least selected members) in the project from the earliest days of idea creation. At least they will understand the decisions, trade-offs and compromises made during the idea creation. This strategy also resolves the first issue above because it normalises the time distribution across business and technical folks.

Detecting and Correcting BizDebt

We can take our cues for detecting and correcting BizDebt from the broader sphere of Organisational Debt. Here are some of the symptoms. Spotting organisational debt can be difficult because it often lurks beneath the surface. Does your project exhibit any of the following symptoms:

- **Inefficiencies**: Redundant or cumbersome processes that were once deemed efficient,
- **Employee Morale**: Lowered satisfaction, high turnover rates, or increasing conflicts among departments,
- **Reduced Adaptability**: Struggles to pivot in response to market shifts or new initiatives,
- **Reliance on Workarounds**: Overdependence on temporary fixes rather than addressing root causes,
- **Signs from Growth**: Are your project teams suffering from broader organisational policies such as uncompetitive compensation, poor training, or dissonance between corporate message and the lived experience of company culture.

If you're seeing any of these symptoms, the fix may be outside of your project's control, but if you're aware of these things then you have a chance of mitigating them:

- **Hiring and Training**: Clearly define job roles, ensure apt training, and align each role with the company's mission.
- **Salary and Compensation**: Regularly assess and adjust salaries based on industry standards, valuing employees with critical expertise.
- **Reevaluate and Adjust Roles**: Some initial hires might need role realignment to match the company's evolution.
- **Company Culture**: Periodically assess and align the company's culture with its size, objectives, and market positioning.
- **Communication**: As organisations grow, adapt communication strategies ensuring clarity and cohesion.
- **Feedback Systems**: Encourage platforms where employees can suggest policy or process changes, taking inspiration from software "bug bounty" systems.
- **Avoid Over-regulating**: Refrain from adding rules for every minor incident and avoid reactionary policy-making.

The Bottom Line

Beware of the creation of "BizDebt" in your project – normalise the activities between "business" and "technical" folks by including some folks from the "technical" team right from the beginning of the project, e.g., the "Idea Generation" phase.

The Tags

#technicaldebt, #projbizdebt, #functionalrequirements, #non-functionalrequirements, #decisionmaking

On Assumptions

I'm sure you've heard this aphorism about assumptions:

> *"Assumptions make an Ass out of U and Me"* — Unknown.

The first time you hear that it sounds helpful, if a little too clever. But it becomes useless through repetition. In projects, at least, it is only unmanaged assumptions that cause problems. Assumptions are a critical element of the project process: every project has them. All assumptions need to be dovetailed into a risk management approach, otherwise you'll end up like Mitch Hennessy.

Samuel L Jackson played Mitch Hennessy as a down-at-heels private investigator in the movie "The Long Kiss Goodnight" and mangled the saying. Or does Mitch's version show a deeper understanding of the planning process?

> *"Everyone Knows When You Make an Assumption, You Make An Ass Out Of 'U' And 'Umption.'"* — **Mitch Hennessey** (The Long Kiss Goodnight)

38. Use assumptions to plug any hole in your planning.

I love assumptions. You can create an assumption to plug any hole in your planning fact base.

You can assume that the laws of physics don't apply if it helps your planning construct.

That's all fine ... until you forget which type of assumptions are which ...

The Axiom

Assumptions can plug any hole in your planning but don't fall in love with them.

The TL;DR

I love assumptions! They can plug any hole in your project narrative. At the extreme, you can use unvalidated memories, professional guesses, or creative speculation. You can even consider ideas that may contradict the laws of physics. Anything is acceptable to develop a project narrative. But don't fall in love with your assumptions or forget their origin. They are only temporary support structures. You must progressively attack each assumption or find a way to live with it.

The Back Story

When you find a gap in your project narrative that cannot be filled with a known fact, you need to find an assumption. You can find your assumptions from various sources, ranging from mundane to pseudo-facts. "Pseudo-facts" are the facts proposed by stakeholders that represent either unvalidated recollections or conventional wisdom about your project environment. If you can't find a "pseudo-fact", then you'll have to invent something. In some cases, it can be challenging to differentiate those assumptions from creative fiction. But it doesn't matter, for now.

Overall, there are two types of assumption:

1. Type 1 Assumptions ("Plausible");
2. Type 2 Assumptions ("Creative").

Let's explore these types of assumptions in more detail.

"Plausible" Assumptions (Type 1)

"Plausible" assumptions are more likely to be true than not.

People making these assumptions know the assumption's general domain and context and may recall various facts in discussions as "pseudo-facts. For example, a team member might confidently state, *'I believe we produce 5,000 invoices per month, although I don't have any supporting documentation.'* While this statement is technically an assumption, it can be easily verified through a simple email or phone call.

A different form of Type 1 assumption emerges when someone uses the word "assume" instead of "conclude". For example, a new project manager says, "If you are doing a formal requirements document before your solution architecture document, then I assume you are also a Waterfall style project, and the next step is a Design Document.".

Another type of Type 1 assumption arises when someone uses the word *'assume'* instead of *'conclude'*. For instance, a new project manager might state, *'If you are creating a formal Requirements Document before your Solution Architecture Document, then I assume you are following a Waterfall style project approach, and the next step would be a Design Document.'*

With "Plausible" assumptions based on a deduction, we progress from a known fact to a hypothesis that flows from a logical conclusion. If such a conclusion can be immediately validated, then it becomes a fact, and not an assumption.

Many Type 1 assumptions exist in our context, masquerading as facts. Things like conventional wisdom or out-of-date documentation can feed incorrect information into our project. As project managers, you must recognise the assumptions hiding behind pseudo facts, so they are correctly identified and targetted for validation.

"Creative" Assumptions (Type 2)

Type 2 assumptions extend beyond the plausibility of Type 1 and can be any hypothesis that fills gaps in the project narrative. They could be accurate but are more likely flat-out wrong. They also take more time to validate.

For example, *"We need a solution with 5 9's reliability/uptime"*. While this requirement is commonly used in the IT solutions industry, those who assert it often fail to fully consider its implications, such as high-cost.

Is this a fantasy that will never be implemented once the sponsor sees the costs? Or is it a "pseudo-fact" that is wrong but close to the mark? If it is a fantasy but something that the stakeholder believes, how long will it take to unpack that belief and converge on the real requirement?

Beyond the well-held fantasy, we can use extreme Type 2 assumptions that are the placeholders within the narrative that will require further work. A team of juniors can replace a team of experienced specialists? Sure, no problem! Get ten months of work done in a week? Done! The software delivered from the vendor will have zero bugs. Easy!

I call these "creative" assumptions because they live in the fuzzy zone between fact and fantasy. Some are plausible but highly uncertain. Others are undoubtedly whacko, but they are the only way to sustain the project narrative. Essentially you are saying, "We have a plan, but it can only be achieved if you <some whacky Type 2 assumption>."

Type 2 assumptions are helpful when you are struggling to establish your project narrative and start exploring what might happen to make that narrative whole. When putting together your project narrative, it is essential to "suspend disbelief" until finished. Remember how important it is to have a story that provides your "bridge to an unknown future".

Assumption Guidelines

These guidelines for making assumptions cover both how to validate your assumptions and how to use your assumptions

Validating the Assumptions

The fact that I love assumptions as an element of practice doesn't mean all assumptions are equally loveable. Assumptions are but a tool to help bridge gaps in our project narrative when envisaging the future state. In some cases they are a necessary evil to support our vision of the future.

> *"Statisticians, like artists, have the bad habit of falling in love with their models."*
> — **George Box**, British Statistician

And likewise, Project Managers and stakeholders have a bad habit of falling in love with their assumptions.

Every assumption must be loved (included in your project narrative) but also suspected (so we subject it to validation or risk management).

Every assumption represents a risk you must manage in your project - perhaps more than one. Every risk has a minimum overhead of validation or treatment. We need the assumption, but it is not cost-free, and the cost increases as long as the assumption remains unvalidated. Therefore we must ruthlessly assess and retire our assumptions as quickly as possible.

All assumptions must be validated, but some are more urgent than others. It is crucial to regularly revisit these assumptions and either replace them with verified facts (preferably) or refine them to be more precisely defined.

Your assumptions shape your discovery process, investigating these aspects of the problem or solution in more detail. If you can't make the assumptions more credible, you need to construct a new narrative or move forward, knowing that these assumptions must be addressed later in the project.

Using Assumptions

The primary purpose of all assumptions is to support the development of a project narrative. Your project narrative is your "bridge to the future" that supports your project vision and enables practical planning.

By articulating your implicit and subconscious yet uncertain thoughts about the project, you add value. Your project becomes viable through the assumptions you incorporate into the project narrative. The value is that you've explicitly identified where the focus needs to be so the project can survive. They help address fundamental questions that determine the feasibility of your project.

All assumptions, especially highly implausible ones, should be promptly removed from your project narrative, by validation. You must attack these aggressively, even to the point of abandoning the project. If the assumptions are not critical to the project's viability, they should be formulated as hypotheses that inform experiments or further research. Discovering early on that your project is not feasible is preferable to facing a mid-project disaster due to overlooked issues.

By exposing and structuring these unvalidated assertions, you've created a checklist for your project's "kill switch" that you will use to terminate the project if necessary. See the Axiom ***"# 81. There are only two kinds of successful projects!"*** for a description of the "Kill Switch" project by Mike Cohn.

The Bottom Line

Assumptions are what you need when you don't have facts, but make sure your "facts" are real, and not "pseudo-facts". Use assertions freely, but don't fall in love with them.

The Tags

#planning, #projectplanning, #assumptions, #risk, #georgebox, #mikecohn, #killswitch, #validation, #riskmanagement, #plausibleassumptions, #creativeassumptions, #projectnarrative

39. Supporting the bridge to an unknown future.

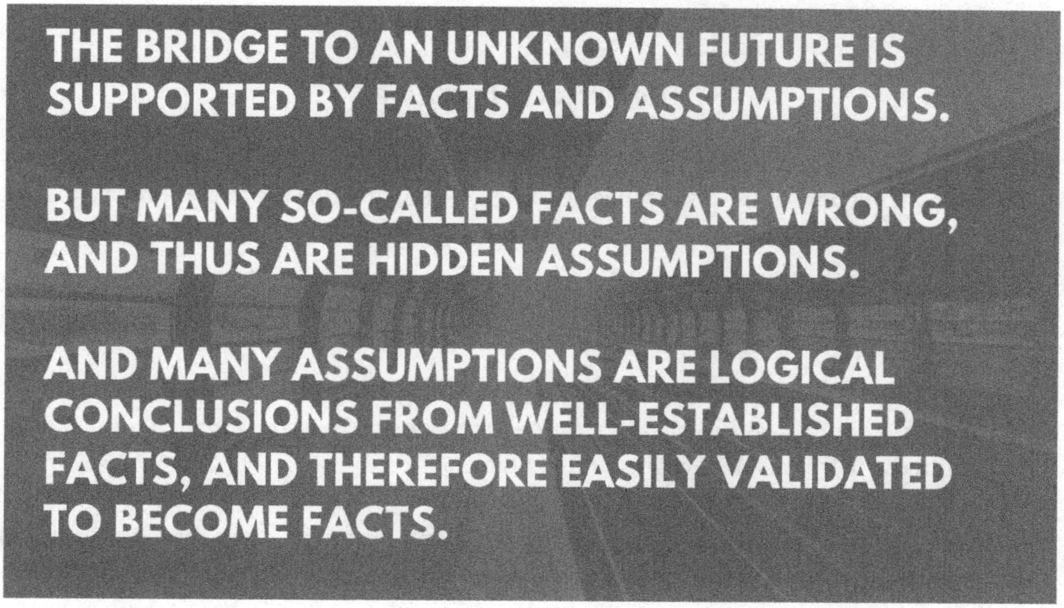

The Axiom

Both facts and assumptions support your project narrative.

The TL;DR

Facts and assumptions support the bridge to an unknown future — this is represented in your project by a "project narrative", which is a story that describes the desired goal and the pathway to success. Many so-called facts are wrong and thus are hidden assumptions. And many assumptions are logical conclusions from well-established facts and, therefore, easily validated to become facts. Recognising the interplay between facts and assumptions is crucial in building a solid project narrative that guides your team toward success.

The Back Story

One of the critical objectives for a Project Manager (PM) is to ensure the team creates a project narrative – a story that takes the team from wherever they are to the end goal.

The Project Narrative

The project narrative is an integral part of project planning in that it allows us to envision the beneficial outcome of the project despite (or even allowing for) the many things we don't yet know and the many blockages that might get in the way.

John F Kennedy provided a famous and concise project narrative on 25th May 1961, describing a human-crewed expedition to the moon.

> *"[Congress] should commit itself to achieving the goal, before this decade is out, of landing a man on the Moon and returning him safely to the Earth."* **John F Kennedy**, 35th President of the United States

A clear and concise project narrative, such as this one, sets the stage for a focused and goal-oriented approach to project management. Although extremely short, JFK's statement described the task's objective, timing, and nature. The mission was to have a human crew.

Over time, as the mission parameters emerged, the narrative for the Apollo missions could have been progressively elaborated. I don't know if it was, but that original statement could be extended to describe the various stages of the mission and which crew members would be involved. And each Apollo trip could add specific locations, distances, experiments, and similar factual differences.

Even if the narrative expanded to a few paragraphs from that marvellously succinct original, it would still be short enough to be retained and repeated easily. Compared to the actual plans and mission execution complexity, the narrative is still a simple encapsulation of the real thing.

From the first statement by JFK, the moon project narratives assumed many significant things that would be essential to success: technological advances, manufacturing, and mathematics.

Creating an end-to-end narrative

So, you can see how assumptions allow us to create the project narrative by supporting it where we lack knowledge.

These assumptions can be either of two types of assumptions - fact-based or fantasy. For creating the narrative, it doesn't matter which kind of assumption you use. What's important is that we end up with a project narrative that "works". Each assumption answers the question: *"What would I have to do to make this work?"* or *"What would have to happen to make this work?"*.

Wherever there is a gap in your project narrative - your "bridge to the future" - you either fill it with a fact or an assumption. In the early stages, it doesn't matter what is plugging the gap, as long as it leads you to an end state.

Depending on your chosen lifecycle model, you may stop with just the initial project narrative. Or you may choose to refine the narrative towards a more concrete plan.

Figure 28. Supporting the Bridge to an Unknown Future

Elaborating the narrative

As we develop the narrative we cycle from the "sponsor" of the project narrative to the "critic". Each assumption is a risk, and the risk rating must reflect the intrinsic qualities of the assumption, including whether it is Type 1 or Type 2. If the narrative doesn't hold up at any point, then you probably have the wrong narrative.

As a PM, you need to drive this cycle of evolution of our project narrative - from sponsor (or author) to critic — to revise the narrative and assumption set as you work through the risk process. That could involve running "experiments", finding needed information about the “as is” situation, onboarding people into the project, or finding a software package ... anything that resolves the risks and solidifies the project narrative.

The Bottom Line

The project narrative is your ’bridge to an unknown future’ — it provides the foundation for your project’s success. It ensures your team can navigate the complexities and uncertainties during the project lifecycle.

The Tags

#planning, #projectplanning, #assumptions, #risk, #facts, #narrative, #projectnarrative, #johnfkennedy, #bridgetoanunknownfuture

40. Assumptions have Boxian qualities.

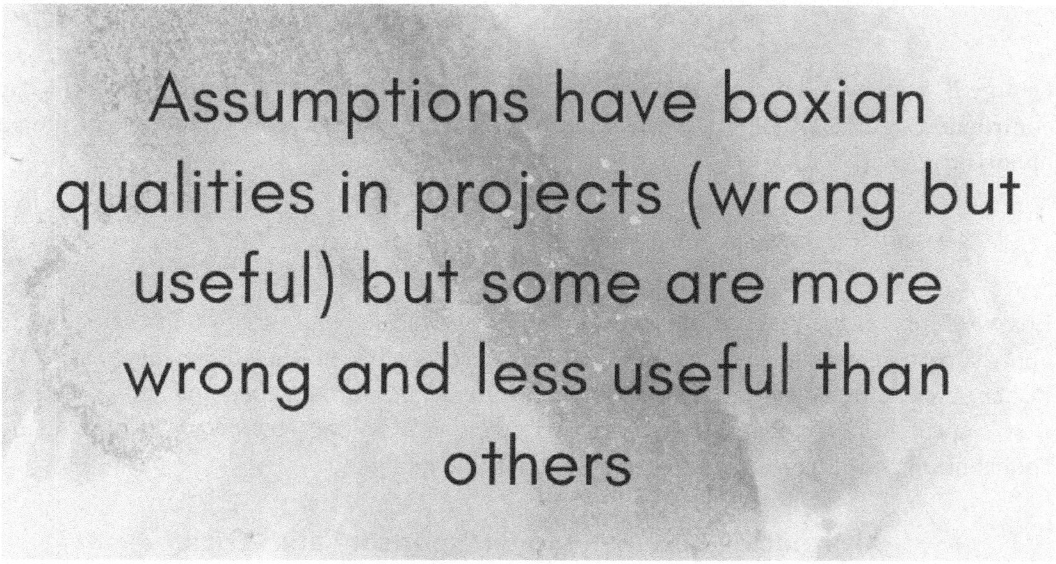

The Axiom

Project assumptions have Boxian qualities (wrong but useful), but some are more wrong and less useful than others.

The TL;DR

Assumptions are a part of any project and must be tracked carefully and progressively retired as either unnecessary or converted to facts by additional research or experimentation. As long as they remain assumptions, they have the Boxian quality of being wrong but useful. Applying Box's iterative approach to discovery in the project management domain can lead to more robust and adaptive project plans.

The Back Story

Assumptions are an important part of every project, and, as I outlined in the previous axiom "**# 39. Supporting the bridge to an unknown future**" are critical to success, if managed correctly. An assumption helps create the narrative, which is an early model of the end-to-end project.

All models are wrong

George Box is the celebrated 20th-century British statistician who died in March 2013. He contributed significantly to statistical science but is more generally known for his oft-quoted aphorism:

> *"All models are wrong. Some are useful."* – **George Box**

Box wrote extensively about the twin problems of experimental design and the ability to apply correct analysis to problems. He was influenced by his one-time father-in-law, Ronald Fisher, an accomplished but obscure English statistician. In fact, the paper in which Box first coined the *"All models are wrong"* statement is a 10-page review of Fisher's many contributions to statistical analysis and the scientific method.

Alternating between model "sponsor" and "critic"

Box described an iterative process for scientific problem-solving that oscillated back and forth from theory to practice and, at each iteration, identified the gaps or conflicts between the theory and the observed facts.

At each iteration, Box wrote, the scientist switches roles, from the "sponsor" of the model, which is subjected to analysis of experimental data, to the "critic" of the model, working on the assumption that the model is "seriously faulty".

Applying this to project management

In project management, adopting Box's approach of iteratively switching roles from the "sponsor" to the "critic" can lead to more robust and adaptive project plans. As a project manager, you are both the sponsor and the critic of the entire project plan, which includes assumptions, tasks, timings, issues, and risks. The cycle of "switching" varies with the lifecycle approach for each project, e.g., adaptive or predictive.

With predictive approaches, during the planning and execution phases, the project manager, as the "sponsor," champions the project plan, communicates the vision and objectives to the team, and ensures that resources are allocated efficiently. They must embrace the uncertainties and make assumptions to move the project forward. However, it is equally crucial for the project manager to take on the role of the "critic," regularly examining and scrutinising the project plan, assumptions, and progress. This role involves questioning the validity of assumptions, evaluating task effectiveness, assessing timeline accuracy, and addressing emerging issues and risks.

With adaptive approaches, the cycling speed between the 'sponsor' and 'critic' roles is increased and should be performed each sprint (or equivalent in non-timeboxed methods).

Facilitating a learning-first project

By adopting this iterative approach, the project manager can foster a dynamic, learning-driven environment within the project team. This process enables the continuous improvement of the project plan as it adapts to new information, addresses unforeseen challenges, and capitalises on emerging opportunities. Moreover, it encourages the project team to be more proactive and accountable as they constantly refine the project plan and respond to evolving project circumstances.

In project management, assumptions are critical elements that help bridge the gap between known facts and uncertainties. They are essential in establishing a project narrative and developing a plan. However, it is crucial to recognise that assumptions can be beneficial and detrimental, depending on how they are managed.

Assumptions are critical elements that help bridge the gap between known facts and uncertainties, especially when applying Box's iterative approach to balance embracing uncertainties and evaluating the plan. Project managers should treat assumptions as temporary placeholders that must be tested, validated, or replaced with facts as the project progresses. By doing so, they can minimise the potential negative impact of incorrect assumptions on the project's success.

The Bottom Line

Incorporating Box's iterative approach of switching roles from the "sponsor" to the "critic" in project management can lead to more resilient and successful projects. By embracing uncertainties and assumptions as the "sponsor" and rigorously evaluating the project plan as the "critic," project managers can create a dynamic environment that fosters learning, adaptation, and growth. This balance between sponsorship and criticism ultimately helps ensure that project plans are continuously refined and optimised to achieve the desired outcomes, even amid uncertainty and change. From a Boxian perspective, we understand they can be useful, even if wrong.

The Tags

#assumptions, #boxian, #models, #georgebox, #wrongbutuseful, #boxianqualities, #projectassumptions, #wrongassumptions, #risk, #riskmanagement, #riskassumptions

On Planning

Planning is a future-oriented activity designed to give each of us a way to achieve our goals. Planning is constant in every human brain. According to one researcher, intelligence is the ability to predict, and planning is a quintessentially human activity.

And yet, planning is downplayed by many proponents of agile project approaches. Maintaining a plan is wasteful when you must keep changing it in the face of changed realities.

Like many other comparisons between agile and traditional plan-based approaches, this is often a Black Hat / White Hat comparison.

Black Hat (therefore "bad") project management creates overly detailed and hard-to-maintain project schedules as a matter of professional practice. In contrast, White Hat ("good") agile either minimises planning or avoids it altogether.

Like all Black Hat / White hat comparisons, they are inaccurate, often disingenuous, and don't serve us well in our quest for improved project outcomes.

Everyone plans just as everything evolves.

Planning is not bad in and of itself, and the problem is when the level of planning is not matched to the project's context. Overplanning a project creates unnecessary overhead and is inefficient, and under-planning a project is a naïve and poor practice.

41. To plan is to be human.

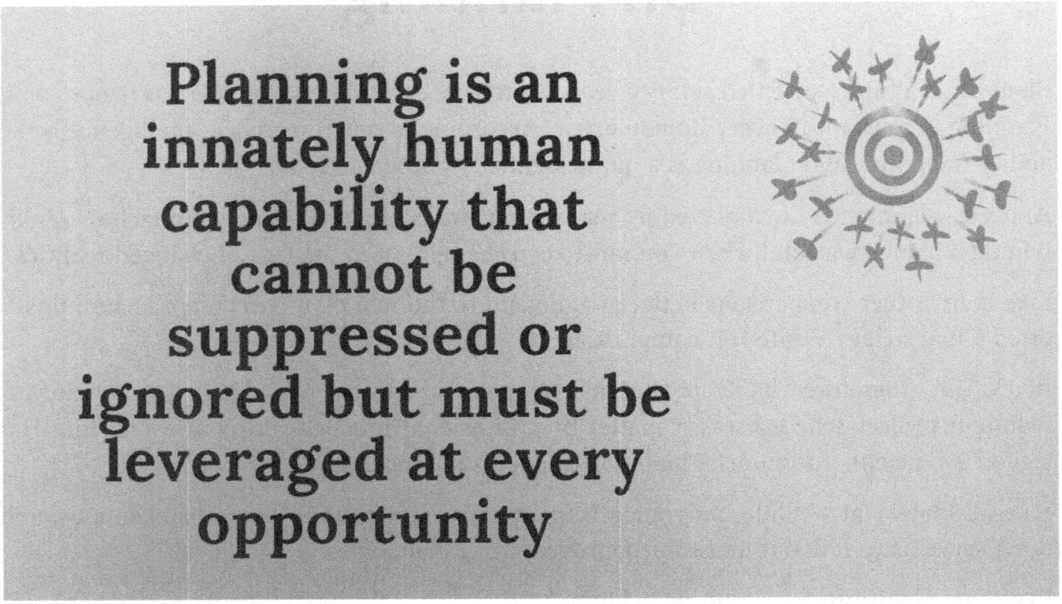

The Axiom

Planning is an innately human capability that we cannot suppress.

The TL;DR

Some pundits say that we don't need plans of any form. In this point of view, plans are "waste" and should be eliminated. But in projects, some types and levels of waste are like friction: the only way it can be completely eliminated is if nothing moves. Even so, it is impossible to suppress or ignore the innate human capability for planning. Other practitioners (and stakeholders) expect very detailed and firm plans from the earliest stages of the project. There's no single right answer. But there are some clear heuristics. One is human cognition: everyone plans all the time about almost everything. We constantly create plans and rework them as the real world dictates. So it's better to have one plan, no matter how rudimentary, than to have dozens of tacit plans in the minds of stakeholders. Don't throw away this most human of abilities.

The Back Story

Planning lost its street cred.

The arrival of the Agile movement brought about a wholesale rejection of many traditional project management concepts, including—at various levels—planning. Some parts of the Agile movement conflated the planning practice with the "big upfront plan" associated with most predictive project management philosophies. Or more precisely, they conflated the artifacts resulting from big upfront planning activities with the general practice of planning.

Many babies were thrown out with much bathwater as part of that process, as agile practitioners and thought leaders experimented to find just how lightweight they could make their project approaches. Project managers were either shown the door or had to transform themselves into Scrum Masters or Iteration Managers if they were lucky enough to have the opportunity.

The "**#Noestimates**" movement arose from this. Their mantra is that estimates are always wrong, and take much time, so they are waste. I disagree with this thinking.

Perhaps the Lean community enabled the "**#Noestimates**" movement by pushing the broad concept of *"waste"* in projects. Lean thinking holds that any work that does not visibly end up in the final product is *"waste"*. By that definition, all process overhead is *"waste"* that we should avoid or eliminate. The logical conclusion is that planning is also *"waste"*.

I understand that waste can be bad, but, like friction in physical systems, the only way to avoid it is to do nothing. The concept of waste works well if you think of projects from a manufacturing paradigm, in which the "means of production" are built and tested. But projects are not manufacturing or any other stable operating environment.

But plans themselves are not the biggest problem with the "no-or-minimal-plans" approach. The real problem in this case is the lack of planning.

It's the planning, stupid!

So, from all the different perspectives, we have a spectrum of planning paradigms, from "big up-front plans" to "no plans" at all, and with different groups staking out areas on that spectrum as the right—if not the one-and-only way to do things. What these perspectives lack is balance. On the one hand, the traditional project management narrative of "big up-front plan" over-invests in creating planning artifacts in the belief that they represent good practice and predict future success. On the other hand, we have a view of projects that is a series of stochastic events, each treated independently, with no requirement for a plan.

But planning - in the sense of designing the future and how to get there - is not about artifacts. Planning is about leveraging human cognitive resources. As General Eisenhower said:

> *"Plans are useless, but planning is everything."* — **General Dwight D Eisenhower**

In all lifecycle models, the primary value of plans is in the planning process. Big plans require significant cognitive effort, fact-gathering and getting mental alignment. In agile practices, relative estimating helps drive out dissonance amongst the team on the features they are planning. Relative estimation is the best example of the primacy of planning over plans. In traditional project models, planning and estimation can achieve the same, and is an essential process for getting stakeholder alignment.

In any group endeavour, it is reckless to remove this activity from the plot. But each project is different. There are few absolute "right" and "wrong" ways of doing things. There are only two considerations:

1. How much planning is needed (planning duration and depth, and the nature of the planning artifacts)
2. The extent to which the team refers to the planning artifacts during execution.

For more information on this, see the two axioms, **# 81. There are only two kinds of project documents** and, **# 113. What is your approach to documentation?** in **"Adam On: Projects (Volume 2)"**[1].

Plans are everywhere and unavoidable.

All projects have a plan because all projects include human beings. And, every human plans all the time about everything.

Planning is natural and instinctual for human cognition and survival. Recent research into the neocortex indicates that the primary purpose of the human cortex is to enable thinking about the future.

> *"Prediction is not just one of the things your brain does. It is the primary function of the neocortex, and the foundation of intelligence. The cortex is an organ of prediction."* — **Jeff Hawkins and Sandra Blakeslee** in "On Intelligence".

[1]https://bjl.ink/aopv2

Humans automatically tear down and rebuild their plans whenever the cortex detects a gap between the current plan and the information they receive via their senses. So, there is nothing intrinsically wrong with having a plan that we continually revise as we receive new information.

Projects are a future-oriented goal-seeking endeavour and, therefore, require future-oriented thinking. Once you reduce or remove planning capabilities, you lose the benefits of the many cognitive skills essential to completing goal-oriented endeavours.

You can throw out planning activities and artifacts, but you'll still have a plan - multiple plans, most likely because every team member and stakeholder will have their own version of the plan based on their knowledge and desires.

"Goldilocks plans"

The key to project management is to leverage the combined team member's planning abilities to develop shared plans that are realised in "goldilocks" level detail: not too much or too little, but just the right amount of detail to match the information and the rate of change in the project.

The level of detail in the plan and the time spent planning should be appropriate for the context and project approach.

A "plan" could be a few bullet points and a diagram. Or a plan could be a project narrative. See the axiom, "**# 39. Supporting the bridge to an unknown future**." for a better explanation of a project narrative.

It is the act of collaborative planning that generates most of the value, not the plan itself. What we need in projects are people good at planning—thinking about the future and adjusting current activities to maximise future opportunities. We don't need the artifacts of planning—we need the ability to plan.

The debate about plans and planning is one-dimensional. Even when if we agree on the concept of "**Goldilocks Plans**".

I've outlined another dimension in the axiom, ""**# 42. Keep planning until you start making shit up.**".

Sliding Windows

Another dimension again is to look at the project context and work out the relationship between four time windows.

1. **Planning Window**: over what time period are your plans set down and considered "solid"?
2. **Change Event Window**: considering the rate of change in all aspects of your project, what time period are you experiencing, or expecting to experience change? Is it daily, weekly, or monthly?
3. **Change Effect Window**: once you know you need to make a change, what is the time window within which this can occur?
4. **Monitoring Window**: what is the frequency of you checking on the status of your project elements?

These windows are relative, and there are few fixed rules on how to relate them. But with some thought and experimentation, you can use these windows to determine the time horizon for your planning, and the way how you monitor and update the plan.

For example:

1. If your **Planning window** is significantly longer than your **Change Event Window**, then you may be over-planning. The plans could become outdated quickly and require re-planning. If it's the reverse, then you're probably under-planning and your plans won't reflect reality.
2. If your project's **Monitoring Window** is significantly shorter than your **Change Event Window**, then you are potentially being inefficient.
3. If your **Planning Window** is shorter than your **Change Effect Window**, then you're not going to be able to avoid an impact.

If you think about these four windows and how they relate to each other, you can optimise your investment in planning against the rate of change and benefits. We can also draw on other domains for guidelines. For example, in sound analysis (analog-to-digital conversion), a heuristic is to use a sampling frequency of twice (2x) the frequency you're converting. If your **Change Event Window** is daily, this heuristic suggests we set our **Monitoring Window** to twice per day. If you're conservative and you don't mind the effort, you could check early morning, lunchtime and later in the day for extra coverage.

And keep in mind that these windows may have different durations for different stages of the project, and for different components.

The Bottom Line

Let's not debate the plans and planning anymore. There's no point - zero - zilch - nada. Humans plan about everything all the time. What we need is the right amount of planning and plans. Debating the need for plans and planning is not a useful exercise. Rapidly figuring out the appropriate planning regime and the optimal breadth and depth of your plan artificats is priceless. We need the fruits of our natural human capabilities to be part of the project team's shared understanding. Because if it isn't, then individuals will form their own plans, naturally, and they may not be aligned.

The Tags

#planning, #agile, #projectplanning, #prediction, #plan-based, #predictive, #abundance, #neuroscience, #cognition, #mentalmodel, #dwightdeisenhower, #noestimates, #estimation

42. Keep planning until you start making shit up.

The Axiom

Keep planning until you start making shit up.

The TL;DR

How much time and effort should you invest in planning? There are many prescriptive answers but none of them scale to all scenarios. Each planning situation is different. My rule of thumb is to keep planning until I start making shit up for lack of knowledge or factual data. Then you either do some fact-finding, run an experiment, or create an assumption. You can't avoid the most basic level of planning in any project, even if it's just creating a project narrative. Without at least a project narrative, you don't have a "**North star**" to guide your project. You can read more about the necessity for a Project Narrative in this axiom: ***"# 39. Supporting the bridge to an unknown future."*** It is definitional that projects are unique, and so forcing a specific level of planning according to an arbitrary external rule is just dumb.

The Back Story

A common question in projects is *"How much planning should I do?"* or *"How much planning is enough?"*. It doesn't matter whether you are in a predictive (plan-based) project or agile: there is always some level of planning that goes into the project.

Two strategies for answering "how much planning"

"How much" depends on many things, but mainly on the availability and accuracy of information. Two strategies for planning provide stopping points for your planning activity.

Strategy 1: Plan until you feel confident to take the next step(s) towards your intended outcome. *Strategy 2*: Plan until you run out of factual information to base a plan.

If you adopt strategy 1, you probably won't have a plan that covers you until the completion of the project. You'll have enough for the next steps. It depends on your planning horizon. If you adopt a short planning horizon, you'll have to repeat the planning process once you've exhausted the boundary of your plan. This strategy is used in many project approaches, including agile and plan-based ("predictive"). The difference is that agile mandates a short planning horizon, and predictive mandates a planning horizon that includes the entire project.

If you're in situation #2 above, regardless of your project approach, you don't have enough information to reach or exceed your planning horizon. If you need to continue planning (e.g., you don't have the option to proceed without reaching your planning horizon), try using assumptions instead of known facts. Using assumptions is a perfectly valid method for increasing your planning horizon.

But, as mentioned in the axiom, "**# 38. Use assumptions to plug any hole in your planning.**", there are two types of assumptions. As you continue planning, you'll eventually run out of reasonable assumptions. If you keep going, you'll start "making shit up", by which I mean writing complete unstructured fiction.

Creating Type 2 assumptions is close to "making up shit" but is specifically different because Type 2 assumptions are identifiable in your narrative, plan, or logic model. Planning fiction is not identifiable and is on the crazy side of professional practice.

At this point, stop planning — there's no point.

Attack the risks

Take note of your assumptions — they have become risks you need to work on (i.e., by finding the information to replace the hypothesis).

The other way to get more information (or bolster some of your assumptions) is to run an experiment. Steve Blank in Lean Startup says (about experiments):

> *"... a hypothesis means we have an educated guess that requires experimentation and data to validate or invalidate. These hypotheses span the gamut from who's the customer(s), to what's the value proposition (product/service features), pricing, distribution channel, and demand creation (customer acquisition, activation, retention, etc.)"* — **Steve Blank** - Why Build, Measure, Learn — isn't just throwing things against the wall to see if they work — the Minimal Viable Product[2]

The Bottom Line

Planning isn't some monolithic process that must be completed before you stop. Your ability to plan depends on reliable information, your willingness to use assumptions, what types of assumptions you're willing to use, and the "planning horizon" that is expected of you. But stop planning when you start making shit up.

The Tags

#planning, #projectplanning, #plans, #eisenhower, #planningprocess, #assumptions, #projectassumptions, #planvalidation, #steveblank

---

[2]https://steveblank.com/2015/05/06/build-measure-learn-throw-things-against-the-wall-and-see-if-they-work/

43. That unforeseen crisis your project is having?

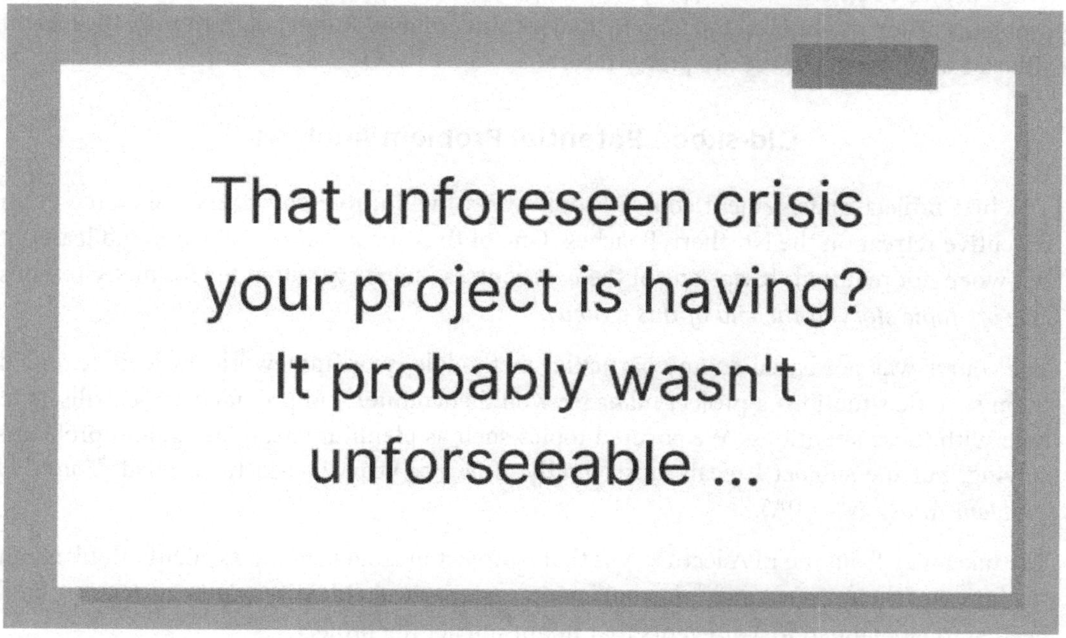

The Axiom

That unforeseen crisis your project is having was almost undoubtedly foreseeable.

The TL;DR

Sure, *"Black Swan"* events in the real world sometimes impact your projects. But such events are, by definition, rare and primarily unforeseeable. Most events that trigger change or impacts on your project are predictable in their nature and (less so) in their probability. You don't have to spend endless amounts on detailed planning or risk management plans. Just a bit of effort envisaging potential problems and their impacts will help you build resilience in your approach.

The Back Story

When projects run into trouble, project managers like to talk about risk events and unforseen problems. They might even talk about "Black swan" events. But, by definition in the case of "Black Swan" events, these are pretty rare.

Old-skool: Potential Problem Analysis

The first project management course I took was a live-in, five-day course delivered at an executive retreat on the Northern Beaches. One of the oil companies owned it and leased it out when not required. It was one of the best courses I have ever attended for many reasons *(see off-topic story at the end of this axiom).*

The course was not based on any particular methodology or framework. Instead, it zeroed in on specific situations a project manager would encounter and provided some skillsets to help with those situations. We covered topics such as planning, negotiating, and problem-solving, but the subject I recall most vividly after 30+ years is a lecture called *"Potential Problem Analysis"* (PPA).

The takeaway from the PPA lecture was that a project manager should explicitly think about the future of their project and "play out" various scenarios to identify what was missing (and needed to be planned for) or events that might impact the project.

PPA is simplified risk management

In retrospect, PPA was about Risk Management - I'm not even sure the word "risk" was mentioned - but it was risk management shorn of all its processes.

In fact, PPA is predicated on the idea that identifying a thing - like a future problem - is the biggest part of dealing with it, and once you've identified the thing you may not need all the detailed processes. Just as the act of planning might be the most important part of a plan, identifying a future problem in may ways is the most valuable part of risk management.

PPA is continually envisaging future scenarios and the problems that could arise, and thinking about what you might do if that situation arose. It was far more valuable than almost any formal risk management content I have since experienced because the focus was on the outcome, not the process.

PPA is prospection

PPA was the first time I'd encountered the idea of prospection in work. "Prospection" is a mental process that anticipates future events, looks forward to the future and considers what might happen. Prospection is both an unconscious and natural process in human cognition and an explicit method of visualising goals and the pathways and obstacles to achieving those goals.

If you think about the potential problems, you'll find that they fall into three buckets, which include events that are:

1. Highly likely and common to most projects.
2. Extremely rare and are likely to affect more than just your project. For example, "Black Swan" events.
3. Very specific to your project and fit into the mid-ranges of probability but have much less obvious trigger events.

Rissues, Black Swans and Project-specific risks

I call events in the first category (common and high probability) "Rissues". And events in the third category are the ones that should receive your attention. Not so long ago, a global pandemic would have been an example of a "Black Swan" event — these days, not so much.

An example of a "Rissue" might be *"a key team member will leave the project"* — generic and high probability. An example of a similar problem in the third category is *"Fred Bloggs, our Solution Architect with critical skills in the Acme solution, resigns to go to a startup".*

Although the actual future states of a project are unknown to us at any given time, there's not a lot that is truly unforeseeable. And it doesn't take much work or imagination to consider them in your problem analysis.

The Bottom Line

Our brains are wired for prediction, and even with a minimum of experience as a project manager, it doesn't take much effort to envisage a wide range of future problems. Leverage that uniquely human capability, and it will build resilience in your plans and your mindset.

The Story

Earlier in this axiom I mentioned my first Project Management course, at which I learned about *"Potential Problem Analysis"*.

There was one other thing I remember from this course, which has stayed with me for over 40 years.

It was a fully residential course held at purpose-built training centre situated in the hills above Sydney's Northern Beaches - if I recall correctly it was owned and operated by an oil company. The course was fully catered and the training centre had a small but comfy lounge area where we could sit or play pool or whatever after A> dinner.

On the first night, we discovered that the lounge had a fully stocked bar. Someone at the workshop said they'd been at a course at this facility previously, and during his last stay the bar was fully restocked A> daily.

Most of us didn't believe it, but decided to put this rumour to the test. Sure enough, after a pretty solid night of drinking on the first night, we found the bar was fully stocked when we came in after dinner on the second night. This discovery triggered a competition to drink the bar dry each night. I can't remember whether this happened every night, but there was undoubtedly some severe destocking. Then, like *"The Magic Pudding"*, the bar was wholly restocked the next day.

Even more remarkable is that one of us didn't drink alcohol at all, and I happened to be mid-way through a "dry January" at the time and drank nothing but mineral water. I think there were eight people on the course, so the damage A> A> was done by six men.

I heard later that when the invoice was sent for the course, it was so large that it bubbled up to our General Manager (GM), who was something of a drinker himself, but well-known to be very tight with money.

He had a fit and started an internal investigation to find the culprits, although I didn't hear any more after I told someone I didn't drink any alcohol. The GM later banned alcohol from all future classes.

We probably couldn't have foreseen this event, but had we thought for a few minutes, we easily could have envisaged that crisis with our GM.

The Tags

#planning, #riskmanagement, #risk, #principlesofprojectsuccess, #abundance, #axiom

---

44. Planning is linear, but execution is non-linear.

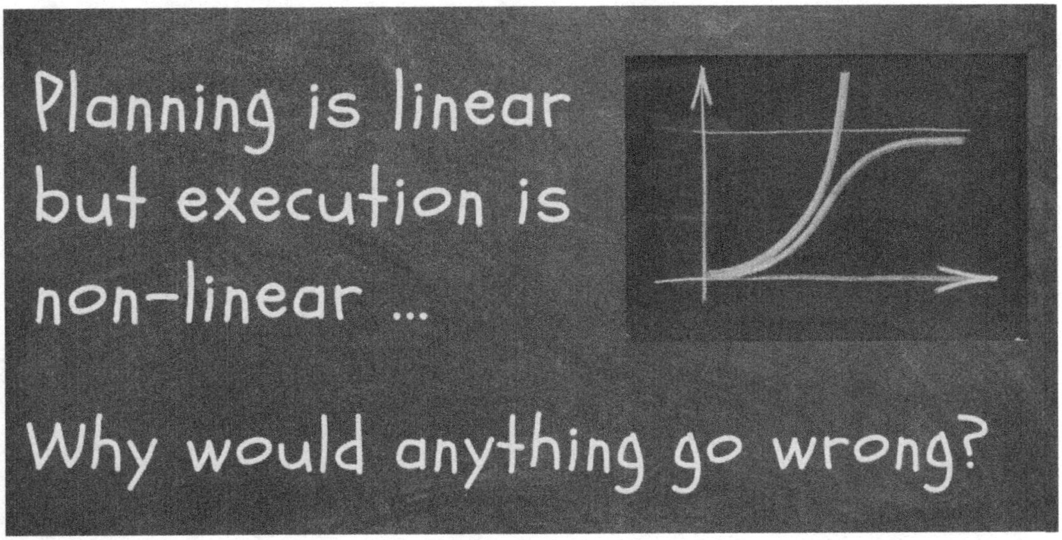

The Axiom

You must understand and manage the project paradox: planning is linear, but execution is non-linear.

The TL;DR

The great paradox of all project management is that planning is linear, but execution is non-linear. All modalities of project approach, whether lean, agile or waterfall, use the same basic techniques for representing activity over time. There are very few ways to express time in a non-linear way or how task execution is variable in unpredictable ways. This paradox creates dissonance in the project teams and amongst stakeholders, because the reality of project execution is very different to how our tools track and communicate progress and status. And rapidly reducing time-cycles introduce a sort of "Heisenberg Uncertainty" to project reporting.

The Back Story

Almost all the standard project planning concepts, models and tools have a linear construct at their hearts.

Planning is linear, and clean

Since the 1960's management theory and practice have progressively morphed away from number-crunching and non-human factors and toward a more significant consideration of human factors.

However, this transition is not universal, as some management philosophies persist from the first half of the 20th century and earlier. At the core of the standard project management narrative, these philosophies are still prominent, if not still dominant. An example of this thinking is "Taylorism", which is still alive and well today.

Taylor wanted intelligent robots, but the technology and even morality of the day prevented such an idea from spreading. Methods were needed to shape the human into a reliable and predictable automaton that would perform the same tasks the same way day in and day out.

One would be hard-pressed to find another description when examining practices in some large logistics and manufacturing organisations.

In project management, practices such as detailed scheduling, task decomposition, organisational hierarchy, and pervasive measurement are still present in project management practice today. Such processes are all extremely linear: in fact, the primary goal of Taylorism (to drive out the variability injected into business processes by human beings) was to create linearity.

One specific example is the 'Gantt Chart' - still the most recognised and probably the most-used management tool in Project Management by far — which a disciple of Taylor's popularised.

Even if we don't use Gantt charts or something similar, we struggle to present uncertainty to our stakeholders in professional and communicable ways. When you show anything "plan-like" to stakeholders, they interpret it as activity over time. And as soon as time enters the discussion, the obvious question becomes, *"When will you be complete?"*. And, as soon as any date is mentioned, even if heavily qualified, it is locked in memory and will forever be a comparative baseline.

Execution is non-linear, and messy

However, when it comes to execution, people are not intelligent robots and do not execute plans linearly.

So, what happens when we move from the planning phase to the execution phase?

Executing a plan depends on how people interact with each other and their mental models – this is highly non-linear. Their skills and experience interact with the probabilistic outcomes of various foreseen and unexpected risk events. In the real-world detail of actual execution, there are orders of magnitude more considerations than at the planning level.

Michael Wolfe writes an epic description[3] of this process. Wolfe's narrative explains in atrocious and painful detail the "plan to execution" dissonance of *"...a hike on the coast from San Francisco to Los Angeles to visit our friends in Newport Beach. I'll whip out my map and draw our route down the coast."*

As the hike gets under way, the low-fidelity plan meets high-fidelity real life. What seemed like a fairly straight route on the map is an irregular curvy track along the coastal headlands an inlets, with bypasses and blockages due to weather, repairs and new buildings. The anticipated average speed is blown away, and people respond very differently to the problems that reality throws in their way.

We could undertake a plan-based project in which almost everything is mapped out in advance. Or we could be doing an adaptive project, in which whatever planning is being done is disaggregated and spread across the timeboxes or iterative processes.

Using the same tools for planning and execution

Regardless of our chosen approach, we still oscillate between planning and execution or between the linear and the non-linear.

The problem is that we use the same tools for both modalities: spreadsheets, Gantt charts, forecasts, or whatever. And project managers must maintain the mapping between their plans and what is happening.

Here is an example of what happens, in this case, in MS Project several months into execution. I'm trying to make my plan match reality (this is a real relationship I built between several tasks in an old schedule I dug up from my archives)

---

[3]https://www.quora.com/Why-are-software-development-task-estimations-regularly-off-by-a-factor-of-2-3

> ***"81FS-10 days,92FF-5 days,99FS-10 days,118FS-10 days,128FS-10 days,144SS+5 days".***

Perhaps you're the project scheduling genius who can understand that deeply. I can understand it by tracing through the tasks, but ensuring it gives the correct overall effect and aligning it with changes is problematic. This dependency structure looks like something created to make the schedule match reality rather than the other way around. Either way, it is brittle, hard to maintain, and easy to embed hard-to-detect scheduling errors into the schedule.

The Bottom Line

Planning is linear, while execution is non-linear, raising the question: What could go wrong? Despite using the same tools for both modalities, the key lies in project managers' ability to adapt their approach and maintain a balance between detailed plans and the flexibility needed to navigate the complexities of execution. Acknowledging and addressing this paradox can help project managers and teams create a more resilient and adaptive environment, leading to more successful project outcomes.

The Tip

I've approached the problems of non-linearity in the last ten years or so by using generic business tools (mainly Microsoft Powerpoint) to present high-level plans with little detail. At the right altitude, non-linear and linear approach each other. I can use the low-constraint tools to illustrate non-linear concepts, or at least call out areas of concern.

In my early-stage plans, I obfuscate timelines explicitly.

I use the "OfficeTimeline" (OTL) tool to create high-level Gantt charts in Microsoft Powerpoint.

OTL allows me to use other Powerpoint tools (mostly callouts) to provide a narrative and highlight assumptions and risks. The distinct advantage of this approach is that the highlights are right there on the same page as the timeline and not buried in a table on a separate page. See the example below.

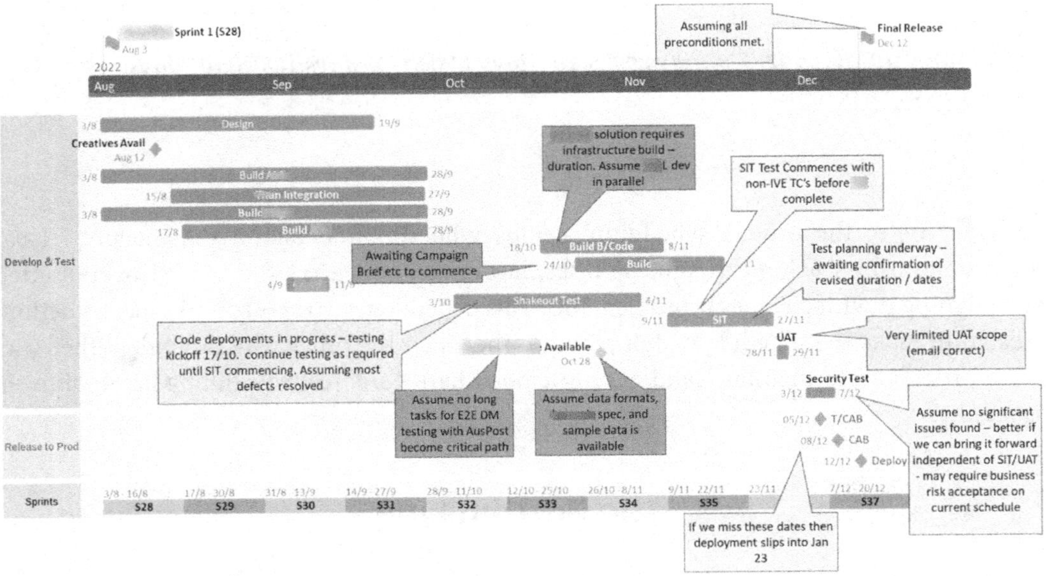

Figure 29. A High-level Schedule in OfficeTimeline

I also use other Powerpoint shapes to help avoid inadvertently setting expectations on delivery timelines. Another example is below.

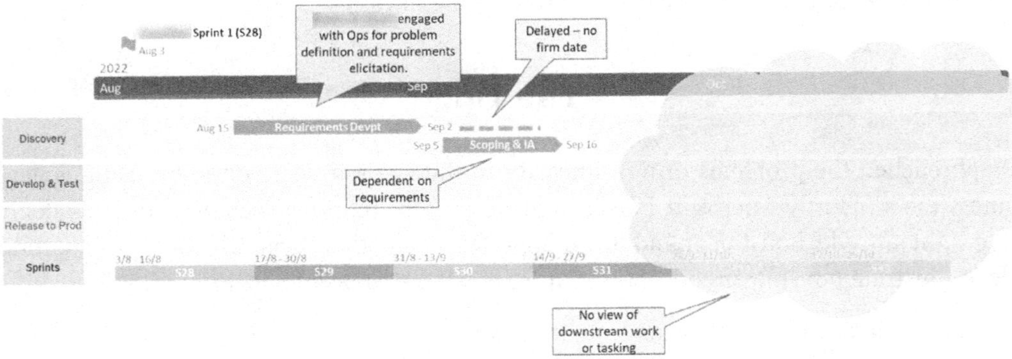

Figure 30. Masking Future Dates in OfficeTimeline

In the above example, I use the standard Powerpoint "Cloud" shape to cover the years and months in the timeline at the top of the chart. I've experimented with different approaches, including not having the timeline, or creating a manual timeline.

But this approach I like because it's very obvious that I'm hiding the dates and this always triggers the discussion we need to have: why are you obscuring the dates? Stakeholders have been very reasonable to accept these reasons until there's enough certainty to put the dates back.

The Tags

#planning, #nonlinear, #gradientofterror, #linearplanning, #humaninfluence, #projectmanagementparadox, #paradox, #righttoleftplanning

45. The false foundation for detailed forecasts.

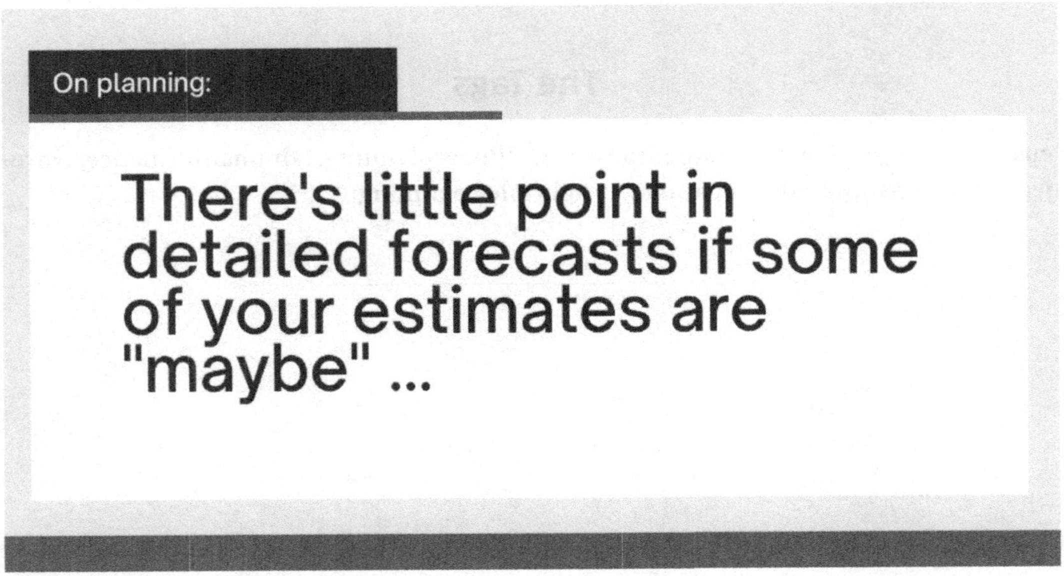

The Axiom

If your detailed forecasts are supported by estimates including "maybe", then you've gone way too far.

The TL;DR

It's easy to get carried away with planning and forecasting, particularly when supported by generic tools such as MS Excel. Your assumptions or guesses are values qualified by *"maybe"* or *"perhaps"* but gain false concreteness as a value in a spreadsheet cell. Unless you are extraordinarily diligent in identifying such estimates, this vagueness and uncertainty are lost, and the resulting forecasts have a false legitimacy.

The Back Story

Using available data and a few assumptions makes it possible to create a project narrative that takes you to the end of the project.

With the narrative and a few facts, Project Managers can create fairly detailed forecasts about the project, such as resource and funding requirements. With spreadsheets, you can make wonderfully detailed forecasts at the week and even day level. And from the data sheets, you can create more analyses with pretty charts and graphs.

These forecasts look like the real deal. But are they telling you anything?

What does this have to do with our forecasts? Well, the estimates are based on both known and assumed values. Even if the assumed values are calculated, they are still the results of an assumption.

All assumptions have probabilistic outcomes. In other words, with assumptions, you posit an outcome that may come true. Depending on the assumption, there may be a range of effects. And you must consider the accuracy of the inputs to your assumptions.

The bottom line is that in any assumption-based estimate, some of your inputs will reduce to "maybe".

And if even one of your terms is "maybe, " the result is the same.

Thus, two issues with this must be accommodated in your forecasts.

1. The presumed accuracy of the estimates.
2. The range of actual performance.

Let's cover those in the sections below:

The supposed accuracy of the estimates

If I remember my school arithmetic lessons correctly, there are rules governing the precision of a result in a mathematical expression.

> *"The calculated result should have as many significant figures as the least number of significant figures among the measured quantities used in the calculation"* — **Significant Figures (Wikipedia)**[4]

For example, calculating the area of a circle with a measured radius of 1.2 meters. If we use the value of Pi to 7 decimal places, we might get the calculated result as follows:

[4]https://en.wikipedia.org/wiki/Significant_figures

$$A = \pi r2 = (3.1415927 \times (1.2\ m)^2 = 4.5238934\ m^2)$$

But to avoid the "propagation of error," we can only use an answer to the precision of the radius. Therefore, the correct answer is 4.5 metres squared (4.5 m^2).

In other words, the decimal precision is one significant digit because of the least accurate term.

So, what is the accuracy of the terms in your forecast?

Range of actual performance

Consider a resource forecast on a project or a portfolio of projects. You might assume someone has worked half-time on your project for over two months. The first questions are about "half-time": is it 50% of the working day? Or are 50% of the available time after routine activities like non-project meetings, administrative tasks, and breaks considered? Is the working day 8 hours or 7.5 hours, or 7 hours?

The person may end up with actual behaviour from 0 hours (because they didn't work on your project) to 8 or more hours daily. Most organisations balk at forecasting overtime because it legitimises lousy practice, but most projects involve longer hours than the norm. Extra work means extra productivity (to a point). So, the actual number of hours could be more than full-time.

These values are just "finger in the air" estimates and shouldn't be shown at a precision of more than the nearest 10%. You don't interpret them as "*so and so the developer is overloaded 250% for the month of November, so we need to hire another couple of devs*". You interpret them as, *"Looks like there might be a spike in demand in November; what can we do to mitigate this?"*.

Those estimates are not gospel, even though you can calculate to fractions of a percentage point.

The Bottom Line

Basic arithmetic tells you the accuracy to read into your forecast calculations. With most forecasts, the precision is very low. Don't fall in love with your projections and misuse them, i.e., as anything more precise than their least accurate input term.

The Tags

#planning, #planninghorizon,#planningdetail, #forecasting, #axiom

On Teams

Although individuals conduct many projects, the full benefits of a project approach come from doing them in groups.

I'm not sure the opposite is true: can you have a team without a project? Regardless, we introduce complications as soon as we transition from one to multiple people, and almost all the narrative about projects is generated from how we resolve these complications.

How do we marshal the collective resources of multiple people whilst reducing the impacts of the same thing?

These axioms reflect my experience and philosophy on teams and teaming.

46. A project is a lifeboat.

AT THE BEST OF TIMES, A PROJECT IS 12 PEOPLE IN AN 8-PERSON LEAKY LIFEBOAT AT SEA. WHEN THE STORM RISES, I DON'T WANNA HEAR PEOPLE ARGUING ABOUT WHOSE JOB IT IS TO PICK UP A BUCKET AND BAIL!

The Axiom

A project is like 12 people in an 8-person leaky lifeboat at sea.

The TL;DR

At the best of times, a project is like 12 people in an 8-person leaky lifeboat at sea after a shipwreck. It's a delicate balance in a time of great peril. Everyone needs to cooperate and look out for each other. Whatever was going on in that ship doesn't matter anymore. And neither does who you were nor what you did before you boarded the ship. It doesn't matter about your role, your title, or how much money you have. That's all in the past. So, when the storm rises, I don't wanna hear people arguing about whose job it is to pick up a bucket and bail.

The Back Story

What would you say if a forward in a UK soccer team was right next to an opposition player near their own goal line, and they stepped out of the way, letting in a goal. What would you say if that player said, after the game *"I'm an attacker - it wasn't my job"*?

Trouble at the mill

This axiom goes originated in my first project, and it's been with me for years. Its genesis was arguments in that project about who should take on specific tasks.

There were two contributors to this problem.

Firstly, the company growth was snowballing and had many initiatives happening simultaneously. There were never enough people, so people made many decisions about their work. It was great in one way, but this created many different versions of people's roles.

Secondly, the project broke new ground for my employer, and some tasks had no attachment to any specific role in the company: we were literally making things up as we went along.

And so, we repeatedly argued about who should do what. We argued about whether tasks or deliverables were assigned to the right person and when things didn't get done because nobody owned them.

So, I came up with this metaphor to illustrate how we were all responsible for the project's overall success, and we had to take a more holistic approach to project completion.

I started using this metaphor in our project meetings, and it at least got people focused on what was important. Once we gave up the "not my job" whining, we were able to have useful discussions about who was best placed to take on different tasks.

The source of this axiom

I was inspired with the lifeboat metaphor by the 1957 film *"Seven Waves Away"* directed by Richard Sale and starring Tyrone Power. In that movie, a group of survivors from a sunken ship must confront extreme conditions and difficult decisions in a lifeboat.

The ship's Executive Officer, Alec Holmes (played by Tyrone Power), had to organise the survivors to perform essential tasks, regardless of what people thought they should or could do. He had to make harrowing choices of whom to save and whom to abandon, where they were deemed less likely to survive. In the crowded lifeboat, he could only put those decisions into effect if he had support from at least some of the remaining passengers and crew. As time passed and they survived storms and other problems, they began to see the wisdom of Holms' hard choices.

"That's not my job" doesn't cut it

At the very least, we shouldn't be squabbling about who didn't do what or who should have done something. This type of argument wasn't productive.

I've seen this situation in less extreme circumstances - when people cling to their job descriptions or roles to determine what they should and shouldn't do. "That's not my job" was the most common statement. This scenario is like a soccer striker refusing to stop a ball on the goal line when the defenders are out of position. "That's not my job" doesn't cut it.

While personal well-being and safety come first in a project team, project success is the top priority. We all need to look for tasks that are getting behind. We all need an objective discussion about delays or work not being done as required. The behaviour we need is that if you notice something needing work, get in and do it.

The Bottom Line

So, pick up the bucket and bail unless you want to go swimming.

The Tags

#projects, #projectcharacteristics, #teams, #teamwork, #analogy, #responsibility, #theseventhwave, #jobrole, #clingtojobrole, #processcompliance, #flexibility, #adaptability

47. How do teams self-organise?

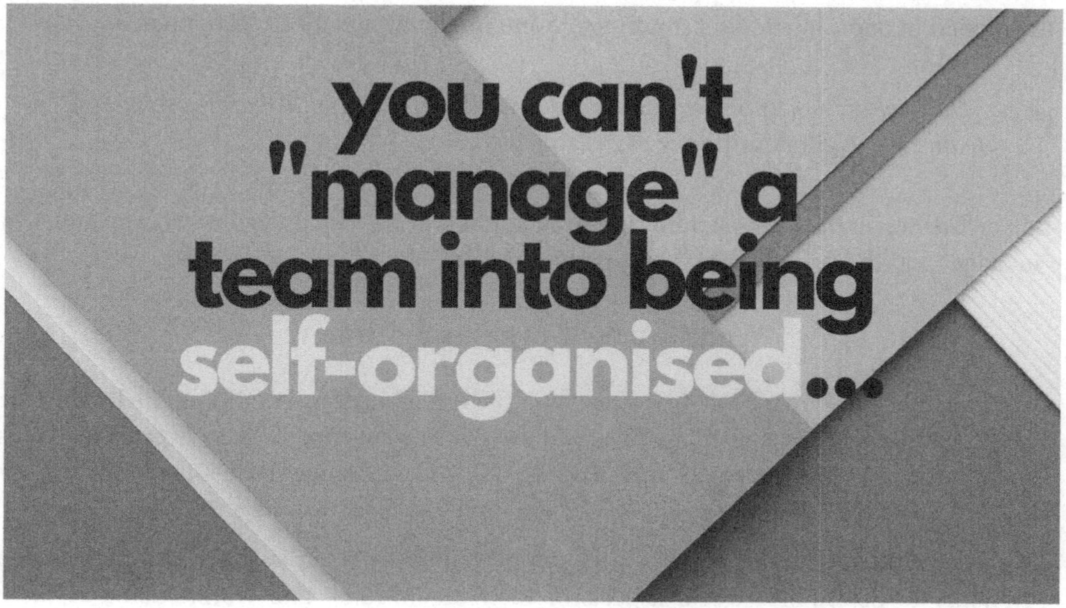

The Axiom

You can't "manage" a team to be self-organised.

The TL;DR

Self-organising teams are essential in the agile project management landscape. Given the lightweight process, self-organisation and the forces of social bonding provide guiderails that channel the team's behaviour. However, successfully forming and nurturing these teams can be difficult. Many managers cannot resist the temptation to try to "manage" the team formation and activities. The manager's job is to create the right environment for self-organisation while resisting the temptation to intervene. How do teams self-organise? Naturally. You can't "manage" a team to be self-organised.

The Back Story

The self-organised team occupies a big piece of the Agile zeitgeist. These teams are explicitly mentioned in one Agile Manifesto principle and implicitly in at least two others.

> *"The best architectures, requirements, and designs emerge from self-organizing teams."* – **Agile Manifesto**[1], 11th Principle

But before we unpack this axiom, we need to look at two components: the meaning of "manage" and the definition of "self-organising team".

What is a "self-organising" team?

Given the interest shown by at least drafters of the Agile Manifesto in the Toyota Production System (Sutherland, Schwaber and Beedle at least) it's no surprise that self-organising teams - mentioned as one of six key elements of the "New New Product Development Game" by Hirotaka Takeuchi and Ikujiro Nonaka - made it into the Scrum Guide.

There are numerous terms used in the agile narrative to describe teams that have some autonomy to determine certain aspects of their organisation and work. Some of these terms have been in use since the 1960s and over time their meaning and significance has changed. Terms such as "**self-organising**", "**self-managed**" and "**self-directed**" are defined and used differently. The Scrum guide moved away from "self-organising" in its 2020 version, preferring the term "self-managing" for the same level of autonomy.

Many research papers refer back to a landmark study by Richard Hackman in 1986 who looked at different types of teams (Hackman's term was "performing units") and their authority to determine their operation. In particular Hackman looked at the distribution of authority between workers and managers, which is illustrated in the diagram below.

[1] https://agilemanifesto.org/principles.html

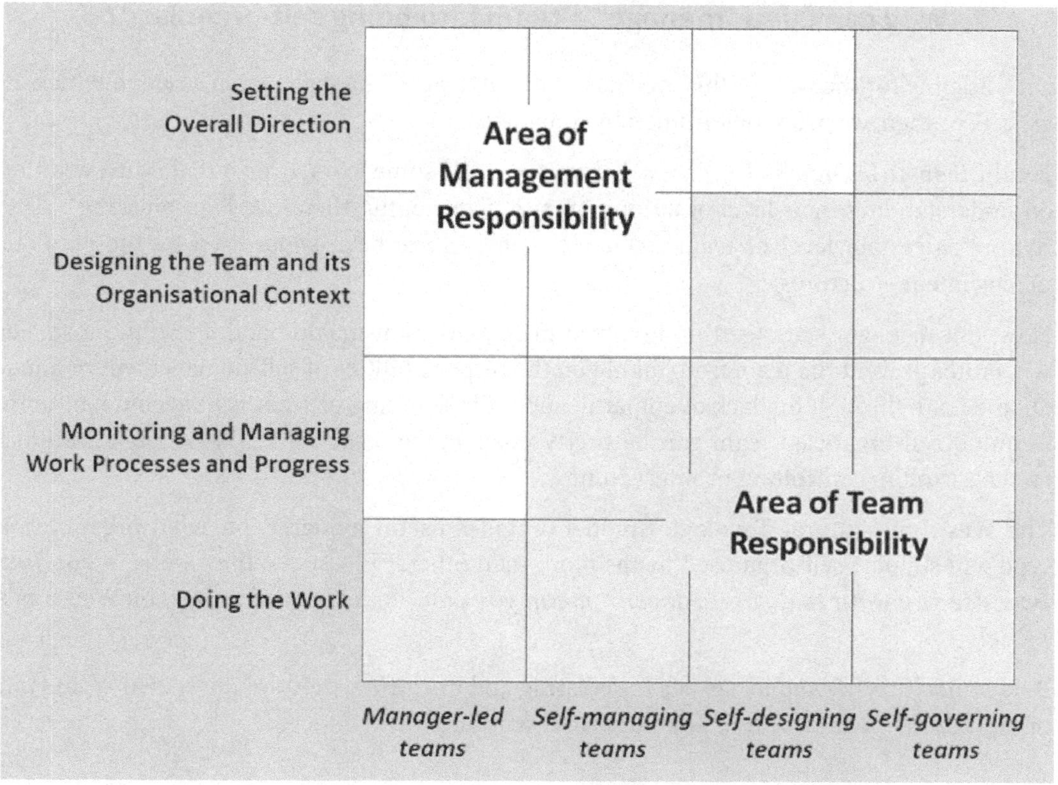

Figure 31. Hackman's authority matrix (Hackman 1986)

This matrix sets the team context for this axiom.

For simplicity, I'll use the term "self-organising" simply because of its historical context.

What is "manage"?

In the context of this axiom, by "manage" I mean "intervene" as outlined in the axiom "# 8. **Practice Minimal Responsible Intervention**", meaning for a Project Manager to *"inject themselves into the day-to-day working of a team".* In essence this means changing, by direction or influence, the way in which the team goes about its work. As you can see in the Hackman Authority Matrix above, "doing the work" is the exclusive responsibility of the team.

In the above definitions, not only is the goal defined in or outside the team, but also the means of achieving them: their "ways of working".

Why can't you "manage" a team into being self-organised?

Let's assume for the sake of this analysis that you have a "managed team": one in which all aspects of their work are determined by a manager.

For the team to become self-organised, they have to do some work, even if that is just working on understanding their level of autonomy and determining their "ways of working". This requires a certain level of team Agency that may have been suppressed by the previous management structures.

Now, if a manager starts getting involved in that decision-making and work, the manager will either prevent the team from taking on the responsibilities of self-management or alienate the team through the lack of empathy and understanding of what is happening, or both. Forming self-organised team can be pretty challenging, especially if your organisational context is more controlling or intervening.

The Westrum Cultural Topologies model provides useful guidance on what organisation type will support self-organised teams more than others. Please see the axiom ***"# 26. Just because you want to do agile doesn't mean you can"*** for additional context on Westrum's model.

Ask yourself: What support exists for creating and nurturing "self-organised teams" in your organisation? What Cultural Topology am I working in?

How not to do it

In one project a very senior manager called an existing project team to a meeting and instructed them to self-organise. We were told: "You are now a self-managing team. Off you go and manage yourselves".

There was little support on how to do this for the team and little support for managers who continued to be responsible for the team's work. They might be much nicer about it and use different vocabularies, but directive management intervention remains as strong as ever.

To clarify, teams created by management and provided with a rulebook do not qualify as self-organising.

Agency can support this process

If we look at the concept of Agency in projects, it is a fundamental component of success. High-agency people and teams have the following attributes (Bandura, 1999): self-organising, proactive, self-regulating, and self-reflecting

People with high agency are not merely reactive organisms influenced and guided by external events. In his book "Drive: The Surprising Truth About What Motivates Us", Daniel Pink describes the difference between extrinsically and intrinsically motivated people.

Extrinsically motivated people do things for an external reward, such as pay or bonuses, whereas intrinsically motivated people do something more to satisfy the task and its achievement.

Pink lists three main factors that motivate intrinsically motivated people:

1. *Autonomy*: *"over task (what they do), time (when they do it), team (whom they do it with), and technique (how they do it)."*
2. *Mastery*: *"becoming better at something that matters."*
3. *Purpose*: *"The most deeply motivated people—not to mention those most productive and satisfied—hitch their desires to a cause larger than themselves."*

Pink identifies several factors that can hinder this type of motivation. Sadly, most of them relate to the outdated control-focused "carrot and stick" strategies in most corporate environments today. Pink used these terms more for individuals than teams, but if you expand the context of these three factors to the team level, they work equally well.

Intervention doesn't help

Although you can facilitate or enable team formation by providing the right conditions, you cannot "manage" a team into existence. If team building is not occurring in a project environment, this simply means that something or someone is preventing it.

One of the managers' most prominent mistakes (after not being sensitive to this issue) is trying too hard to make the team concept happen. In some ways, this is not surprising, given how vital team building is and considering how much material exists on the need for and the mechanisms to obtain good teamwork.

But books or courses rarely recommend doing nothing in the face of a threat to team building. Most advice urges management to intervene (perhaps to justify their existence). They think that "doing things" to get the team rolling is management accountability. It's much easier to point out something you did than you didn't do.

Please also refer to the axiom "**# 8. Practice Minimal Responsible Intervention**", for more information.

The Bottom Line

As a thought experiment, envision your team as a circle. The circle's circumference marks the boundary between the team and the rest of the organisation. Management can create what's inside the circle and the environment and conditions within the circle. Once the team has been set up, managers should "do nothing" within the circle unless invited or extreme circumstances require it.

The Tags

#teams, #selforganisation, #teaming, #teamorganisation, #agency, #principlesofprojectsuccess, #agilemanifesto, #selfmanagedteam, #self-directedteam, #emergentteam, #managedteam, #albertbandura, #reflectiveemergentagency, #danielpink, #motivation30

48. Stop rolling around in broken glass!

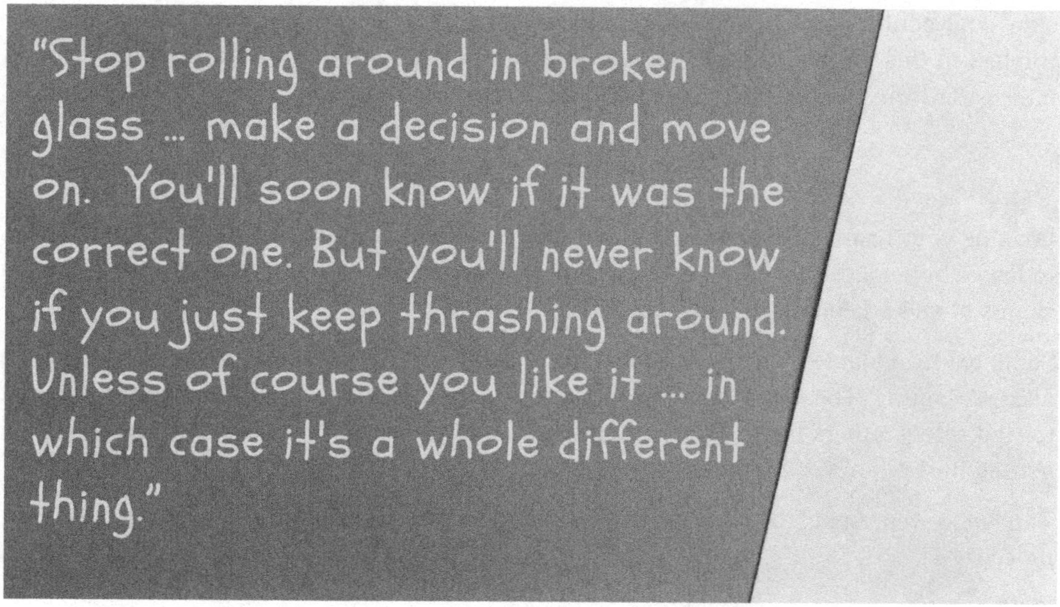

The Axiom

Endlessly worrying and bickering is like enjoying rolling around in broken glass.

The TL;DR

There's nothing more tragic than a team that is indecisive or thrashing between decision alternatives. It's painful for the team and a huge waste of time. I know we're all under a lot of pressure these days to get things done faster and cheaper, which leads to more decisions made under conditions of uncertainty. But those conditions mandate better and faster decision-making, not bad decision-making. Just stop rolling around in the broken glass. Make a decision and move on. You'll soon know if it was the correct one. But you'll never know if you keep thrashing around. Unless you like the pain, in which case it's a whole different thing.

The Back Story

During challenging times, team interactions can devolve into a continuous loop of discussions and conflicts without making any progress. People may not even realise they are trapped in this unproductive behaviour — they don't know how to escape it. The pain of indecision seems preferable to confronting the issues and moving forward.

Explaining the Metaphor

Imagine your team is in someone's living room, and a brick is thrown through the window, followed by a volley of gunfire. Everyone throws themselves to the floor, ignoring the broken shards of glass. People yell and panic.

Some want to blame. Others want direction. And some people roll around in the broken glass screaming. The chaos is intense — but what happens afterwards? Some people attempt to find safety, others try to bring order, while some continue to scream and blame others, getting hurt but never ceasing.

This image represents the unproductive cycle project teams can fall into when they become indecisive.

Team interactions during challenging times

During challenging times, team interactions can devolve into a continuous loop of discussions and conflicts without making any progress. People may not even realise they are trapped in this unproductive behaviour — they don't know how to escape it. The pain of indecision seems preferable to confronting the issues and moving forward.

Perhaps people are overwhelmed or unable to deal with the current project situation. Maybe they have problems outside work that are affecting their work context. They may simply not be suited for project work.

Do people prefer the pain to the solution?

Whatever the root cause, people "rolling around in broken glass" often cannot deal with any rational argument or discussion. This situation resembles the axiom ***"# 51. Actual activity vs displacement activity"*** because it relates to unconscious behaviour that you must deal with as a PM.

Alternatively, the situation may not be as extreme. Have you ever repeatedly experienced a series of project meetings in which the team hashes over the same issues? Or team members trigger negative behaviour in each other, resulting in passive-aggressive behaviour.

The team goes back and forth without reaching a resolution or defining a course of action to implement changes. They feel like one long session if you have enough of these meetings.

You begin to wonder if people are actually enjoying them. If not enjoying them, they might see these meetings as an acceptable alternative to addressing the underlying issues.

The Way forward

The only way forward is to reframe the situation so that they perceive themselves as not under the threat or stress that triggered these symptoms. Or, at the very least, trigger a reassessment of circumstances.

Tactics may include involving a person's line manager or trusted peer in discussions about the situation or progress. Sometimes, even just arranging some time off can improve things. In some cases, providing additional tasks as a distraction can help. Or, in the most egregious cases, finding them a role in another project.

The Bottom Line

Despite the pain, some team members may find "rolling around in broken glass" more appealing than getting up. Being aware of situations where your team becomes trapped in dysfunctional behaviour is crucial as a project manager. So, either act to reframe the situation, or you may as well get down and roll around with them.

The Tags

#teams, #groupbehaviour, #projectteams, #suboptimalbehaviour, #teambehaviour, #agency, #principlesofprojectsuccess, #displacementactivity

---

49. Project teaming happens quickly or not at all.

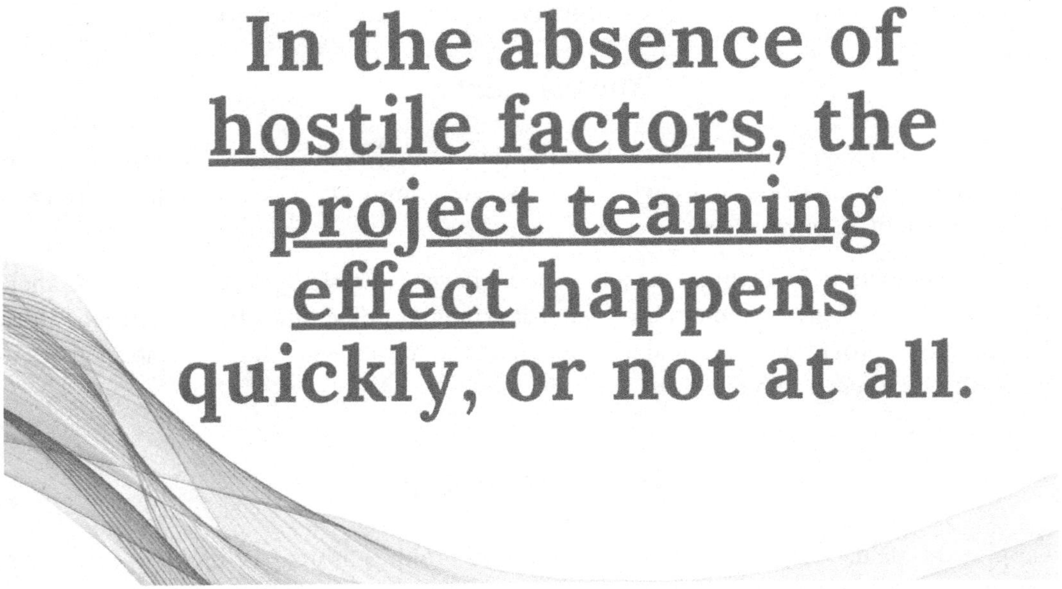

The Axiom

In the absence of hostile factors, the project teaming effect happens quickly or not at all.

The TL;DR

Without hostile factors, the project teaming effect happens quickly or not at all. The Tuckman model of team formation (Forming, Storming etc.) has become so embedded in management culture that it is accepted as gospel, despite its lack of original research and replication. Most of the discussion is focused on what can be done to facilitate teaming. But this misses the point that teaming is an almost automatic process when you get a group working together on a common goal. We shouldn't be looking at how to facilitate teaming but at what prevents or impacts the natural teaming process.

The Back Story

One of the cornerstones of successful projects is a good team. In adaptive approaches, the team construct is critical to success, whereas, in predictive methods, other constructs can mitigate the issues associated with teaming problems: for example, a organisational structures and roles that result in explicit team assignment.

How do good teams form?

How do good teams form? Is it more than luck?

Do the teams that are created by management assignment bond any better or worse than teams formed organically or through other means?

You'll find plenty of advice and recommended techniques in the literature. In all likelihood, the Tuckman model of team formation will be trotted out as a conceptual framework or even as a roadmap for team formation which is measured and reported.

But like many things in project management, having an extensive toolset doesn't help if you don't know what tool to use in what situation. In messy real life, advice that reads easily from a book or rolls off the tongue of a consultant is not always easy to follow.

So, let's abstract the complexity and look at the teaming problem from "20,000 feet". At this level, we see two forces:

- Pro-teaming forces; and
- Anti-teaming forces.

Let's look at those below.

Pro-teaming forces

Pro-teaming forces facilitate a group and create a predisposition to become a team. Mainly, they result from social and psychological evolution - the result of millennia. Humans are social animals and share a basic tendency to form groups driven by various needs, for example the need for affinity and affection, security and so forth.

Pro-teaming forces are powerful innate human forces which will express themselves naturally if given a chance. They can be amplified by facilitation, but you need to be careful.

In a project, common goals naturally enable teaming. Identifying common goals automatically facilitates the interaction between team members. Further down the line, shared successes and the feeling of overcoming adversity as a team are powerful pro-teaming forces.

Anti-teaming Forces

Anti-teaming forces prevent or impact teaming. There are many anti-teaming forces and they range in prevalence and strength. You'll probably experience only a handful in any project — or at least I hope you do.

So many things can get in the way of teaming, including loss of trust, lack of respect, lack of cooperation, selfishness, lack of maturity or misaligned social cognitive development, poorly constructed KPIs, past experiences, personal circumstances or illness, poorly executed team facilitation exercises, miscommunicated expectations, low-level intervention by managers or supervisors, cultural differences, and the environment (e.g., office location and makeup).

The list of anti-teaming factors is long. See the below breakdown from Yavuz Kozak in *"Barries against better team performance in Agile Software Projects"* (2013).

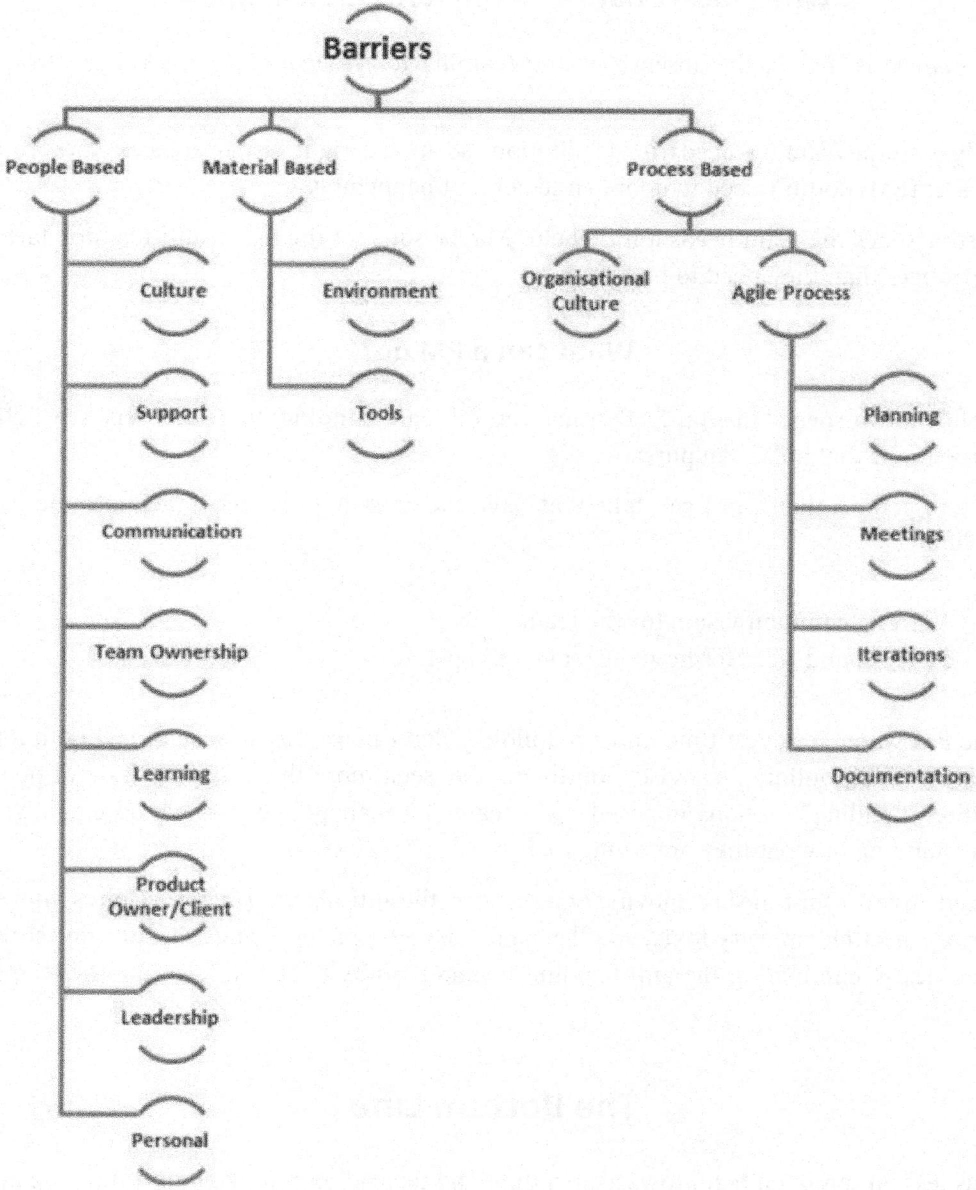

Figure 32. Barriers to Team Formation Kozak (2013)

It's very hard to find organisations or team contexts that don't have some of these barriers.

Why doesn't natural team formation happen?

My premise is that in the absence of anti-teaming forces, teaming occurs naturally and quickly.

Purely natural teaming needs no facilitation, so in the right circumstances, the project manager (PM) doesn't need to do much to get that happening.

But sometimes the team needs a little help. Maybe some of the many anti-teaming factors are stronger than they need to be.

What can a PM do?

If you want to spend time on facilitating natural team bonding, there are very few active interventions that a PM can pursue.

The two actions that a PM can take that have the most impact are to facilitate the team developing:

1. A strong common vision for the team.
2. Basic ground rules for how the team will operate.

If the PM wants to invest time in team building, don't make the mistake of trying to force so called "team building exercises" on them. I've seen more than my fair share of poorly handled "bonding" sessions imposed upon teams by managers who have no empathy or understanding of what they are trying to do.

Instead, invest your time in removing or mitigating the anti-teaming factors. Unless things in your organisation are very toxic, you'll get a much better payoff from your time investment by ruthlessly eliminating the anti-teaming factors than by trying to facilitate the teaming process.

The Bottom Line

Focus less on forcing a team towards bonding and instead on removing or mitigating anti-teaming factors. Be ruthless in eliminating anti-teaming factors — your project success depends on doing so.

The Tags

#projectteams, #teams, #teaming, #teamformation

---

50. Every human action has a reason behind it.

Every human action has a reason behind it, no matter how dumb or destructive it might seem.

A PM must find and understand that reason in time to stop it damaging the project.

The Axiom

Every human action is triggered for a reason, no matter how dumb or destructive it might seem.

The TL;DR

Every human action is triggered for a reason, and if the behaviour is harmful, you need to identify it quickly to prevent project impairment. There's always a reason, no matter how dumb or destructive it might seem. In fact, there may be multiple triggers, and other folks can only guess what those reasons might be if they only rely on observed behaviour. A project manager (PM) must be able and willing to quickly identify and understand the root cause of such behaviour to prevent it from negatively impacting the project.

The Back Story

In the rough and tumble of IT projects (or any project, I guess), it's too easy to become frustrated or even angry because someone in the team or the broader stakeholder group did something you think was dumb. Or even counterproductive. Or, worse, destructive.

Be careful with quick judgements

As a Project manager (PM), you should be careful about forming judgements of blame. I should know – it's my biggest weakness and something I must work on. I can be impatient and quick to judge.

The adage "there are two sides to every story" is true in multiple senses.

Firstly, everyone has their perspective on a situation, and someone else could see things differently.

Secondly, almost everyone has blind spots and cognitive biases, and most of us have psychological weaknesses that we compensate for in various ways.

Thirdly, just because you think that what somebody did was "dumb", it could be that your concept of "dumb" means *"I wouldn't have done it that way"*.

Sometimes we don't do or say the things we intended or even know why we took specific actions. Occasionally we don't even notice that we said them.

Recognise the legitimacy of other people's actions

Therefore, as a PM, you must recognise that individuals' actions often stem from various factors, including miscommunication, lack of proper training, personal issues, stress, or competing priorities. Understanding these motivations allows you to address the root causes, leading to better team dynamics and productivity.

To identify and address the root causes of harmful behaviour, project managers can adopt strategies such as active listening, empathy, clarifying expectations, and providing constructive feedback.

Also, ensure that individuals can access the organisation's support and resources.

By addressing the root causes of harmful behaviour, project managers can foster improved team dynamics and enhanced productivity.

Ok, Tough Guy - Enough, Already.

But, most importantly, as a PM, you must ensure — as much as possible in any given situation — that the human beings involved in your project are not in a potentially harmful situation. Too many PMs decide that this is not a necessary skill — that their job is to be challenging and "demand performance".

Sometimes you'll hear things like, "You can't make an omelette without breaking eggs". It's worth reminding them of the people who used that saying to justify their actions and the consequences: Napoleon Bonaparte and Joseph Stalin. These are not always the role models I consider helpful for a PM.

I have been in tough situations where that mindset was prevalent and damaged me in multiple ways. It's unacceptable for project managers to completely disregard the feelings and well-being of the people they work with or who are under their care.

There's always a legitimate reason.

The one thing I think is true — and if it's not, then it's safer to treat the world as if it's true — is that there is a reason behind every human action, even if they don't know themselves why it occurred. As a project manager, you are responsible for understanding and attempting to mitigate such issues.

The Bottom Line

As a PM, you need to recognise this fact and not respond to immediate action but truly understand why it occurred. It's not easy, but it is necessary. By taking the time to understand the reasons behind actions and addressing the root causes, you can foster a more productive and harmonious team environment, ultimately increasing the likelihood of project success.

The Tags

#humanmotivation, #motivation, #projectmanagementskills, #humanbehaviour, #humanemotion, #behaviour, #emotion, #behaviouraltriggers

---

51. Actual activity vs displacement activity.

YOU NEED TO BE ABLE TO DIFFERENTIATE BETWEEN *REAL ACTIVITY* AND DISPLACEMENT ACTIVITY

The Axiom

You need to be able to differentiate between actual activity and displacement activity.

The TL;DR

Displacement activities arise from tension or confusion and appear unrelated or don't directly add value to the main action within which they occur. Many displacement activities are simple and harmless, such as a person scratching their head when confused. But in sophisticated environments, displacement activities can be complex and camouflaged as legitimate project activities. Although, as a PM, you need to be able to differentiate displacement activities from productive activities, it's often worse to try to stop them; instead, attempt to minimise their wasteful impact on the project.

The Back Story

Not all activity is useful or productive.

Displacing a lot of jungle

I first heard of "displacement activity" at university in Psychology 1, and I can remember the context today. My lecturer was a Michael Sandel-style educator who mixed the course material with stories and analogies. He cut a much larger figure than Sandel, a hugely obese Scot who was also very loud and animated. His name was Dr Dalziel, and he was legendary for his lectures: he performed to a packed house – standing room only – at 10 am three times a week. Often many of those in the classes were not Psych students at all.

Dr Dalziel described the displacement activity of the mountain gorilla in Africa who beats its chest, grabs large handfuls of foliage (grass or bushes – whatever is to hand), and throws it around. I remember Dr Dalziel saying this behaviour *"displaced a lot of jungle in the process"*.

A displacement activity is an activity that humans and some animals perform when agitated and confused about the options available to them. I'm sure you've heard about the gorilla above, who reveals this activity when confused about whether to flee or attack. Classic human displacement activities include scratching one's head or putting one's hand on one's chin as if thinking.

Project displacement activities

Project displacement activities occur in precisely the same situation: when one person (or, more usually, a group) is unsure about what option to take. Examples of project displacement activities are things like:

1. Having a meeting;
2. Making a list;
3. Activating a process, like an issue review;
4. Picking an argument with someone.

These are pretty simple displacement activities. There are many others. The kind of projects I'm most experienced with – Information Technology (IT) projects in enterprises – operate in sophisticated and complex environments with many overlays, process interactions, and highly-trained people. Consequently, the types of displacement activity seen in these projects can be complicated and have a superficial patina of legitimacy.

Examples of complex displacement activities include:

1. Redoing a plan;

2. Redesigning a progress reporting format;
3. Reworking a table in a database;
4. Reformatting a presentation into a new style;
5. Rewriting a code module;
6. Buying a new tool;
7. Hiring a consultant.

I'm not saying every instance of the above is a displacement activity generated by confusion or stress. But I am saying that these activities could be, despite their apparent legitimacy.

How to identify displacement activities

The test is simple: do they materially improve the project or make progress towards the project's goals? If not — if you're pretty much at the same point when they complete as you started - then they hold little value and are displacement activities other than temporarily reducing tension or agitation.

And this is the key to handling them: displacement activities are intended to release tension and assuage agitation — this is of value to the people or group that initiate them, even if it is unconscious. The problem, of course, is whether you can avoid them.

Imagine trying to stop the gorilla from ripping up the jungle foliage and getting a big hug instead. Unlikely. And the more sophisticated a project displacement activity, the harder it will be to stop. It will have momentum, it will have the triggering tension or agitation, and it will have superficial legitimacy.

You will probably find it more wasteful and stressful — trying to stop it instead of letting it run. The best you can do is try, and if that fails, to minimise the investment in time, people or money.

The Bottom Line

Displacement activities are waste, but sometimes trying to stop them is more wasteful; sometimes, it's best just to let them run. Either the person will release enough stress to abandon the work, or you can intervene part way through. But you need to understand the difference and how to find out which activity type it is.

The Tags

#projectmanagementskills, #projectactivity, #displacementactivity, #projectstress, #teamstress, #stress, #projectpsycology

---

52. Business people make lousy solutions architects.

BUSINESS PEOPLE MAKE LOUSY SOLUTION ARCHITECTS.
TECH PEOPLE DON'T ENGAGE WITH BUSINESS PROBLEMS.

YES, THESE ARE STEREOTYPES, BUT IGNORE THEM AT YOUR PERIL.

The Axiom

Business people make lousy solution architects.

The TL;DR

Business people make lousy solution architects, and yet many insist on giving solution requirements or even making architectural decisions. There are many potential reasons for this behaviour, but it impacts their projects and can lead to dysfunctional solution results. Is it because information technology in the 2020s has been part of people's lives for so long now that they feel comfortable talking in solution terms? Or is it because the business problems are intractable or messy, and they feel safer dealing with concrete software capabilities? Neither of these answers feels quite right, but when project managers observe this behaviour, they must do whatever they can to have business people spend their time speaking for the business and not the solution.

The Back Story

In any project team, even and agile *"Cross Functional Team"* (**CFT**), we need access to understand the business problems and how the business should operate after they have solved those problems. The Agile Manifesto calls this out explicitly, but it's an absolute requirement in any project, regardless of the lifecycle model.

> *"Business people and developers must work together daily throughout the project."*
> — **Agile Manifesto, Principle Four**[2]

This is a valuable principle, but let's break it down.

What are these roles, and how do they work together?

By *"business people"*, I mean those people who will use the solution to capture value in their organisational context, together with their respective stakeholders (e.g., direct managers or executives). This term doesn't mean that those people have no other skills, but that their role in the project is primarily to represent the problem domain.

The term *"developers"* is a general one covering anyone who speaks for the solution domain. In Information Technology (IT) solutions they are drawn from organisational IT team members, vendors and other consultants.

The idea of a CFT is a team which has all the skills necessary to deliver the project. In many real-world projects, obviously depending on the scope and context, some skills will not live in the team, but must be sourced from other departments or organisations.

That's uncontroversial; what's the problem?

The problem arises in project teams when those primary responsibilities become blurred.

At least in advanced economies, most working people in 2023 have extensive exposure to computers and IT. Gen-X, Millennials, and Gen-Z — who made up approximately 75% of workers in the USA in 2020 — have tracked at least the boom in personal computers, and at least half of them have tracked mobile computing through their school and work lives. They acquired computing skills from at least work age and most likely during school. A solid proportion — I honestly don't know how many — have some level of exposure to software development and a much larger proportion to computer-based content development.

[2] https://agilemanifesto.org/principles.html

So, for most "business people" we encounter in IT projects, IT is a generic/horizontal skill set. If not second-nature, then IT awareness and confidence are pervasive.

The problem with this is that pervasive skill as a user does not translate to the ability to design high-quality IT solutions, or to understand the compromises made when making design decisions or trade-offs between design alternatives.

Although we want there to be cross-functional interaction, there are also specialities. Coders make their living by developing software; other people have core expertise in other domains. It doesn't matter if it's Accounts Payable, Waste Removal, or High-speed bond trading; all professions are highly complicated and technical these days.

There are at least three strong reasons the non-IT folks should "stay in their lanes" as the default position in any interaction:

1. Divide and conquer the problem!
2. Put domain capability where it is sorely needed.
3. Expose the problem/solution mapping for the entire team.

Divide and conquer the problem!

Business representatives understand and explains the problem space to the other team members.

So, who speaks for the problem space if business people use their brainpower on technical issues? Who can articulate the current value chain problems and desired behaviours?

These are non-trivial issues and need focus and time to understand, articulate, and prioritise. These things are critical if a project is to succeed.

A project should already have technical subject matter experts (SMEs) who can speak to the architecture and design of the solution. If these people are missing from the team, this is a problem in its own right and not solved by having a business domain specialist act in the role. (See below for a discussion on domain capability.)

Put domain capability where it is sorely needed.

Solution architecture and software design are deep technical specialties that take most people a long time to get right. Not all technical choices are similar; making the wrong decision can significantly impact system performance.

For example, on a past project of mine, the primary business person for a function dictated the distribution of functionality between two integrated components, without architectural guidance.

The result was a spaghetti-like data flow that tightly coupled the two systems, resulting in poor performance and numerous integration issues. This design will need to be wholly unwound post-launch.

Many a project sees business representatives who are overly focused on the solution's functionality and design, but unconcerned about non-functional characteristics. Their world is ever full of "sunny day" options. They are not familiar enough with architectural vulnerabilities and so don't dig into all the corner cases and exceptions that enable the solution.

The biggest issues in many projects are design/architectural. Most architectural decisions are concerned with Non-functional capabilities that are not always obvious or understood. Arbitrarily determining functional placement or system topology without understanding the non-functional impacts is a big enough problem with professional solutions architects, leave alone someone who is primarily concerned with functionality.

Please refer to the axiom **# 31. Non-functional requirements are a secret weapon**. for more information on "NFRs".

Expose the problem/solution mapping for the entire team.

The core job of a project is to map the problem space into the solution space. Thus, we emerge with a system optimally tuned to solve specific project constraints, e.g., time, money, or people.

If business people over-invest their time in technical design/feature description, it's a problem. Perhaps, they are not explicitly considering the problem space in those technical inputs.

Or they are hiding that mapping in their heads. It's probably a combination of both. It is important to note that, unlike many other professions, software developers need access to the core business problems to hear directly how those problems are articulated by the business teams.

Hiding the problem/solution mapping prevents developers from building the mental models to produce optimum software solutions: concealed mapping results in poor solutions.

The most important factor

All three of these factors are critical to the success of your project, but if we had to focus on only one, I would focus on exposing the problem-solution mapping.

Concealing the mapping between problem space and solution space leads to "BizDebt", a much bigger problem. If business users do that mapping in their heads to dictate a technical solution, the project has to guess, often wrongly

Please refer to the axiom "**# 37. There's a bigger problem in your project than TechDebt!**" for more information on "BizDebt".

If we have a flawed business model, we will almost certainly have a flawed architecture, even with good quality technical people on the project. We almost certainly have a flawed product, which puts the whole project construct at risk.

The Bottom Line

Solution architecture is a critical element of a successful project that is best left to professionals. There are few enough skilled solution architects available as it is without introducing dilettantes to the mix.

The Tags

#teams, #teamroles, #playyourposition, #projectresources, #skills, #agilemanifesto, #businesspeople, #problem/solutionmapping, #problemdomain, #solutiondomain, #bizdebt, #techdebt

53. Beware the one-person "team"!

BEWARE THE ONE-PERSON "TEAMS" EMBEDDED IN YOUR PROJECT ...

THEY WILL SCREW YOUR PROJECT JUST AS BADLY AS AN EMBEZZLER WILL SCREW A BUSINESS!

The Axiom

Beware of the one-person "teams" in your project.

The TL;DR

Beware of the one-person "teams" embedded in your project. These people claim unique expertise or knowledge and grab anything that touches 'their' area. They never say 'no' to more work, yet they are always so busy that they can never finish anything, but they give assuring reports on progress and lack of issues. It's tough to leverage that unique experience, and you will always have nasty surprises when the actual situation becomes known. These people will screw your project just as severely as an embezzler will screw a business!

The Back Story

Some people are great team players from the start. And other folks start as lone wolves but join the team over time. Some people are never able to bond with the team. All these are clear-cut situations with obvious and detectable symptoms. The fourth category, however, is the most problematic and the hardest to spot and deal with. This category includes folks who appear to be teaming but only ever "team" as individuals.

The one-person team within a team

These are the people I call "one-person teams". Another term is "team 'black hole' ": work approaching them disappears, never to be seen again without some cataclysmic event.

People in this category will always take on more work, even if — at the exact moment — they are discussing how busy they are. They always appear to give importance to team-related activities, but somehow it never works out that way. They are reluctant to work collaboratively and tend to want to work on things alone. A collaborative session may start with the appearance of teamwork, but somehow nothing gets done in the meeting, and one person grabs all the actions, either through claims of specialised knowledge, alignment with current activities, or brute force. These meetings often end with other team members scratching their heads and saying, "What just happened?".

Often, they will be asked, "How can you take on more tasks"? The answer typically trades on this person's unique experience or knowledge: "Who else is going to do it?".

But the work never materialises. These people are often apologetic at standups or when asked about progress: they have so much work and couldn't get any time on the weekend to work due to family activities. But it will be different this week; wait and see. And they rarely provide anything specific about progress or completion dates in status reports. You'll hear from them "no update" or "still working on it — should be done soon".

It's as if work gets sucked into these folks and never escapes until a cataclysmic event: the classic "black hole" analogy.

Blowing up the black hole

One of two things happens to blow up this situation — you'd better make sure one occurs because the third option is that you'll be left high and dry.

The first event that triggers the unravelling of this situation is that the person goes on leave: either they get sick or a planned holiday comes around that they cannot avoid. Interestingly, there's a "red flag" in the white-collar fraud industry that experts warn managers to look out for: someone who never goes on holiday.

> *"The profile of a typical fraudster is a long-serving, trusted employee who works long hours and is reluctant to take their annual leave."* – **Jonathan Middup**, Partner at Ernst & Young's Fraud Investigation & Dispute Services practice. – cited in "Vacation Fraud"[3]

This axiom is not about office fraud, but the same thing occurs with "one-person teams".

The problems surface when this type of person goes on leave for more than a few days or when they leave the company. The team sees the actual situation. Some things will likely be done very well, but for some reason, the "black hole person" has kept working on them and hasn't released them. These people are sometimes very competent and professional in all other ways. Other work tasks are probably badly behind schedule or just items on a "to-do list". The overall level of progress is likely to be far worse than implied.

The second event that blows up the one-person team is that they are put on the equivalent of a "Performance Improvement Plan". Usually, the project manager realises what is happening and forces a scenario in which the "one-person team" is forced to spend formal time working through a status-checked work plan with someone on a very tight review cycle. Usually, this is the project manager, but it may also involve the person's direct people manager or another seasoned manager. This situation is a considerable overhead and requires significant focus and detailed record-keeping. The reviewer must keep detailed notes of each meeting and highlight repeated performance failures and excuses. It's a time-consuming, usually unpleasant, and wasteful process. But it has the effect of exposing the problem in a structured way. The only thing harder than getting it set up is to keep it going: the person under review will wriggle and squirm and try to get out of the review cycle as quickly as possible. They'll typically promise anything to get the review process suspended.

It's analogous to addiction scenarios and the activities that an addict takes to avoid rehab interventions. In a way, this is an accurate description. The person is usually very nice and genuinely wants to help. They are addicted to taking on work, and perhaps there's a narcissism of being in the spotlight, even though it can't be enjoyable.

Ruthlessly eliminate "one person teams"

As a project manager, you must be vigilant of work "black-hole" situations - you must watch out for the symptoms and take action to ensure these one-person teams don't cripple your

[3]https://glanalytics.ca/vacation-fraud/

project. Don't hesitate to act on the "performance improvement plan" type required to monitor such people's work. A big part of this is to trigger the scenario where everyone — including the individual concerned — recognises they are at total capacity and cannot take on any more work. Where there are more critical tasks than this person can handle — even though they might be the only person who can perform the job — you must trigger a prioritisation process or otherwise find a relieving tactic, such as extending timelines.

Ensure there's a clear timeline for these activities and that you don't create interdependency between multiple tasks within the same person.

Otherwise, you'll end up in the third scenario: the time comes when the work is required, but the cupboard is bare: there's nothing to deliver. This scenario is when the whole team can be impacted.

The Bottom Line

Suppose people have a legitimate set of unique work experience or knowledge and the project's best interests at heart. In that case, they will readily share the knowledge and ensure it is leveraged for the project's benefit. Any other behaviour may signify that you have a 'one-person team' and you'd better sort it out.

The Tags

#teams, #teaming, #teamroles, #individualagency, #nonteaming, #lonewolf, #work-management, #pip, #performanceimprovementplan, #whensomeoneneversaysno, #onepersonteams, #projectfraud, #narcissism, #vacationfraud, #jonathanmiddup, #blackhole, #neversaysno

54. When your project team complains.

When your project team complain about too many emails or too many meetings, it's almost certainly not about emails or meetings ...

These are among the many common symptoms of excessive WIP

The Axiom

A team complaint might be the tip of the iceberg - or it might just be a lump of ice.

The TL;DR

When your project team complains about things that appear relatively superficial, e.g. too many emails, meetings, or the office environment, it could be either a deeper root cause or a genuine problem. Don't jump to the conclusion that it is one or the other. And just because it might be superficial doesn't mean it will be easy to fix. Be prepared to surface these deeper issues. It's often a tricky task to parse the symptoms without inadvertently upsetting the team.

The Back Story

There are two reasons people complain about something. The complaint might be a genuine issue or it may just be a *"displacement activity."* For more information on displacement activities, please refer to the axiom "**# 51. Actual activity vs displacement activity**".

A genuine issue is obviously more straightforward to diagnose than those that trigger displacement activities - at least you know the issue and can tackle it directly.

A displacement activity - by definition - is a clue to some other problem. Some other area of your project is stressing the project team and it is surfacing as trivial complaints. But finding the root cause of the tension or conflict can be problematic because displacement activities are almost always unconscious.

In a project, there are a few immediate and apparent candidates for the occurrence of displacement activities, but surprisingly these may not be the root cause.

Excessive Work in Progress (WIP) - trying to do too much simultaneously - is the an obvious potential problem. Overworking the team is a guaranteed way to generate stress, which indirectly then may contribute to displacement activities.

But what is the root cause?

Sources of excessive WIP

A common cause of excessive WIP is a mistaken - or deliberate - misunderstanding the current team can achieve.

Some managers cannot escape the mindset that everyone naturally has a "Theory X" personality which lacks motivation and drive. In this mode, managers will load teams up with work to see the "real" WIP boundary.

Sometimes the cause originates top-down, with management demanding results faster than they can be realistically achieved. Perhaps senior managers are unable, or just unwilling, to prioritise between competing initiatives.

Or maybe the cause originates bottom-up, for example, teams not wanting to say "no" or wishing to appear "gung ho" about their ability to deliver. Other times inexperience leads them to underestimate the work required.

But in all these cases, excessive WIP is just another symptom, not the root cause.

Diagnosing the root cause ... or not

Excessive WIP is just one example of an underlying symptom that is compelling, but not the root cause of the observed issues.

How do you work out what it is?

Unless you're 100% or more sure about the root cause behind a complaint, you must make a good-faith effort to investigate and resolve it at face value, even if it's slightly goofy.

For instance, how do you define "too many emails" in today's context of "always on" communications? But you can't afford to dismiss it. You must scrape away symptoms and let the root cause expose itself.

A Case study

In a project a while back, the team began to complain about "too many meetings". We had already noticed how jammed people's calendars were when trying to schedule project meetings.

I suspected there were multiple causes for this, including working on other projects or "business as usual" (BAU) activities or leaving "phantom bookings" - old invitations to meetings that had been cancelled or expired, but remained in a calendar.

We tried a few things to cut this down, including consolidating a couple of meetings and asking people to explicitly remove "phantom" bookings or other non-essential meetings. Most of the team was notionally assigned to this project 90% or 100%.

Around that time, the department held an "all hands" meeting at which many folks objected to the number of meetings they attended, asking, *"When are we supposed to do the actual work?"*

In reality, the number of meetings for our projects was now pretty low. But we went ahead and cancelled them all temporarily as a gesture of "good faith". I suspected this wouldn't resolve the situation, which was proven true. Within a week, the empty timeslots had been filled with new meetings for other activities.

The number of project meetings wasn't the root cause, it was excessive WIP.

The organisation assigned people to the project nominally as dedicated but in fact was management still expected them to work on business as usual tasks like period end consolidation and reporting, as well as other projects.

That gave us something to work on, but it took another delayed launch to trigger real action.

The solution was for key business people in every functional area of the project were taken out of their roles temporarily and dedicated totally to the project.

Complaints about meetings was just surfacing of a deeper problem of excessive WIP, but the root cause was management not wanting to take on a serious prioritisation call.

The Bottom Line

In many ways, your team is like your customers or other stakeholders. Figuring out what they want or understanding their behaviour can be messy and troublesome. But it's worth it, and you must take the time to understand why they do what they do. Unlocking the secrets of your team is almost certainly a more complex problem than any mere technical dilemma.

The Tags

#teams, #projectteams, #overload, #wip, #displacementactivity, #complaints, #team-complaints, #inexperience

55. What expectations does your team set for themselves?

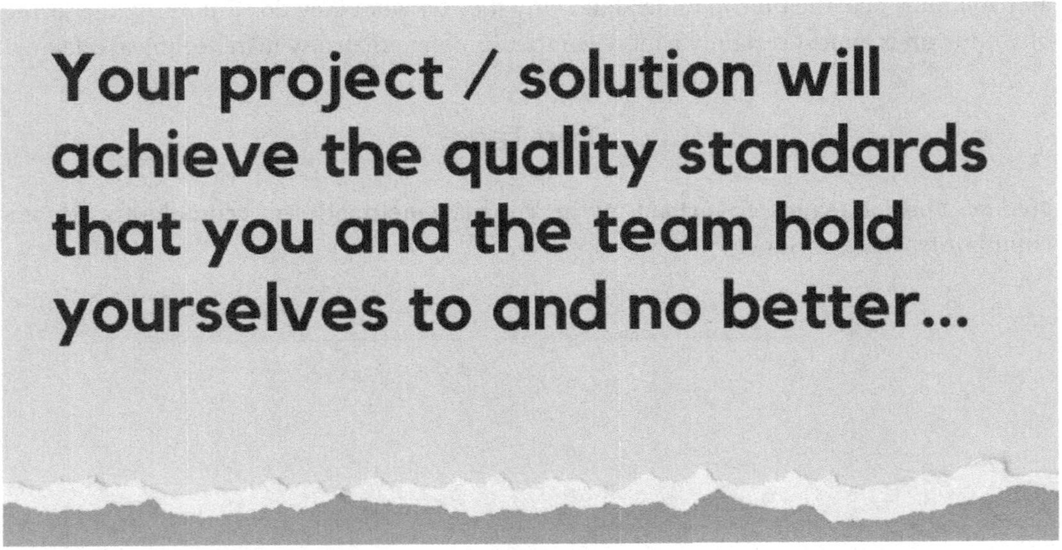

The Axiom

The results of your project won't meet any higher expectations than those you and your team set for yourselves.

The TL;DR

Regardless of how big or complex your project objectives are, they will never exceed the standards the team sets for their performance. Technology won't achieve anything beyond your expectations for yourselves - nor will toolsets or methodologies. Your project could be large or small in its goals, but the only way you achieve them is by setting standards of performance and quality that exceed your goals.

The Back Story

The project you're working on is not some abstract entity.

The team members' and stakeholders' expectations and actions make up a dynamic and living system. The project and its results will reflect these expectations and actions.

What do you want the experience and results of that project to be? Ordinary to define, boring to execute or *"Ho-hum"* or *"Meh!"* to its stakeholders? Or are they exciting, extraordinary and exhilarating? Anything above average is pretty good. But top-end performance will absolutely change your life.

The standard you walk past

How does a project team set "top-end" expectations? By remembering this quote:

> *"The standard you walk past is the standard you accept."* – **Lieutenant-General David Morrison** (Chief of the Australian Army)

If a project team *"walks past"* average performance or dysfunctional behaviour, i.e., doesn't call it out or seek to correct it, the project outputs will be poor or worse.

If the team is sloppy, they will have a disorganised project. Let the team accept lateness, and then the project will be late. Accept poor knowledge management, and the project will be incomplete when the team forgets or misremembers vital facts. If people lack energy, they will slow down the project's momentum. If the products coming out of the project are of poor quality, people will likely care less. And so forth.

This principle operates at all levels, right down to the most minute actions, e.g., if your team is habitually late to meetings, it may seem like a tiny thing, but it has a powerful impact.

The project and its results will be reflected in everything the team collectively does, and vice versa. There is a symbiotic relationship between the team and the project, which deepens with time. For example, people will lose energy and commitment if the project slows.

The primary input to this interdependency is the team's collective performance expectations.

Transforming standards

As a PM, the team's performance and yours are inextricably linked. Regardless of your managerial mode, you lead by example and are influential in setting team goals. You may have little explicit authority, but your behaviour defines your actual power.

> *"Action expresses priorities"* – **Mahatma Gandhi**

A project is a transformative endeavour — to bring about beneficial change — so we must aim high. We must set aspirational goals and work to achieve them. Because if we don't, then the natural forces of entropy will drive the project towards lower-quality outcomes. If you're not trying to improve, then you're going backwards.

Excellent performance comes from within and can't be enabled from the outside. Please don't fall for the idea that using some funky tool, process, or hot technology will increase the project's performance in and of itself. The tool, process, or technology needs people to drive it and bring it to life.

A project is supposed to be a transformative endeavour to bring about beneficial change. And to have that happen means we must aim high. We must set aspirational goals and work to achieve them. Because if we don't, then the natural forces of entropy will drive the project towards lower-quality outcomes. That's just life - that's the second law of thermodynamics.

Funky tools aren't the answer

So, please don't get the idea that using some funky tool, process, or hot technology will increase the project's performance in and of itself. The tool, process, or technology needs people to drive it and bring it to life.

The project manager's role must show leadership in this above all else. You must demonstrate that an abundance mindset to believe the project will succeed - abundance gives you the pragmatic optimism that drives performance.

The Bottom Line

There's one question that everyone on the team needs to ask every day: "How can I do this better?". It's not optional. You must maintain standards from day one and then incrementally improve. If you want your project to succeed, you know what to do.

The Tags

#quality, #projectmanagermindsets, #teamefficacy, #selfregulation, #agency, #principlesofprojectsuccess, #davidmorrison, #mahatmagandhi

56. Invest in alignment!

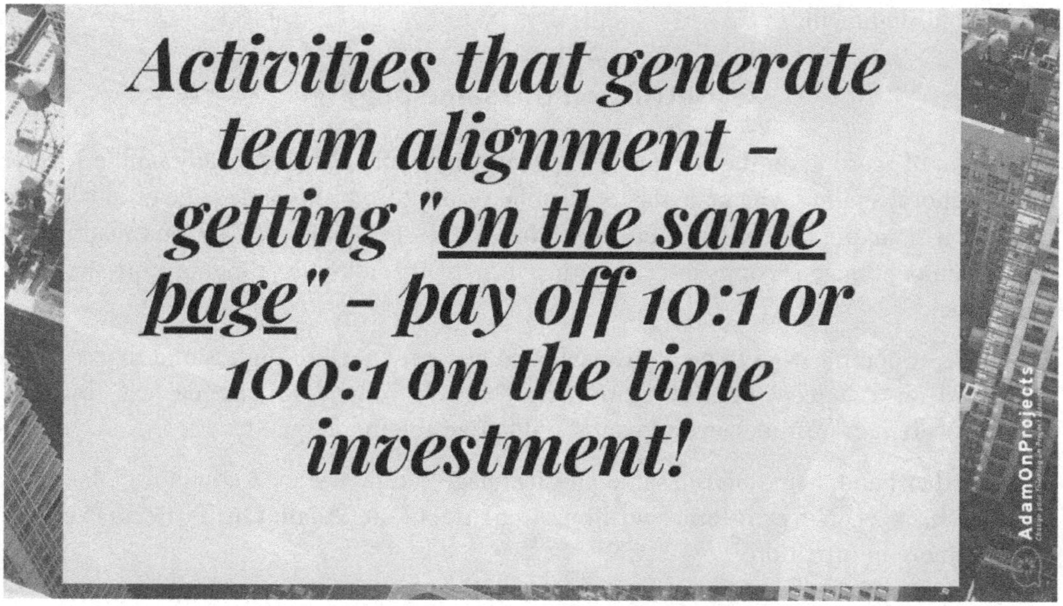

The Axiom

Investing time to get "on the same page" pays off at 10:1 or 100:1 or more.

The TL;DR

Activities that generate team alignment - being "on the same page" pay off spectacularly. If you're driving a project to a schedule, nothing can undermine your progress more than having different team members with varying ideas about what is being developed or how the team will do its work. I acknowledge that meetings with large attendee lists often include people with areas of responsibility not directly or immediately related to the meeting agenda and may consider this a waste of time. But from a project perspective, it is critical.

The Back Story

In a project team, alignment is everything. But it has to be genuine, validated, and sustainable alignment.

Getting on the same page

The origin of "getting on the same page" appears uncertain, although many online sources refer to choral singing when all singers must be reading from the same page of music. But whether it's singing education or business, the concept (or quality) of a group reading the same document page is compelling. Another form of this idiom is "Singing from the same hymn book".

Of course, it doesn't need to be a physical page; we only need to understand that a group is aligned on a concept or idea. Given how easy it is to be unaligned (e.g., by poor communication or attitude), every team should prize alignment quality.

On the other hand, being on the same physical page is a pretty good situation. Check out the Axiom, "**# 79. Never interact without an artifact!**" in "**Adam On: Projects (Volume 2)**"[4], for more information.

Alignment is not static

In a project, alignment is not a static quality and is hard to achieve and maintain. Given the many information gaps in most projects, team members constantly absorb new information, ideas, and concepts and evolve their knowledge.

And yet alignment is crucial, at least on core objectives and directions. Projects rarely prosper when teams are out of alignment.

I'm not saying everyone must think and say the same things all the time: projects are not the same as the sport of synchronised swimming. But on critical matters, alignment is the backbone of success.

As a project manager, one of your primary responsibilities is to promote and validate the existence of alignment amongst your teams.

Investment in alignment pays off big time

And so, any activities that promote alignment are precious and result in an excellent payoff.

[4]https://bjl.ink/aopv2

Investment in time spent on such things as Kick-off meetings or workshops (whether on the whole project or a specific sub-task or deliverable) are important set pieces to establish a baseline of alignment. Various team members have communicated (whatever it is), and everyone there knows they have. People can ask questions, and the presenters can validate understanding by asking their questions.

The problem arises when key stakeholders believe that the time spent in alignment meetings is a waste and that folks have too much to do. Such objections are often a sign of either micro-optimisation or overloading the team. Micro-optimisation occurs when people think purely at the transactional level. A manager might say:

> *"Those ten people are all busy, and could use that time to do productive work!".*

This observation may be valid at a surface level, if we only take into account the theoretical opportunity cost of 10x30-minute timeslots. If meetings aren't defined well or the wrong people are invited, such opinions are only emphasised.

In projects I hear this type of complaint all the time:

> *"I'm too busy to be stuck in meetings all the time!"*

Figure 33. Too busy for meetings?

But it's not possible for a team to converge on a successful outcome if they aren't interacting. Not only that, but continued resistance to meetings is an indicator of "one-person teams" in your project. Refer to the axiom # 53. **Beware the one-person "team"!** for more details.

Let's do the math. In the if the payoff multiple is true, the attendees collectively lose 300 person minutes are lost if the alignment meeting delivers zero value. But a meeting would have to be spectacularly bad to have no value whatsoever for all attendees, so we have a double payoff — at least partially.

On the other hand, we need to consider all the potential impacts downstream in a project. What if, because of not having the meeting, people don't understand what we are doing, have different views of what is required, or arrange multiple other meetings because they didn't know who needed to do what tasks — or worse, assumed incorrectly. Due to the many direct and indirect problems that this meeting prevents, I view their investment payoff as at least 10:1 and possibly higher.

If this hypothesis is true, then we're saving at least 300 minutes per person in wasted activities by having the meeting.

I believe that the payoff is higher, given that there are both positive upsides and preventing negative ones. A well-run alignment meeting becomes a shared experience and a baseline for the next set of activities.

The Bottom Line

There is a tendency these days to treat meetings as wasted time; in many cases, they are. Any communications event can be a waste if not managed carefully. Teams can communicate information in myriad ways, and we have a huge number of tools and platforms to do that. But, ultimately, direct, real-time interaction cannot be avoided. It builds the team and shared understanding, and it's the only way to establish a baseline of common knowledge.

The Tags

#teams, #teamalignment, #alignment, #mentalmodels, #samepage, #productivitypay-off, #microoptimisation, #nonlinearresults

On Risk

Risk is how people deal with the uncertainty of the future in a structured way. Projects are all about risk, so we couldn't let this subject area go untouched by axioms.

The problem that many project managers face with risks is that the practice has been institutionalised to such an extent that teams can fall into a blind rote practice that adds no value.

> *"Most of our industry pays more lip service to risk management than it actually performs."*—**Tom DeMarco and Tim Lister** in *Waltzing with Bears: Managing Risk on Software Projects.*

Project managers need to step up and step into an intentional engagement with risk, regardless of the processes used to capture and manage them. Risk should be incorporated into every facet of a project, not sequestered into a stale and stand-alone practice.

57. It's great to be the first penguin off the ice!

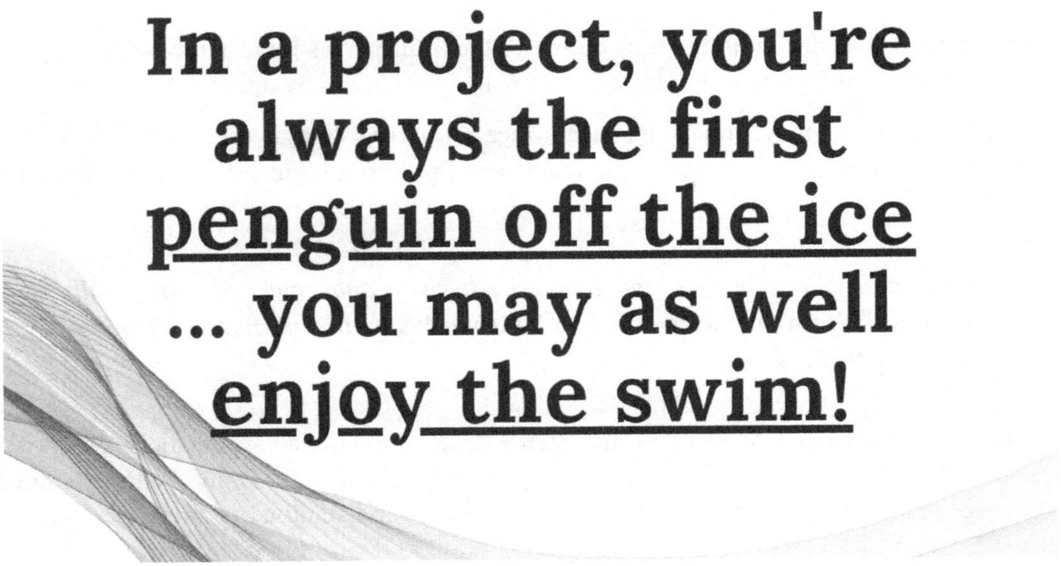

The Axiom

In a project, you're always the first penguin off the ice, so you may as well enjoy the swim.

The TL;DR

The "first penguin off the ice" metaphor seems less widely understood than ten years ago. The idea that goofy penguins could display complex behaviour that involved a future-oriented concept such as risk is what makes the metaphor so striking in my view. So, whether you're familiar with it, check out the "Back Story" below.

The Back Story

One of my favourite metaphors - if only more people know about it.

The Adélie penguin

For those unfamiliar with the Adélie penguin's social behaviour in Antarctica, here is a short sidebar for context.

Adélie penguins care for their eggs in pairs: while one parent minds the eggs, the other forages in the sea for food. Feeding penguins approach the sea in groups and have a distinctive behavioural pattern at the ice edge.

The group hangs around the entry point to the sea, pushing and shoving other penguins to try and get them to dive into the sea first. They show great reluctance to be the first in the water, presumably due to the predators who often wait, like leopard seals and killer whales (orcas). Even after they are all in, they immediately jump right out again. There is a vital element of play in this behaviour and survival instinct. This jostling might go on for a few minutes or much longer. At some point, the group behaviour changes, and one will dive into the sea deliberately. Immediately after this first penguin, all the other penguins will swoop in from the same point.

There are benefits to being first (access to food with less competition) and significant risks (getting eaten).

The First Penguin Award

Dr Randy Pausch at Carnegie Mellon University set up a technology innovation event and established an award for the team that took the most significant risk on a new idea or technology, even if it didn't work. He called it the "First Penguin Award."

> *"The title of the award came from the notion that when penguins are about to jump into water that might contain predators, well, somebody's got to be the first penguin."* — **Randy-Pausch**[1]

Projects mean risk

Projects exist in environments that are at least partly hostile, and while there may not be orcas, there are risks of failure and impairment. We can do things that reduce the risk, but this is a given; there's no way around it.

Risk is a part of our lives — it's endemic to existence. It equally applies to food as it does to the penguins.

[1]https://www.post-gazette.com/local/city/2009/10/30/Walk-on-CMU-campus-honors-Randy-Pausch/stories/200910300294

> *"I've long believed that good food, good eating, is all about risk. Whether we're talking about unpasteurised Stilton, raw oysters or working for organised crime 'associates,' food, for me, has always been an adventure"* — **Anthony Bourdain** in Kitchen Confidential: Adventures in the Culinary Underbelly cited on goodreads.com[2]

Don't be confused

I'm wondering, at this point, if you're confused. "What's Adam on about penguins and celebrity chefs?" The purpose is to break you out of your closed, narrow mindset on what makes projects tick. I apologise if you feel that you're not in that category; I find many project managers to think of project management as a set of unique knowledge and practices that live outside of anything else.

Understand that everything is connected and derivative; the more analogies we can find in other disciplines and life experiences, the deeper we'll understand our chosen profession.

So, there's no point in worrying about this — don't do projects if risk isn't part of your work profile.

The Bottom Line

Just like the Adélie penguins, have fun and enjoy the swim.

The Tags

#projects, #risk, #abundance, #principlesofprojectsuccess, #fun, #enjoyment, #firstmoveradvantage, #firstmoverrisk, #randypausch, #firstpenguinaward, #firstpenguinofftheice, #anthonybourdain, #analogy

---

[2]https://www.goodreads.com/author/quotes/1124.Anthony_Bourdain

58. Everyone is fine with your risk management plan.

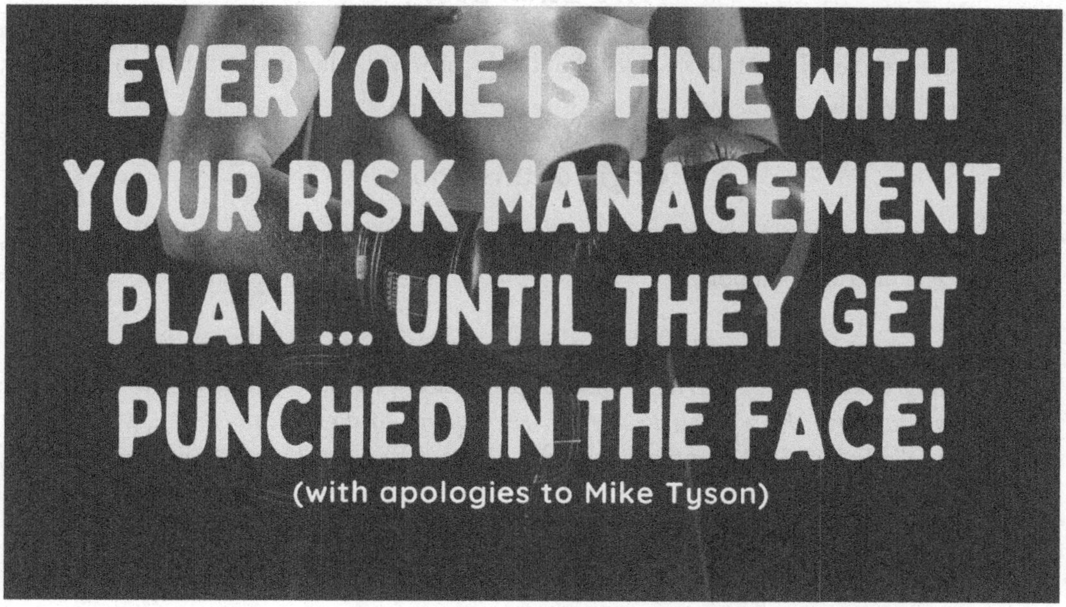

The Axiom

Everyone is fine with your risk management plan - until they get punched in the face!

The TL;DR

All projects entail risk. The collective project management body of knowledge includes significant time and spec to the study and practice of "risk management". But this focus on codifying risk management doesn't change the fact that sometimes things will blow up. And when things don't go right, you will experience strange reactions to risk. There are always one or two stakeholders in a project who have no concept of risk or uncertainty and assume that everything will always be "just fine". You get punched in the mouth (figuratively) when things go wrong, but it's often not just once but twice: once when the event happens and the second time in your stakeholder's adverse reaction to the event. There's not much you can do to prevent this, so you'd better get used to it.

The Back Story

Many project stakeholders talk casually about risks, as if just talking about them makes them go away. They don't

Origin of this axiom

Yes, I'm riffing on Mike Tyson's famous line, but more illuminating — and relevant to this axiom — is a later explanation:

> *"People were asking me [before a fight], 'What's going to happen?.' They were talking about his style. 'He's going to give you a lot of lateral movement. He's going to move, he's going to dance. He's going to do this, do that.' I said, "Everybody has a plan until they get hit. Then, like a rat, they stop in fear and freeze.'"* — **Mike Tyson**, quoted in "Mike Tyson explains one of his most famous quotes"[3], 9th November 2012

Projects entail risk

Projects entail risk — it's axiomatic.

To help deal with project risk, a broad discipline of "risk management" is used to identify, categorise and work to reduce the likelihood of risk events and their impact. Risk management plans range from qualitative and short — perhaps only bullet points — to large and quantitative, with spreadsheets and simulations. There may even be a person dedicated to maintaining the risk management plan.

But no matter the size and scope of risk management activity in a project, it is not a guarantee. Plans are not some magic wand that makes projects risk-free.

Risk management is not a magic wand

Unfortunately, that's not always the perspective of all stakeholders, who hold high and unrealistic expectations of the project manager's ability to avoid the impacts of risk events.

[3] https://www.sun-sentinel.com/sports/fl-xpm-2012-11-09-sfl-mike-tyson-explains-one-of-his-most-famous-quotes-20121109-story.html

And because the risk events are described in general terms in a future state, they seem to have more effect when they happen.

As a PM, you can pretty much guarantee that you'll get punched in the mouth at some point. Then, no matter the quality of your risk management plan, you'll have to justify the impacts.

As a project manager, you will experience some strange reactions to risk.

There are always one or two stakeholders in a project who have no concept of risk or uncertainty. Perhaps they've always worked in stable environments where nothing has gone wrong. Or do they have a mindset that devalues risk? Some stakeholders aren't familiar enough with the projects in their organisation, so they are unaware of what can go wrong.

It's like a gambler who won't accept that losses do occur. S/he can't quite get their head around events when the cards (or balls or horses) don't go their way.

Risks are pre-excuses for failure

In the project world, you'll experience stakeholders who look at the risks you identify and see them as "excuses for failure written in advance". Others see them as reasons to "pad" your budget or timeline.

Some won't accept that the event you might identify is something that might happen. I remember one senior manager telling me that the risk — a plain vanilla one — "Key personnel change projects or leave the company" was an event that was even possible. "They love it here and are completely dedicated. They'll never leave".

Others believe using a particular methodology, application, or technique will guarantee success. Some people believe that Agile removes all risk from a project and won't accept any mention of risk — *"Risk management - that's a Waterfall thing, isn't it?"*

And then you have some stakeholders who know what can go wrong but aren't prepared to admit it's possible — they want a magic wand that eliminates all risk.

Just don't be late

I remember a reasonably large digital project I babysat for another project manager while s/he was finishing a delayed project. My presentation at the first stage-gate approval meeting was balanced: I only covered a handful of particular and material risks relevant to that project. But it wasn't enough — our sponsor's comment:

> *"Adam, that's all fine, but just don't be late."* — **Anonymous Project Sponsor**

The Bottom Line

Projects are risky; there must be an expectation that some will fail and others (more others) will suffer some impairment that doesn't meet the initial parameters. I guess they expect the PM to get punched in the mouth (as a proxy for the stakeholder team) and deal with it. Nice idea. Mike Tyson's 2012 explanation is more appropriate to quote this lack of preparedness and emphasise the last sentence.

The Tags

#riskmanagement, #risk, #riskmanagementplan, #stakeholdermanagement, #miketyson, #appropriation, #projectrisk, #stakeholderresponse, #riskevent

59. Why should every project succeed?

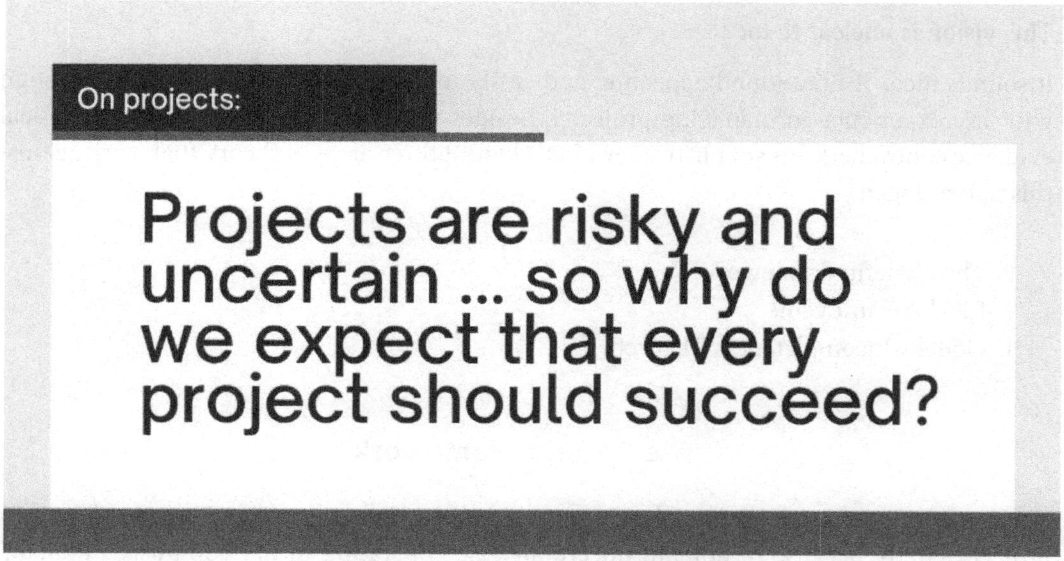

The Axiom

Projects are risky and uncertain, so why do we expect every project to succeed?

The TL;DR

Wishful thinking, unrealistic expectations, or attempts at brand management do not alter the inherent risks associated with any project. A project manager needs to balance risk management processes against the need to have all stakeholders on board for the journey. Finding this balance can be challenging. Project managers must be able to navigate this dynamic tension. You must also be prepared to handle situations where stakeholders are unhappy, regardless of your diligent risk approach.

The Back Story

I saw a couple of years back in the Association for Project Management (APM) in the UK — their strategy vision paper had the tagline:

> *"A world in which all projects succeed with project management as a life skill for all."* – **Association for Project Management** in Vision / Strategy Statement[4]

This vision is unclear to me.

It sounds nice. It may sound appealing and easily understood. However, it does not align with my experience in managing projects. Besides my experience compelling theoretical evidence contradicts this simplistic view. Let's look at three areas of theory that work against this naïve slogan

1. The Cynefin Framework
2. Black Swan Events
3. Gödel's Incompleteness Theorem

The Cynefin Framework

The Cynefin framework best highlights how unrealistic the expectation of success for every project. Firstly because of domain uncertainty, i.e. operating in the "Confused" domain. Operating in this domain happens because the project team doesn't know what domain applies to their situation. Secondly, due to misdiagnosing the domain, or misapplying the operating strategy for the relevant domain.

And lastly, even when the project manager, team and stakeholders correctly identify the domain and the operating strategy (practice), the nature of some domains works against decision-making.

Projects operating in the "\Complex"\ and "Chaotic" domains are exposed to the impacts of "unknowable unknowns". By definition, there are no specific actions that a project manager can take to address the unknowable. There is only an approach to "Emergent Practice and "Novel Practice", which have no guarantee of success.

Black Swan Events

The theory of risk contradicts the APM's slogan. Risk Management can mitigate a wide range of potential effects on a project, but it is challenging to mitigate high-impact, low-probability events known as 'Black Swan' events. Black Swan events are rare, unpredictable, and have significant consequences, making them particularly difficult to manage in a project context.

[4]https://www.apm.org.uk/about-us/apm-strategy/

These events are a stark reminder that unforeseen circumstances can dramatically impact a project's outcome, regardless of the project management approach employed. Project managers must recognise that they cannot anticipate every possible eventuality, making the notion of a world where all projects succeed implausible.

Gödel's Incompleteness Theorem

I don't know any practicing project managers who apply theoretical mathematics to their everyday projects. But that doesn't mean they are immune to the impacts of mathematically-derived situations. Gödel's incompleteness theorem implies that methodologies and knowledge frameworks we use to understand and manage projects will always have inherent limitations and uncertainties.

If we cannot rely on our frameworks to be consistent and complete, then the expectation that every project will succeed is not only unrealistic, but it also overlooks the core aspect of project management.

The purpose of project management is to adapt and work in the presence of uncertainty.

What Does all this mean?

Considering the insights from the Cynefin framework, Black Swan effects, and Gödel's Incompleteness Theorem, the APM's vision of a world where every project succeeds oversimplifies the complex reality of project management.

Instead of pursuing an unattainable ideal, project managers should prioritise building resilience and adaptability in their projects, which can increase the likelihood of success in the face of unpredictable challenges.

This does not imply that we should not strive to improve the success rate of projects. There is significant room for improvement, as described in the axioms "**# 3. Why do projects fail?**" and "**# 2. Successful projects? We've got both kinds!**".

Claiming that we can achieve a situation where all projects succeed is not only naive but also reckless.

I do not intend to direct this criticism solely at the APM, although they should have a better understanding. Many project stakeholders share a similar perspective on risk.

Many perceive a risk management plan as a collection of pre-emptive excuses — see the axiom ***"# 58. Everyone is fine with your risk management plan"***, for a personal example.

Undoubtedly, project teams can improve their ability to anticipate potential impacts and develop project approaches to control or mitigate them.

Simply articulating a specific event and asking 'what if' can be enough to create a response plan, even if the event probability cannot be mitigated. As I outline in the axiom ***"# 60. Happy with your stand-alone risk management process?"***, intrinsic approaches are more effective than extrinsic ones. However, for 'Black Swan' events, there are limited intrinsic options.

Projects are risky, and risk means loss. Some projects will fail absolutely and disastrously. Others will deliver reduced benefits or have some stakeholders believing they are failures, regardless of what happened. Thus, a subset can be deemed wholly successful. I don't know what that percentage is — it must vary significantly across different environments.

But the quantum of unsuccessful or impaired projects doesn't matter for this axiom.

Project sponsors and senior stakeholders must be taken on a journey that allows them to understand what will be considered a partial success and what will be considered an abject failure.

The Bottom Line

Striving for a world where every project succeeds is unrealistic and naïve. Recognising the limitations of our understanding and control over projects allows us to prioritise building resilience and adaptability. Project sponsors and senior stakeholders must be prepared for the potential of partial success or failure, and collaborate with project managers to navigate the complex and unpredictable journey of project execution, wherever it leads.

The Tags

#risk, #riskmanagement, #projectsuccess, #projectfailure, #cynefinframework, #cynefin, #blackswanevents, #apm, #gödelincompletenesstheorem, #franzgödel

---

60. Happy with your stand-alone risk management process?

Having a stand-alone risk management process in a project is like hosting a dinner party and ensuring that your guests stop and discuss their digestive processes every few minutes.

In a project, everything is risk-based: everything you do has a probability function of < 1.

You can't stop the world while you have a meeting.

The Axiom

Organic risk management structures in your project approach eat formal risk management processes for breakfast.

The TL;DR

Invest more time setting up implicit risk management processes in your project than executing explicit risk management procedures. Having a stand-alone risk management process in a project is like hosting a dinner party and insisting your guests stop and discuss their digestive processes every few minutes. One of the problems with the way project management is written about and taught is the deconstruction of the lived experience into stand-alone discrete processes. Everything is connected — you can't split the real world into discrete streams and prosecute them independently. Risk management is a case in point for this axiom, but it could be an issue management process, a benefits management process, or any other process recommended for universal use.

The Back Story

Perhaps a common theme of this book is that I do not advocate stand-alone processes unless their use is specifically required by the needs of a particular project. I've used risk management as the example in this axiom, but it could be an issue management process, a benefits management process, or any other process recommended for universal use.

Stand-alone practices are a fool's errand.

Why is this a potential problem?

It's a problem because we can't stop the world while focusing on one thing to the exclusion of all others.

Our lived experiences as human beings occur in a sea of events and activities that surround us and interact with us. We can potentially carve out a small chunk of time to zero in on one thing, but this focus is an illusion. The rest of our lives continue, and things change when we return from our temporary exclusion.

Perhaps we try to partition activities into relatively smaller chunks, like "work", "family", or "hobby". These are still big chunks of our lives and cannot be wholly partitioned from any other aspect.

Anybody in a meeting at work discussing a breakfast table argument with their partner will understand what I mean.

And so it is with projects: our cognitive powers are not differentiated into process-level activities.

The objects we consider in stand-alone processes are not genuinely stand-alone: a risk is connected to assumptions, deliverables, issues, human factors, etc.

This conceptual separation may serve as a training or research strategy. However much this strategy makes sense, it runs the risk of teaching the split along with the core content you are teaching about the process. It doesn't help our project to execute them in independent activities, stand-alone from anything else.

Sometimes, a laser-like focus is required on a particular object, such as defects, issues, or risks. Still, the conversation will never be limited to such things because *"everything is connected"*.

Enter Organic Risk Management

Instead of driving separate and discrete processes (like Risk Management), which a project manager drives explicitly, organic processes are built into the day-to-day project construct, and happen implicitly.

I've written about Organic Risk Management in the axiom "**# 62. You need to manage Rissues organically**", but will expand on this a little here. The axiom "**# 43. That unforeseen crisis your project is having?**", also contributes to the idea of Organic Risk management.

If you look at risk management generically, and thinking about all the problems you might encounter, you end up with two big strategies:

1. Many of the so-called "risks" in most risk management plans can be mitigated by simply running a high-quality project, and that is something very much in the control of a PM. Note: handling your "Rissues" happens here.
2. Of the rest, you decide which ones you want to invest time in (group A), and which of them you'll prepare to respond to (group B - the rest).

Preparing to handle the group B risks - the ones you'll deal with when the time comes - falls into the work you need to do to run a high-quality project.

In most IT projects that I've worked on, the Group A risks are a tiny bunch. There are few risks that you both have some control or influence over, and you've decided to invest time in them. Group A is so small that you can probably just as effectively throw them into Group B and use the time to improve the quality of your project.

All of which leads you to the strategy of running a high-quality project.

So your organic risk management practices are those built into and serviced by a high-quality project. They are built into the things you do daily, weekly, or whatever periodicity is required.

What does running a "high-quality project" mean?

I'd say here that a "high-quality" project is for each project manager to decide for themselves, in their own context. I'm not being coy or vague here - after all, I've written two books of over 100 of these axioms describing what I think represents good project practice. My positions are clear.

It's not about how many "things" - practices, processes, tools and the like - you can include in your project. It's about selecting the right combination of those "things" that represent the right payoff for the investment.

But, having said the above, I'd say there are a few obvious candidates:

1. Focusing on enablement of customer outcomes.
2. Developing and maintaining good relationships with your key stakeholders.
3. Adopting a good knowledge management process in the project.
4. Leveraging the best outcomes for and from your direct team members.
5. Fully understanding all the linkages that your project has into the parent organisation.
6. Prioritise ruthlessly.

Some small things in projects have big payoffs. For example, I've always been amazed and pleased at how many problems a good onboarding document can avoid or solve.

And running a high-quality project has the double payoff of being a place where people want to work - at least the kind of people who want to work on high-quality projects.

The Bottom Line

Risk management is critical: in a project, everything is risk-based: everything you do has a probability function of < 1, and you must build everything around risk factors. But most activity in any stand-alone project management process is done organically by the project team without any explicit method. Remember the next time you want to set up a risk management meeting: maybe that's not the best way to deal with risks.

The Tags

#risk, #riskmanagement, #projectmanagementprocesses, #projectmanagement, #organicprocesses

61. The most common project WOFTAM.

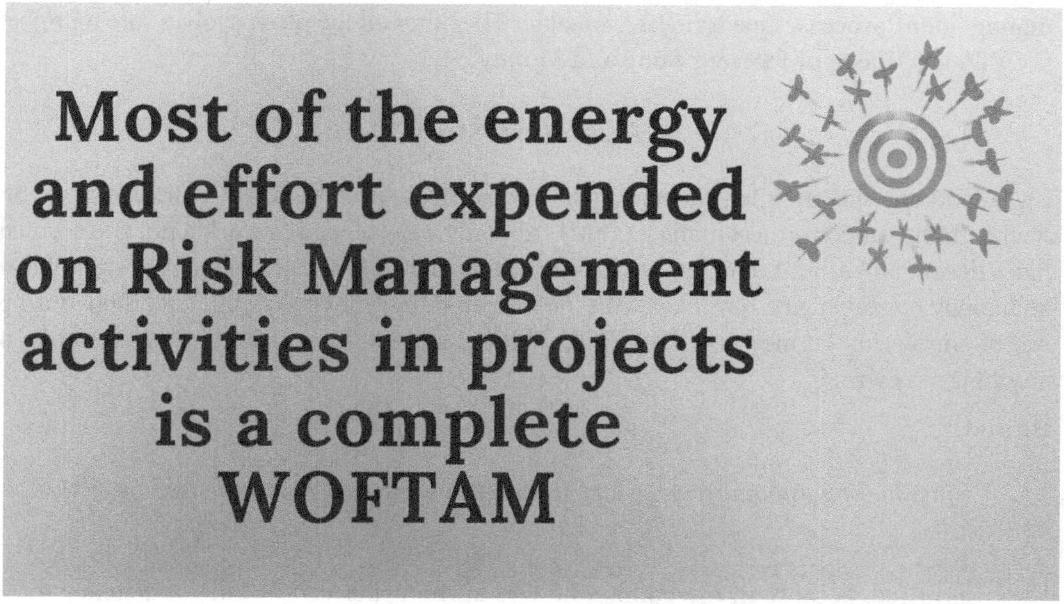

The Axiom

Most of the energy and effort expended on Risk Management activities in projects is a complete WOFTAM.

The TL;DR

Project managers are often judged based on compliance with a formally documented process, regardless of whether the process is inappropriate for the project. This assessment seems most common for risk management processes in enterprise environments. This judgement happens even though the PM may be effectively managing risk in the project through other means.

The Back Story

The first thing to understand about **risk management** is that it isn't the same as a **risk management process**. One is highly valuable. The other all too often evolves into a project WOFTAM (**"Waste of F$%#&g Time and Money"**).

A personal story

I was working with an integration partner for a software package a few years ago. I got on well with the vendor project manager (PM) - not only was he good to work with, and seemed like a decent bloke, but I thought that he was a competent PM. He was usually pretty upbeat and happy to exchange a few jokes with me to keep things moving along. And then, during one of our weekly 1:1 meetings, he seemed a bit flat and not his usual self. So I asked him if anything was wrong.

He said,

> *"I just had my annual review, and it didn't go well. My boss criticised my PM skills"*

I was surprised, because in my opinion he was at the upper end of PM competency for a vendor. So I asked him whether his boss gave any hard feedback.

The PM said:

> *"A few things around my project management documentation; for example, he said that I didn't have enough risks in my risk register."*

I've been given similar feedback from time to time, usually when the PMO audited my process compliance, or when a process-minded boss reviewed my project documentation.

I always respond:

> *"Ok. Tell me, how many should there be? I'll put them in.".*

The usual comeback to my question is:

> *"That's up to you and the circumstances of your project. But I think that you should have more risks in there. It feels half-cooked to me. How many more can you add?"*

That's when I give my '**Mozart Answer**'.

The Mozart Answer

My 'Mozart answer' is,

> *"From where I'm sitting, I have just the right number of risks. If there were other material and actionable risks for this project, then they would already be in the plan. But if you can identify a relevant risk, then I'll be happy to add it."*

The source of my 'Mozart answer' is an apocryphal story about Wolfgang Amadeus Mozart, that I saw in the movie Amadeus. Mozart played a composition to his benefactor, the Emperor of Austria, only to be told there were *"too many notes"* in it.

Mozart replied:

> *"There are just as many notes as I required, neither more nor less."* — attributed to **Wolfgang Amadeus Mozart**, in the movie 'Amadeus'.

Just follow the process

This anecdote about my poor vendor PM and Mozart illustrates that much of the work put into Risk Management processes in projects is pretty arbitrary. It is more frequently based on opinion and preferences of managers and other stakeholders. Some want more, some want fewer, and others want none.

You might say: *"just follow the process,"* but the problem is that most formal risk management processes are defined for the largest projects that might exist in the organisation, usually in very long and complex documents, which take enormous time to understand and implement. Inevitably, especially in large enterprises, the documentation for them is out of date, can have errors, inconsistencies, or broken links to other documents.

Formal processes are highly stylised, procedural and complex to operate. And they bore project teams and stakeholders to death. It's very challenging to get sustainable stakeholder engagement in risk management.

But many project stakeholders - PMs included - don't get the difference between **risk management** and a **risk management process**. They can't accept that we can have one without the other. At the same time, they appear happy to take on board whatever risk management process is mandated by their Project Management Office, and use it slavishly.

Figure 34. Somewhere, deep inside a PMO...

A dysfunctional process

This weird situation results in an artificial and mechanical process that gets little engagement from those who must participate. A typical risk register is full of generic formula-driven risks. Most of these risks are unmanageable and unmitigable. So, we have an environment where compliance is checked off, but almost no value results from the process.

Risk management of this type is a WOFTAM. It is a rare project risk register that doesn't deserve that rating.

The Bottom Line

I fully understand the need for a risk-based approach to projects. More than understanding it theoretically, I live it daily. Risk is everything in a project. A risk perspective must be part of everything you do. But do it in a way that doesn't involve the ritualistic exercise of a complex process.

The Tags

#risk, #riskmanagement, #projectmanagementprocesses, #projectmanagementprocesses, #wolfgangamadeusmozart, #woftam, #pmo, #projectmanagementoffice, #stakeholderexpectations, #stakeholders, #justfollowtheprocess

62. You need to manage Rissues organically.

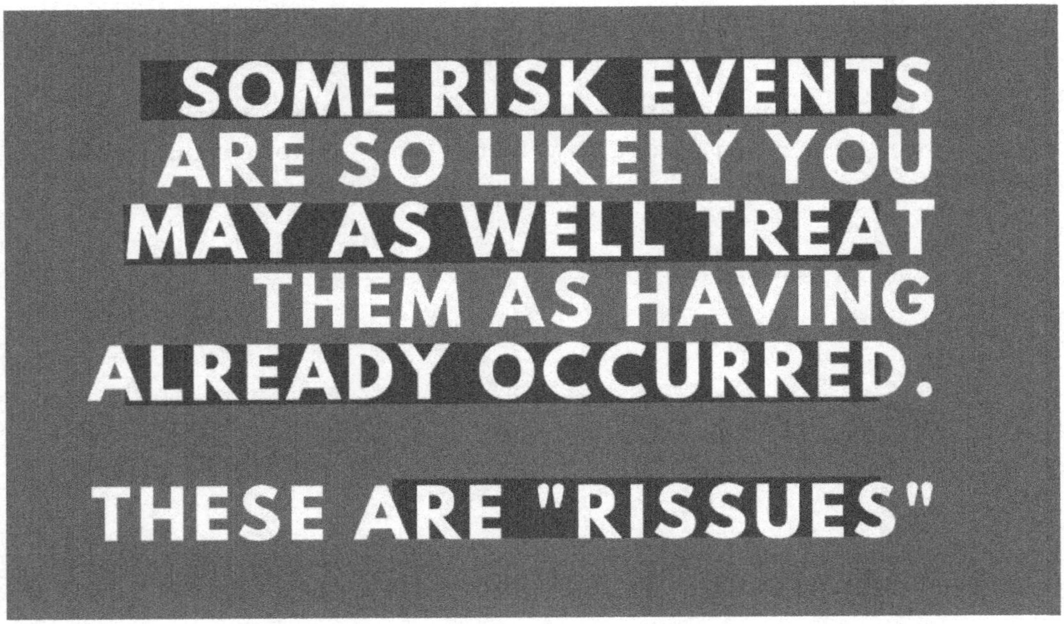

The Axiom

Risk events that are so likely that you may as well treat them as having already occurred are called "Rissues".

The TL;DR

Rissues are risk events that are so likely that you should treat them as having already occurred. Unlike other risks, we shouldn't manage Rissues in a traditional Risk Management process. Instead, they require a different approach known as "Organic Risk Management". This involves designing your project to deal with Rissues as part of your day-to-day activities. This gives you a prioritisation framework to run a high-quality project.

The Back Story

I coined the term *"Rissue"* many years ago during my time at a major Australian Telco, most likely around 2002. It began as a play on words but became a bit of an obsession.

The word is a *portmanteau* word combining **"Risk"** and **"Issue"**.

What is a "Rissue"

Standard Risk Management ("RM") methods split events into two:

1. Risks: events that have not yet occurred.
2. Issues: events that have occurred.

But what about risk events that haven't happened yet, but for which the probability of occurrence is very high - effectively 100%? A Rissue meets the technical requirements for a risk but is so likely that managing it through normal risk management processes dilutes the necessary action required to handle the event.

Rissues require that we act on them immediately. Even though they haven't happened yet, we jump over all the RM pre-work and straight to managing them. And we don't include them in any risk register or risk management plan.

How do we manage Rissues? I'll deal with that later.

What kind of projects have Rissues?

Rissues are present in all projects, whether or not they are noticed. Existing projects may already wrap their Rissues into their risk management plan or they may remain unmanaged. Either way, their existence is a common aspect of project management.

Rissues are part of your project context - the environment in which your project is started and executed. Rissues are common and frequent. Not only are they almost certain to happen, but you'll be lucky if they only happen once in the lifetime of your project.

Examples of Rissues include:

- "A Key team member may leave the project";
- "A Change Request (CR) may be raised late in the project";
- "We may uncover a missing mandatory requirement";
- "A vendor may deliver a component late";

- "Another development team may deliver a component that doesn't meet the specification".

In my experience, such events are almost certain to occur at some point. It's just a matter of when and where in the project and how often.

The Opposite of "Black Swan" Events

Rissues differ from "Black Swan" events, which have a very low probability and a very high impact. In contrast, Rissues are virtual certainties, regardless of their potential impact. Most Rissues have a mid-range impact that can be annoying and inconvenient but cause delays. Unlike "Black Swan" events, most Rissues can be easily planned for and mitigated.

Project teams spend a lot of time on high-impact risks like "Black Swan" events. But focusing on remediating Rissues is much more productive, due to their high probability.

Why Risk Managing Rissues is Counter-productive

I'll answer this by working through an example, which is the risk that:

> *"A Key team member may leave the project."*

(I think this may have been the genesis of the term way back when.)

Standard Risk Management guidelines require us to analyse, track and mitigate risk events in either or both of:

1) the likelihood of occurrence;

2) the impact of the event after it occurs.

Project managers are required to operate a formal process to carry risks in a register that is reviewed discussed regularly during the project.

But with Rissues, this process doesn't help.

Mitigating the probability of someone leaving

What would reduce the probability of a key team member leaving? Maybe we could make sure that "our office environment was nice". Or be "flexible in our working arrangements." Or "show respect for individuals." There are many more. But no matter what we think of, there are three questions:

1. Wouldn't (shouldn't) we be doing these things anyway?
2. What control do we have at the project team level to put these types of strategies into practice?
3. How does it help to manage these strategies in a traditional risk register and process?

Of course, we should create a respectful, enjoyable and flexible project team environment, but there are limits to what we can implement locally and what is dictated by corporate policies. Any good project manager will work on these and also how to do as much as possible within corporate constraints.

Lastly, if a key person decides they want to take another opportunity, it's usually for reasons that far outweigh mundane environmental issues.

Mitigating the impact of someone leaving

If someone leaves and needs to be replaced, this must happen as quickly and seamlessly as possible to minimise the project impact.

There are typically three pathways: new hires, transfers and secondments.

Most organisations and all large companies have very specific and restrictive policies that cover these three tasks. In my experience, most PMs don't know how these processes work. PMs may not know the employment status of each team member, and therefore the correct pathway or process to onboard new people.

Consequently, many PMs are not prepared and often make many mistakes, which slows down the process. Additionally, many PMs aren't great interviewers and/or aren't great at finding candidates.

So the alternate way of dealing with this Rissue is to ensure that the project team can easily onboard new people. This approach is not mitigating a risk through a risk management process - this approach is something you set up in your project establishment checklist.

Another aspect is project knowledge management. At the very least, you need to ensure that critical knowledge isn't quarantined in one person's head or otherwise not available to the team if a person was to leave unexpectedly. Please also see the axiom ***"# 2. Beware the one-person 'team'!"*** for more on this issue.

For example, you could focus on making sure that the project team always records its decisions, and that they keep critical documents up to date. In many projects, this is considered a low-priority task, but mitigating the impact of someone leaving is a high-impact rationale.

You could also set up a backup arrangement for each key role by nominating a second person to track the activities and material covered/performed by the critical role.

Addressing and resolving these deficiencies as early in the project as possible is far more productive than working them through a Risk register.

Organic Risk Management

It's clear (at least to me) that the mechanisms for dealing with Rissues are far better being built into your project "ways of working" so that they are mitigated as an automatic by-product of your team's work.

I refer to this as "Organic Risk management", in which you embed your risk management activities into the operating model of each project from commencement. Organic Risk Management handles Rissues implicitly as opposed to the explicit treatment of standard Risk Management processes.

There are so many tasks and processes that we expect each project team member to know. Still, Organic Risk Management gives you a prioritisation approach for what to do now and what to invest your time implementing.

I don't really want to coin this as a term because the Rissue-management approach is fundamentally about setting up high-quality ways of working for the project team. But, it's important to highlight the counterpoint to traditional risk management for these types of risk, so I stuck with it.

The Bottom Line

Remember that "Rissues" are a virtual certainty, so you don't really have much choice about whether you have to deal with them. Your choice is how. "Organic Risk Management" may only be a minor change to how you usually run your project. I'm sure everyone reading this aspires to running high-quality projects. But knowing what to focus on and why will ensure that Rissue events don't blindside you.

The Tags

#risks, #riskmanagement, #raid, #rissue, #issues, #issuemanagement

---

More from Adam Russell

If you enjoyed this book, check out more of my books and other content at BrainJuice.Media!

1. **"Adam On: Projects (Volume 1)"**[1]
2. **"Adam on: Projects (Volume 2)"**[2]
3. **"Adam on: Projects (Quotations Edition)"**[3]
4. **"Adam On: ChatGPT: The AI Appliance"**[4]
5. **"Adam On: Advanced ChatGPT Application Primer"**[5] (Published in Beta on Leanpub.com)
6. **"Adam On: Advanced ChatGPT for Agile PM"**[6] (Published in Beta on Leanpub.com)
7. **"Adam On: Advanced Excel Table Management with TableWiz"**[7] (Published in Beta on Leanpub.com)
8. **"Adam On: Advanced Excel Outlining with TreeWiz"**[8] (Published in Beta on Leanpub.com)

Building a relationship with my readers is the very best thing about writing. Please check out the page ***"Getting Engaged with this Book and its Author"*** to see the different options. I'd love for you to join my mailing list. You can find details of this and other contact options in the "Getting Engaged" page.

Check out my other content on the **"BrainJuice.Media Titles Page"**[9]

Or scan the **QR Code** below:

---

[1] https://bjl.ink/aopv1
[2] https://bjl.ink/aopv2
[3] https://bjl.ink/aopquotes
[4] https://bjl.ink/chatgptappliance
[5] https://bjl.ink/chatgpt
[6] https://bjl.ink/chatgpt4apm
[7] https://bjl.ink/tablewiz
[8] https://bjl.ink/treewiz
[9] https://bjl.ink/titles

About the Author

The following two sections provide a high-level summary of Adam's extensive project management career and an update of Adam's "Career by Numbers" — a breakdown of experience in work hours.

Career Summary

Adam has lived, eaten, slept and breathed the dynamics of Software Development, Software Project Management and large-scale Systems Integration of IT platforms for nearly 45 years. This experience enables a deep understanding of software projects, which informs his ability to successfully deliver projects of all kinds.

Adam started as a developer and later moved into pre-sales technical support and project management. He managed his first project in 1985 and hasn't looked back.

Adam has extensive enterprise experience on both the supplier and customer sides. He worked for some of the largest companies in Australia, such as News Corp, IAG, Telstra and BHP and numerous large government departments. He has also worked for global vendors such as Hewlett-Packard, Wang Labs and Wipro. This experience resulted in a deep understanding of effective IT governance.

As a counterpoint, Adam's experience in startups and working with smaller software companies have instilled the delight of nimble and agile approaches to delivering customer value. Adam aims to implement governance with discipline and agility: strong and disciplined controls where needed, but with agile independence and flexibility that focuses on customer value in product development.

Adam's strength is bringing together people from all company areas to work on value delivery via software or digital components. Adam loves to solve complex problems in highly dynamic and often chaotic digital environments and thrives on building digital products and bringing them to market.

Adam does this by focusing the team on the outcomes that must be enabled. Although experienced in most traditional plan-based (Waterfall) and Agile methodologies, Adam is not bound to any specific one, preferring to assess each problem on a case-by-case basis and select the minimal tool-set necessary to support each project.

A Career by Numbers

Introduction to a Fetish

Around 2015, I began thinking about defining my expertise, independent of any certifications, academic qualifications or other training. How do I answer the question, *"Why would anyone listen to what I have to say about project management?"*.

The answer came courtesy of Malcolm Gladwell's assertion that an "expert" in anything had accumulated a minimum of 10,000 hours of "deliberate practice".

My question was simple *"Compared to this 10,000 hours benchmark, where did my project management experience sit?"*.

And so I began to reconstruct my working life and codify the various aspects in a spreadsheet. This is the result.

There are doubtless many flaws in this thinking — see next section for more on the 10,000 hours thing. The first flaw is that I'm not comparing apples with apples. I have catalogued work experience — Gladwell and others refer to it as "deliberate practice". These are very different things.

I've outlined some thoughts on this in the section below.

Regardless, there is a weight in numbers; as you'll see, I've accumulated these in spades.

The 10,000 Hours Thing

In the book *"Outliers: The Story of Success"*, Malcolm Gladwell explored the reasons behind highly successful individuals, including their birth and family situation, education and other variables. Ultimately, he focused on a study by Anders Ericsson and two others that looked at the role of "deliberate practice" in acquiring expert capabilities.

> *"In fact, researchers have settled on what they believe is the magic number for true expertise: ten thousand hours."* — **Malcolm Gladwell** in 'Outliers: The Story of Success' 2008

One should keep a couple of cautions in mind comparing the numbers in this analysis with that famous 10,000-hour "expert" calculation.

Remember that the 10,000 hours from the original study referred to as "deliberate practice", which is a particular kind of performance. It is not the same as "doing the job" or "on-the-job training" — learning by doing in a live work environment.

"Deliberate practice" includes several factors, including:

- Structured training: e.g., musicians spend many hours practising scales on a deliberate work plan;
- Supervision by an acknowledged master;
- Practice that deliberately focused on transitioning from one skill level to the next.

However, Gladwell also gave weight to the simple fact of "doing something". For example, he gives the example of the Beatles' early career in Germany when their contract required them to play for 7 or 8 hours on stage per night. This constant repetition — the total number of hours "doing it" also contributes to gaining expertise.

Project Management is not a typical office job with a routine on daily, monthly or annual cycles. During a project, there are rarely quiet times in which one can "goof off" to destress or manage mental health during work. Downtime usually happens between projects. So, a rough equation of "hours on the job" to "real work" is no stretch. The extent of wasted time has been considered via the two discounts described in the previous section.

Interestingly, 10,000 hours of pure work experience equates - in my experience - to a project manager getting to be reliably and sustainably successful in complex organisational contexts. This work hour count roughly equals five to eight years of experience. In hiring and managing relatively large numbers of project managers, this 5-8 years' experience shows a definite "knee in the curve" if plotted against efficacy on the job.

A level of 10,000 work experience hours gets someone "into the game". Considerably more hours of experience/practice are required to become what one might consider a "master".

I believe that attitude counts significantly in how experience hours translate into expertise. Someone who learns a few things and effectively sits on that knowledge, applying it repeatedly to projects, is developing experience in just one thing — perhaps they get more efficient at it, but that's it. Someone else who is constantly learning by reading, discussing and trying new things out in their projects will develop a much more comprehensive range of skills over time.

Lastly, there is an argument I'll make for pure experience, which is just the benefit of having been in and around multiple projects over a long period. Whether they are projects you are directly managing, projects that fit within your portfolio, or even projects that you see run by others, you get the benefit of a vast range of variations of projects and all the parameters that differentiate one project from another. This hands-on experience helps build the mental models that allow the master project manager to see into the heart of any project and rapidly assess its positives and negatives.

Interestingly, this concept called "thin slicing" is the subject of another Malcolm Gladwell book called "*Blink: The Power of Thinking Without Thinking"*.

I also believe that my career has constantly been one of self-learning and trying to improve the strategies and techniques I applied to each new project.

The bottom line is that I believe that the "Experience Hours" contained in this analysis are reasonably associated with the idea of the 10,000 hours and the additional experience/practice required to move beyond an "expert" into the realms of the truly competent.

My Experience by Numbers: Summary

As of New Year's Day in 2023, I've accumulated 67,253 hours of work experience over 174 project roles in 21 industries.

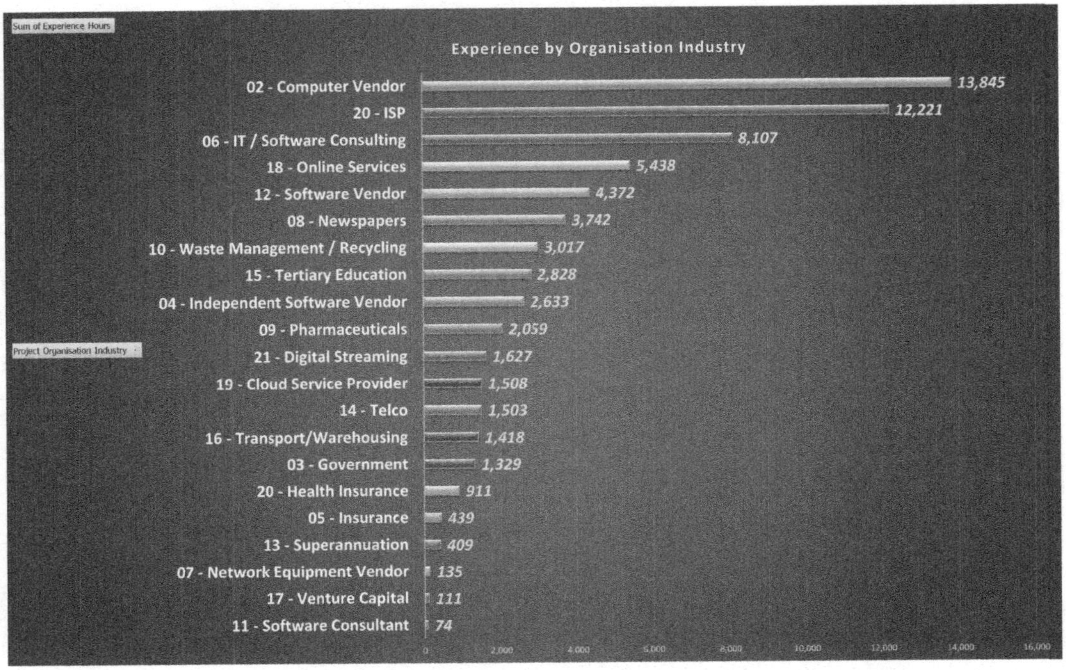

Figure 35. Experience by Organisation Industry

These project roles only relate to those projects in which I've had a direct role in their management, e.g., as a project manager, program manager (where the project managers directly reported to me), portfolio manager or General manager of project delivery. It does not include projects in my portfolio where I did not take a direct role in their management. I don't know how many of these were, but it's a large number.

For example, during my four years as GM of Program Delivery, the department I helped manage delivered approximately 60 projects every six months, or around 500. At that time, the number that I used to calculate my experience hours was eight — 8 projects of the 174. As a working number, I'd estimate that I've been involved in the delivery of approximately one thousand (1,000) Information Technology ("IT") projects projects, directly or indirectly.

The total catalogued Job Role or "Experience Hours" to date is 67,253 hours across all types of activity & initiatives.

All this nearly 70,000-hour work experience has been in IT Solutions Integration (barring a few early jobs).

Thus, I have lived, eaten, slept and breathed the dynamics of software development, software project management and large-scale systems integration of IT platforms for my entire working life.

Of these 67k hours of experience, just over 42,000 (42,272) hours have been in Project Delivery, including 32,265 hours as an individual contributor and hands-on Project Manager. The remaining approximately 10,000 hours in Project Delivery comprise more senior roles, such as Program and Portfolio manager.

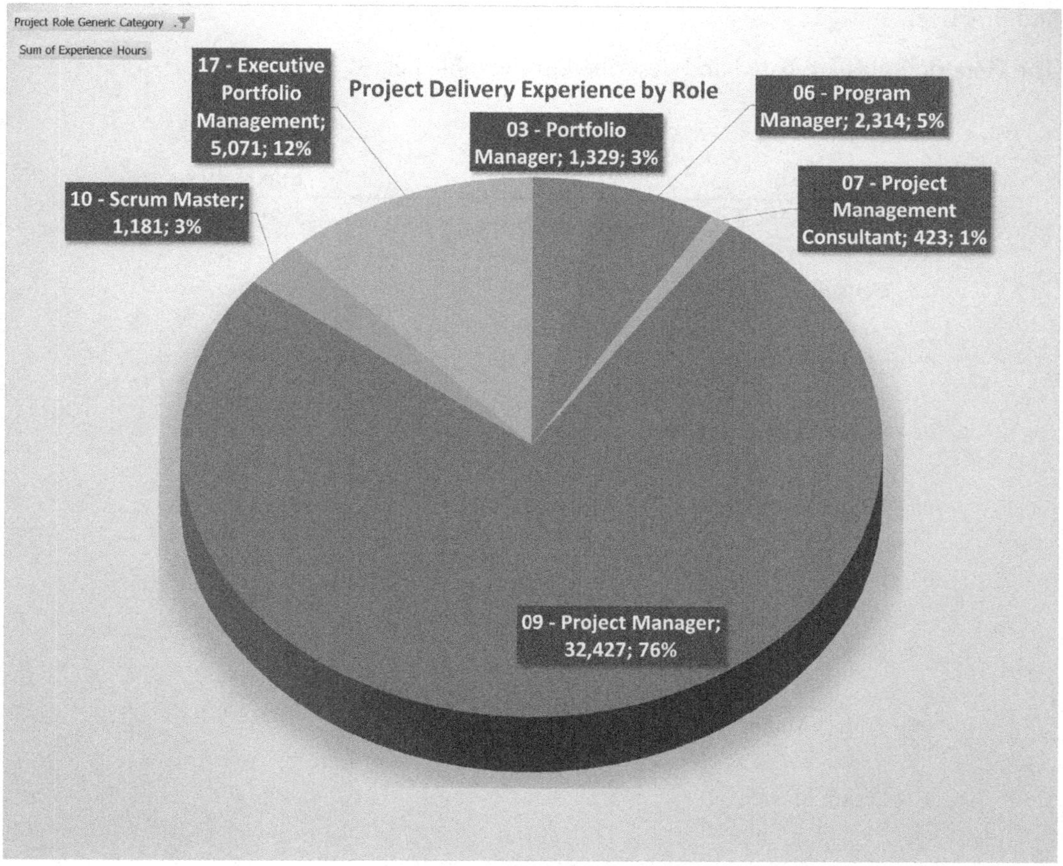

Figure 36. Experience by Role

Other roles make up the rest of the 24,000 hours of experience. Those roles include various kinds of business development and management and the activities related to finding good solutions to customer requirements, pre or post-sales.

Experience Hours by Generic Role

The Generic role aggregates many job titles into a small number of categories based on experience similarity. Based on this high-level activity breakdown, you can see that the bulk of Adam's experience is in Project Delivery. An anomaly of this analysis is that much (but not all) of the consulting experience was related to Project Management (e.g., methods and practice).

The Generic Roles are listed and described in the table below.

Generic Role	Exp Hours
01 - Business Analyst	439
02 - Consultant Developer	324
03 - Portfolio Manager	1,329
04 - Product Consultant	7,506
05 - Product Support Manager	6,912
06 - Program Manager	2,314
07 - Project Management Consultant	423
09 - Project Manager	32,265
10 - Scrum Master	871
11 - Software Developer	3,205
13 - Business Development	410
14 - General Management	381
15 - Management (generic)	3,383

Generic Role	Exp Hours
16 - Software Consultant	1,327
17 - Executive Portfolio Management	5,071
19 - Bid Management	358
99 - Not Applicable	736
Grand Total	**67,253**

Copyright

A BrainJuice.Media publication.

First published in Australia in 2023 by BrainJuice.Media an imprint of Tiligent Pty Ltd